Continui

Journeys Through the Spirit World

Shannon Harwood

ISBN 978-1-7774805-2-3

Publisher: Harwood & Harwood
spiritworldjourney@gmail.com

Cover Photo taken by Shannon Harwood
Cover and interior design by C. Hutcheson

DEDICATION

This book is dedicated with heartfelt thanks to each and every person who has allowed me to share their personal experiences in my memoirs, and to my family, for all of their support.

Also, to Cheryl H., I am beyond appreciative for all that you have done to assist me, and to see my manuscripts completed. These projects would not have happened without you. Thank you!

To Lucretia and to Lynne, a sincere thank you for all of your time and efforts.

I am grateful to you all.

Table of Contents

INTRODUCTION

Thank you for joining me once again as I continue on my journeys through the spirit world!

This book, my second memoir, is a compilation of individually written stories, detailing my personal experiences with the spirit world, and how it has changed not only my life but the lives of so many other people. I share heartfelt, emotional experiences that are made even more impactful by the important lessons that are learned with every visit and interaction. I am also learning with each experience, for no two are the same. I hope, as you are reading, that you will share in my laughter and my tears.

If you have not had an opportunity to read my previous memoir, Journeys into the Realm of the Spirit World, at the risk of repeating myself to those who have, I will say that I was born with the ability to connect with the spirit world. I discovered in my late teens how best to utilize these gifts for what I believe to be a higher purpose, and have spent the rest of my life in service to that. It has been a very adventurous path which I have followed.

Please remember that interactions with the spirit world are "normal" for me, as I have been aware since childhood. Consequently, there can be moments where I have an unintentional, casual familiarity with some of the entities around me, but this is never intended as disrespect for my gifts or the spirit world. There are days when the messages are clear and obvious, and other times when I can struggle to understand what the message is about or who it is for, and I talk about that, too. I think it is important to show all aspects of my spiritual journey; perhaps other people can relate, or learn from my experiences.

Spirituality is heavily involved in my mediumship, and I strongly believe in a Creator, which I identify as God, throughout my book. This is not to say that you must be a believer in Him in order to read these stories. I feel that at the end of the day, it matters not who the figurehead of your faith is determined to be. A spirit world exists, regardless of race, gender, nationality, or spiritual beliefs. I only wish to share in my experiences, the lessons I have learned, and perhaps open your heart and mind to the fact that you are not alone.

I truly believe that I am directed by my angels, or what I refer to as my holy spirit guides, throughout my writings. There are also moments in which this gift is used to teach and elaborate upon important aspects of spiritual growth, and I hope that you can apply this to your own life and experiences.

I do not summon or inquire of those who have departed before me, and I feel that if a message for another person is to arrive in any form, it will come to me when it is appropriate. Messages are usually inspired upon me quite unexpectedly, and in many different ways, through sights, sounds, and emotions. I have never taken on clients for readings as I believe that my gifts are just that: a gift for me to share.

Because of my beliefs, and the fact that I am careful with my energy and try not to actively seek out contact with spirits other than my guiding angels, I can be misconstrued as not wanting my gifts, or shunning them. This is not so. My abilities have always been a part of my existence. I don't know how I would function without them.

All of the experiences recorded in this manuscript are true and have been documented as honestly and as accurately as possible. In some instances, names have been changed in order to maintain privacy, but wherever possible even this information has not been altered.

Enduring the loss of a loved one, be it human or animal, can be very painful for those left behind. Please bear in mind that their journey has not ended with corporeal death. It is started anew in a purely energetic form that is not constrained by the material body, thus granting them freedom from physical pain, suffering, and the ability to move about at will. Take heart in the fact that although you may be unaware of them, they are walking beside you, very often in the times you need them the most. Read on, and you will see!

Shannon Harwood

THE LOVE THAT LIVES ON

It was in September 2007, at our wedding, that I first met a man named Kelly, along with his wife, Violet, and their adult daughter, Priscilla. Ray and I had decided to keep the guest list to the wedding relatively short, with only family and a few close friends in attendance, and Kelly is a cousin to Ray. Although I had not ever met Kelly and his family before, I felt very honored that they would drive all the way down from Northern Alberta to join us in our celebration. A great time was had by all who attended, and it was one of the most wonderful, enjoyable days of my life. I did not have much time to get acquainted with my new family members, of which there were quite a few to meet that day, but Kelly and his wife and daughter had made a lasting, favorable impression upon me. I was looking forward to getting to know them better. It was more than apparent that Kelly and his whole family were fun people with a great sense of humor, who loved to laugh.

Years passed by before an opportunity to visit together would present itself once more. Because the distance between our homes is considerable, it is almost impossible for a casual, unplanned gathering. However, our phone rang early one evening, late in the year 2010, with Kelly on the other end, announcing that he would be arriving in Southern Alberta later that night. It was business that brought Kelly into our area of the province, and Violet and Priscilla had gone along with him for the ride. We happily accepted an invitation to meet, and a time was set.

We met Kelly and his family at a local feedlot and visited while the livestock was offloaded from the trailer. The hour was very late and Kelly had a lengthy return drive home, so we were not afforded much time to visit. What little time we did have was not wasted with silence, however, and some great conversation ensued. I found myself quickly engaged in discussion with Violet, and before the end of our visit commenced it felt as though strong bonds had already been formed between us. Oddly enough, I felt as though I had known all three of them for most of my life, instead of having met them only twice. Ray did not actually know his cousin very well either, but he also seemed quite comfortable with Kelly and the whole family. Our goodbyes were exchanged with promises to meet again, as soon as we could.

As we all know, life gets in the way of our plans, even the best laid ones. This was no different with our hopes for another get-together with Kelly and Violet. Ray's work schedule, and my duties on the acreage with numerous gardens and animals to attend, made it hard to find the time to go anywhere overnight. Kelly and Violet had offered to make the drive to our home when the weather was good, and that was very kind of them, especially since Kelly battled with his own health issues. But I had a little secret that I did not wish to share with anyone: I was embarrassed to have them in my home.

My home is not modern, but it is beautiful, spacious and simple. Comfortable and nicely decorated in a manner that most people find very appealing. It is filled with plants and animals and a few hundred antique tins that are neatly displayed on various shelves within the home. Everyone that visits loves how warm, inviting, and safe the atmosphere feels once they arrive. I am very proud of the house I share with my husband, and I love to be here. But the house has a very obvious flaw that is evident the moment you see my kitchen table and my counters. Clutter.

The chaos never leaves this area, no matter how hard I try. The rest of my home is usually presentable, but the table appears to be a magnet for every piece of paper and paraphernalia that ever enters the house. My husband keeps his gloves and his hats and his vitamins scattered all over the surface of it. I also keep every receipt and household bill I might have use of for the last year, on the table. You can find tape and tools and anything else you might need, all on the table. Somehow this disorder seems to migrate to the countertops as well. No matter how often the mess is removed, it seems to magically re-appear in no time.

Although my unorganized clutter is much better managed now than it was years ago, there was a time when the piles of paper became too much for us to navigate, and they got banished to the basement. This was where the problem had gotten really out of control. Stacks and stacks of household papers, bills that needed to be filed, magazines and newspapers, receipts, all of it made its way downstairs onto an old table that was no longer in use. It had taken some time to achieve, but the papers were stacked to such heights that they threatened to fall over at the slightest disturbance. Actually, so much time had passed that the dreadful mess began to stack and spread under the table, with the piles of paper eventually making their way into clusters on the floor space that surrounded the table itself. My shameful secret. Add to this fact that the disorderly disaster was right outside of the only guest bedroom we had, and you might be able to see my dilemma. It was very embarrassing.

Equally as horrifying to me was the fact that our spare room was extremely outdated with its décor. The bed was a futon mattress on an old wooden frame, it was uncomfortable to sleep on and low to the ground. There were no side tables and the lighting was poor. The walls were badly in need of fresh paint. Not exactly a situation I was proud of. Certainly not a place where I wanted to invite guests to stay that had never been to my home before. However, no one who ever visits my home seems to be uncomfortable with my clutter, for my home is generally clean; just don't ever expect to see the entire surface of my kitchen table at one time. The average person might not have an issue cleaning up the clutter and disposing of the paper in the basement, but I found it overwhelming to even consider attempting such a daunting task. Especially because I have my own health issues which I struggle with on a daily basis, and a very full schedule.

Too ashamed to admit my problems to Kelly and Violet, I found myself suggesting that they wait until the weather was very warm before they drove down for a visit. This way I could house them in our travel trailer, which was modern and comfortable and not in the least bit embarrassing to view. I can only imagine that it must have seemed strange for family members to be offered outside accommodations when we have a house large enough to hold everyone, but no mention of this was ever made.

Concrete plans never were arranged for Kelly and Violet to drive down for a visit, and of course, with my home not up to proper standards, this did not bother me. Although I really, truly wanted to meet up with them, I was actually relieved that they were not coming: this meant that I could keep my secret. Plenty of people have stayed in our outdated spare room before, with all of the paper just outside the door. But those were people that knew me well, and understood that I have physical challenges to deal with. Kelly and Violet knew very little about me personally, and for some reason it was extremely important for me to have my home make a good first impression upon them. I believe that I was also fearful of what they might think of me when they saw the mess. I felt badly about the whole situation.

Kelly and Violet offered once or twice more to make plans to visit, and I was always in agreement with that idea, but would stall them with the suggestion that we wait for warmer weather. It was becoming obvious to everyone involved that I was reluctant to host them, but without an explanation from me, the offers merely stopped and faded into silence. One might think that this would have made me happy, but honestly, I was very disappointed in myself for not explaining my situation. I was frustrated for not correcting the clutter problem and cleaning it up. I began to fret that perhaps Kelly and Violet might think that I had some prejudice against them, which could not have been further from the truth, but I also felt unable to rectify the issues I did have. I found it to be quite a dilemma.

An opportunity to visit with Kelly did not come about again. We learned in 2013 that Kelly was struggling hard with his various health issues, some of which were life-threatening. Even so, I don't think we actually grasped the severity of Kelly's problems, and we were quite surprised and saddened to hear that he passed away in October of 2014. Now I was especially unhappy with myself for not doing more to have spent some time with Kelly and Violet before he had crossed over.

Several months passed by, and February had arrived with its icy blast of howling winds and artic air. The grey skies were dark and dismal, and my mood was not much better. I was curled up on the couch in the living room, alone, blindly staring off into space with very little on my mind. Quite suddenly, the empty room surrounding me was no longer empty, but filled with the warm and unmistakeable presence of Kelly himself. I felt a strong sense of peace and happiness surrounding him. "Ridiculous!" I snapped under my breath, for my mood was foul and I was not feeling very gracious towards myself. "Why on earth would Kelly be here? What would *he* have to say to *me*?" I shook my head in defiance and continued on in my melancholy.

Surprisingly, a strong, masculine voice answered the sharp words that I had directed towards myself. It was the male spirit in the room with me. The words were calm and simply stated. "He would tell you that he understands. He would tell you that now he can see your situation, and he understands your reasons. He would tell you not to be angry with yourself."

These words were followed by a very strong, encompassing emotion: forgiveness.

I was momentarily unable to even process another thought as I sat there in shocked silence, realizing that it was actually Kelly in the room with me. He was speaking about himself and how he felt about me, answering my question in the same manner that it was spoken. Even more beautiful to me was the fact that I understood immediately that Kelly truly did comprehend why I had held him at arms length. Not only did he radiate forgiveness for me, he wanted me to experience forgiveness for myself in this matter.

I was in awe to discover that the spirit world cares so greatly for our well-being that they do not wish to see us carry even the *slightest* of unnecessary guilts. A situation such as my untidiness and shame, insignificant compared to so many other events taking place in the universe, weighed heavily upon my soul just the same. Apparently, that was also obvious in the spirit world, and I am humbled by the effort that was put forth to correct me and encourage me to give up my burden of guilt. Which I was able to do.

Although the visit was very brief and he departed quickly, I am so grateful to Kelly for caring enough about my happiness that he visited me. Despite the fact he hardly knew me, he still cared immensely. Thank you, Kelly. Thank you, God, for alleviating the pain in my heart.

In case you were wondering about my mess and if it still exists, it is here that I should probably relay to you how the clutter problem in my basement got very swiftly resolved. The solution came about well after Kelly's visit to me. One can only imagine the sizeable amount of paper that had accumulated in my basement in the space of time that had passed since he was here. It was considerable. I also found myself somewhat depressed and extremely overwhelmed at the enormity of the task that lay before me. How on earth was a person going to be able to sort all of the paper? How could I ever find the energy needed to take on such an effort? I prayed to God for the strength and ability to tackle the monumental task; it was going to take more than a few days to complete. I knew that it was a ridiculously long overdue chore that needed to be completed, but try as I might I could not bring myself to start.

God, who I have discovered over the years has a great sense of humor, decided to answer my prayers a few days after I had asked for His help.

The day started out innocently enough. I had asked my oldest son, Wayde, to assist me in performing maintenance on one of the big canister filters that cleaned the water in our large, 180-gallon fish tank on the main floor of our home. The tank was 6 feet long and quite tall, perched on a beautiful cherry wood stand. Coincidentally, that tank sat right over the same spot in the basement where all of the paper was stacked.

Wayde was very enthusiastic to assist me, knowing that I was unable to disconnect and lift the heavy filter out from underneath the tank stand on my own. He is quite strong and more than capable of doing so. However, his enthusiasm and strength turned out to be a dire combination in this moment. When he reached below the tank to disconnect the canister filter, in his haste to be helpful, he merely tugged the fitting right off of the hose, instead of actually disconnecting the proper fitting. The very same fitting that was there to stop water from spewing out of the hose when the filter was removed.

Wayde's panicked voice alerted me to the fact that there was an emergency, but it was too late to intervene. I ran into the living room to discover that there was water literally gushing out from the hose that had been inadvertently pulled from the fitting. Water was streaming out from underneath the tank. It was pouring all over the floor, and running in one direction towards an area of flooring that was damaged and missing linoleum. To my shocked and disbelieving eyes, I observed that the water was also simultaneously *disappearing* once it flowed onto that specific section of flooring. Oh gosh, there was a small hole that had been drilled into the exposed wood floor at some point during a renovation, as well as a large split in the wood, and we had never bothered to patch it! The water was now running down that hole and flooding the basement. To be specific, it was flooding right on top of years of accumulated papers. All of it.

I was practically jumping up and down as I urgently begged Wayde to somehow re-attach the hose to the filter. Water was spraying in every direction as Wayde was attempting to force the hose back onto the fitting as quickly as he could. Thankfully, he managed to do just that. But not before the tank had managed to lose over 2 inches of water, which equated to a lot of gallons, and it was now dripping all over my basement ceiling and onto the floor. I could hear it. I made my way downstairs as quickly as I could to turn off the electrical breakers and assess the damage. What a sight to see.

Every square inch of paper clutter, piles and piles of it, was covered in water and completely saturated. All of it. Nothing had escaped the flood. The ceiling was still dripping, the water was still running onto the bundles of paper on the table, and from there down to the mounds on the floor. I could not believe my eyes. As shocked as I was by the sight that greeted me, I still had the presence of mind to observe that, strangely, the water had not spread anywhere else before the flow had been stopped. It literally pooled on the papers, the table, and the papers on the floor under the table. Nothing else, not a thing was damaged. But what was affected was unsalvageable. All of it, without exception, was now trash to be thrown away. No sorting, no decisions to be made, and nothing could be done but to gather it all up and dispose of it into large trash bags. It had to be done immediately before the water ruined the old wooden floor beneath the papers. I had no choice. I might be tired, I might be overwhelmed, but this was an emergency and it had to be managed. I had to muster the strength and energy for the task without exception, but I knew that I could do it. I turned away with a heavy sigh, what a chore.

I had barely cleared that thought from my mind as I headed for the cleaning supplies, when I heard the echoes of my prayer to God just a few days earlier float through my head. *"Dear God, please grant me the strength and ability to tackle the paper..."* and then it hit me - God most certainly had answered my prayer! Not at all in the manner I would have hoped, with a solution I would have preferred, but He had answered me. In the most humorous way possible. Now the paper mess had to be dealt with, I had no choice. The paper would be cleared out. Today. This realization, that God had indeed granted me the ability to deal with the papers, hit me hard. It was then that I began to giggle, then chuckle, until finally I was laughing out loud as hard as I could, scarcely able to stand. He got me good, without a doubt. And He answered me, alright. The stacks of paper have not ever returned since that day.

Kelly did not appear to me again for a couple of years, but it was an occasion to make note of, so I still remember the day clearly: Feb. 11, 2017. It was a Saturday evening.

Nothing out of the ordinary had happened on that particular day. No indication that there was any activity around me in the spirit world, either. I was standing at the stove, preparing supper, and Ray was seated at the kitchen table not far from me, reading a magazine. One minute I was alone in the quiet of my thoughts, the next minute I was very much aware of the fact that I was no longer alone at all. I could hear a ruckus beside me that garnered my immediate attention, and a flurry of activity could be tangibly felt just off to the left side of the stove. I quickly glanced up, puzzled by what I was hearing and sensing. What I saw almost made me drop my spoon.

Not only was it Kelly's spirit standing in very close proximity to me, appearing to me to be very healthy and strong, he was not alone. Immediately next to him stood his cousin, George, who also happens to be Ray's father. George crossed over in 2012. And although I have seen him on occasion, George is seldom very communicative, preferring instead to hang back in peaceful silence whenever I am aware of him. Silence was not the case at this moment, however, as nothing about this moment was quiet.

Although Kelly was right next to me, he was not standing still at all. Rather, he was moving so much while staying in one spot that the air was almost swirling around him. As was George. Together they stood, side by side, sporting comfortably worn western shirts and fading blue jeans. They were laughing hysterically, slapping their knees and digging their elbows into each other's ribs like they had just heard the Best Joke Ever. They looked like middle-aged men with their dark hair and stocky physiques, but they were acting like teenagers. Whatever the joke was, it seemed as though it would remain private, for not a word was said between them, or to me, about it.

The laughter was infectious, however, and their antics played like a comedy show. It went on for a few minutes, much to my amusement. The hoots and howls Kelly and George shared every time they looked at each other had me puzzled, because they were acting so secretive, yet making it so blatantly obvious, that *something* was happening. I was curious beyond belief but had no answers. The scene playing out before me was so odd that I found myself unable to remain silent any longer. With a smile on my lips, I relayed to Ray exactly what I was seeing.

Ray couldn't help himself but to grin as I explained how Kelly and George appeared to have the funniest secret in the world. I told him how they were behaving, and acting so juvenile. I explained that I had no idea what the fuss was about but that there was something happening in the spirit world that appeared to be exciting, or hysterically funny. Something we humans did not know about. Kelly and George did not stick around very long, and soon the hilarious incident was put on the shelf in my mind, momentarily forgotten.

I should mention at this moment that the year 2017, right up to the night I saw Kelly and George, had been a very difficult year. In some regards, it was also a little lonely for me and my remaining dog, Belle. You see, Belle's last remaining pack members, Mystique and Amy, had just died less than 8 weeks beforehand, in December. Belle was devastated, as was I. In her advanced years, Belle had come to rely heavily upon Mysti and Amy. I still struggled with the fact that we had lost 2 dogs in less than 24 hours. The house was very quiet without the happy, vocal presence of my sightless Mystique, and I was at a loss as to how to fix it.

Purchasing another companion for Belle was out of the question as my husband, Ray, had been out of work since December, and funds were low. We had discussed what kind of dog we would be looking for, preferably a younger male dog that might be a little protective of me. We definitely wanted a non-shedding dog, hands down. We have had as many as 5 dogs living in our house at one time, all were smaller, non-shedding dogs. We would have drowned in loose fur had they not been, and we were not interested in that.

Regardless, as I said, another dog was just not in the cards for us, and I was fretting a little about that. Ray had recently picked up a contract in the oilfields of Northern Alberta, and he was leaving on Monday for 2 weeks. I would be left alone out on the acreage with a deaf dog that could not alert me if there were any issues during the night as I slept. It was not a comfortable situation for me. I have always had a watchful dog that could hear well and act as my living alarm bell so that I had no concerns about being caught unawares.

Early in the afternoon on the day following the visit from Kelly and George, my phone rang with an unfamiliar number showing on my call display. Since it was a Sunday and not a business day, I took a chance and answered the call, hoping it was not a telemarketer. It was not. A cheerful voice on the other end of the line was asking for a woman named Shannon, but the woman was not trying to sell me anything. Once I had identified myself, she told me her name. As it turned out, she had a very interesting story to tell me.

Apparently, this lady was calling on behalf of an elderly couple that was looking to re-home a dog. Not just any dog, but a dog that had been badly treated during its life and was desperately in need of an experienced handler. The elderly couple had just come into possession of the dog less than 48 hours earlier, but discovered that they were not capable of dealing with such a poor creature. They immediately began searching for another home for the dog, but with no resources available, could only turn to local animal shelters with the assistance of a friend. The problem was that no one, not a single shelter, was able to take the dog in. Capacity was high in most places, staffing was an issue, and the dog had far too many problems for them to deal with appropriately. The elderly couple was at a loss.

The lady on the phone went on to explain to me that the funniest thing had happened after she had called every shelter she could find, and was routinely turned away. A little voice in the back of her mind suggested that she place a call, for the second time, to one of the small, local shelters that had already said no to her. The voice was persistent, said the lady, so she decided to heed it. With fingers crossed she called the number once more. This time a different person answered the phone, so she explained her predicament anew. Once again, the lady was told that there was no room at the shelter, however, this time the person had a question for her. By chance, had the lady ever heard of a woman named Shannon Harwood? The shelter worker went on to explain that they were very familiar with me, and that I worked with abused dogs. They suggested it was worth the chance for her to call, and gave her my number.

I began to enquire about the dog in question. I was told that it was a young male that didn't appear to be well-fed or house-trained. It sounded like he was a handful for a couple that was unfamiliar with dogs to begin with, and I knew in my heart that I could not leave him there. When I inquired about his breed, I was told that he was a cross between a Miniature Schnauzer and a Pug. I was quite happy about that, for Mini-Schnauzers have always been a breed that I have owned, and I was very familiar with their temperament. I came to the conclusion that he must be non-shedding with his lineage and made arrangements to go pick him up. Even better, this dog needed a home so badly that he came without charge. When I got off the phone, my mouth was agape, could this *really* be happening? Was I truly going to go pick up a young male dog for free, just a day before Ray was to leave for work?

It was a 45-minute drive to the town where the dog was located. We brought Belle along for the ride and left her waiting in the car while we entered the house. Good thing she stayed behind, for the dog that we were about to meet was beyond my wildest imaginations. He was a wide-eyed, hysterical, vocal mess. His fur was long, white and cream-colored, and his tail curled over his back. He raced about the house, barking non-stop and apparently looking for food, according to the elderly couple in possession of him. They told me that no matter how much they fed him he cried for more and they were afraid that he would get sick if they over fed. He did not seem to understand what to do when they took him outside, and he would mess in the house. He was so hysterical I couldn't get near him, but I knew that I could not leave him there for these poor people to have to deal with him.

Finally, I was able to swoop the dog into my arms as he was passing by. He relaxed immediately at my touch and became quiet, stretching the length of his body out and laying his head in the crook of my arm. It was as though he recognized my concern for him, and that he would be going home with me. "Good boy," I murmured, and gently reached out with my free hand to stroke his fur. My fingers stopped halfway down his back as I came to a horrifying realization, *he sheds!* NO!

I stared in dismay at the elderly lady and exclaimed with some panic, "He sheds!"

"Not much," she replied to me with enthusiasm, "look!" She immediately held up a small jacket that had come with the rest of his possessions, it was dark blue in color and absolutely, completely covered in white dog hair. Every square inch of it. I couldn't believe my eyes, and I tried hard to keep my face from showing my horror. While there was no doubt in my mind at all that we would take the unfortunate animal home with us, for who could leave him there, I am fairly certain that for a minute or two I was absolutely dazed. I had not had a shedding dog in years and years. That was one of my biggest requirements whenever I was searching for a new pet: non-shedding. This dog didn't just break that rule a little bit, he blew it right out of the water. One stroke of his fur and your fingers were coated.

At any rate, we took the dog home with us. I christened him with a new name, which was Farley. Within mere days I had added a middle name. Rotten. Farley Rotten. Farley had turned out to be the biggest challenge of all of the dogs I have ever owned. He was so starved that our vet told us he was near death, but you wouldn't have known it. Farley had so much energy and was so hyper, he could run at lightning speed and was always on the lookout for the next adventure. He was also so starved that any indication of food would have him scrambling to try to get on top of the table or the countertop to attempt to eat it. He was very determined to eat whatever he could find, and could devour a bowl of food in three seconds flat. Farley also was not house-trained at all, and didn't seem to understand what to do when he was outside. He was terrified to be in the yard alone. He was petrified of the kennel, having spent most of his life in one, and he howled and screamed in fear and frustration when I put him inside. He was overly rambunctious with my elderly Belle, and would not quit barking at the top of his lungs whenever anyone entered the house. The air in my home was literally swirling with loose fur. I could go on and on forever about Farley's issues, but you get the idea. At the end of it all, we love him as much as any other in our life. I can tell you that he now loves the bed in his kennel, and he doesn't try to steal food off the counter, but he still barks like crazy.

Can you see as clearly as I can, that Farley was a gift? The day before my husband is to leave me home alone for weeks, without the protection and comfort of an alert dog, we get a phone call to go rescue a young, male dog. We had no extra money or resources, yet that too was provided for. Belle was provided a companion. But, can you also see as clearly as I, where the gift came from? And how the individuals giving me that gift would have thought that Farley was the most hysterically funny gift of all? Or perhaps I should say the spirit world found this gift to be the most special, uproariously funny gift, for that is what it was. A gift. From Kelly and George. A gift so funny that they could hardly contain their delight. I think that they are still laughing right up to this day, especially about the shedding fur, and I don't blame them at all.

It was 2020 before I had the opportunity to visit with Violet and Priscilla once more. Ten years since I last saw them at the feedlot with Kelly. Although many years had passed, they fell away instantly the second we reunited, it was as though we had been in contact the whole time. We were at a large family get-together in Northern Alberta, a birthday celebration, and many of the guests had decided to camp in the yard for the night, myself and Ray included. It was a lively function, with much laughter and conversation.

There were a couple of times during that evening when I wanted to pull aside Violet and Priscilla to have a chat with them about the visits I have had from Kelly. I had only told a few people up to that moment, Ray's sister Bonny Lou being one of them. I felt bad for not having shared this information sooner with Kelly's family. The opportunity to speak privately had not occurred however, and I resigned myself to wait for what I felt would be an opportune time. There were so many guests gathered around the firepit at the party, I was not sure if that moment would ever come. Occasionally I would experience some mildly repetitive thoughts about speaking in front of everyone about my encounters with Kelly, but nothing was overwhelming, and I prefer not to be in the spotlight, so I chose to stay quiet.

Apparently, the spirit world had plans that evening, however, if I was not going to speak then they would find someone who would. My sister-in-law, Bonny Lou, appeared to be the perfect candidate. Quite suddenly, and much to my shock, she announced to everyone listening about "the time Shannon saw Kelly after he died" during one of the group conversations being had. She told me later that it was almost as if she had no choice, that the words just tumbled from her lips. She'd only had time to hope that I wouldn't mind before she found herself speaking out loud.

I now had the full attention of everyone gathered around the campfire, most especially Kelly's immediate family members. This had me somewhat horrified because I am very private, but with no time to worry about that, I began to try to explain both of the encounters that I experienced with Kelly after he crossed over. I felt awkward and self-conscious but managed to explain as best as I could. I could see that Violet and Priscilla were very open to what I had to say; they looked calm and happy. We did not stay on the subject for very long before the conversation continued on in another direction, but I felt as though it had been very important that the news of Kelly's afterlife was shared. I was wise enough to understand that Bonny Lou had not acted on her own when she initially spoke out, but was inspired by her own guides to do so. I was happy that she had. I don't think I would have had the courage to do so otherwise, and the opportunity might not have come about again during the visit. I had no way of knowing at the moment, but Violet had chosen to leave the party that night and head for home. Only Priscilla was staying. Who knows when I would have seen Violet again, or had the chance to speak with either of the women?

The remainder of our evening was wonderful. The fire was warm and the conversation was entertaining. One of the aunts started playing a set of spoons, rhythmically slapping them between her thigh and her hand, and my husband Ray had started playing his guitar. It didn't take long before I could hear the sound of what could only be described as bells coming from the other side of the fire. Seated as I was towards the back of the group it was difficult for me to get a good view, but what I did see was Priscilla's head bobbing in time to the music and the bells. It looked as though she was performing some sort of a pow-wow dance, and if my ears were correct, she was wearing a set of native bells on her ankles. I was thrilled to be able to witness this, native culture is very important and interesting to me, especially because my husband and his family are of Metis lineage.

Priscilla came dancing around from the back of the fire, her head was keeping time with the beat and I was craning my neck to be able to see the bells. The closer she came the louder they got, and I was getting very excited. Finally, Priscilla came into my full view, and I was astonished by what I saw. There were no bells. There were, however, short glass jars stuffed into her socks beside her ankles, filled with random silverware spoons, that clanged and rang like bells whenever Priscilla tapped her feet. The perfect pow-wow accompaniment, as far as I could see. I don't know if I have ever laughed so hard in my life. Priscilla was a blast.

The next day left us with little time to visit. We had a long drive home with a few stops to make along the way, but I did find the time to sit and converse with Priscilla and a couple of other relatives for a few minutes before we had to depart. I found it touching that Priscilla decided to share some stories from her childhood with me. I felt our connection growing, and Priscilla especially wanted me to let her know if I ever heard from her dad, Kelly, again. I assured her that I would. She was so happy to have had news of him that I felt some dismay for not having contacted her on my own when he did come through the first time in 2015, let alone the second time.

Although I was not able to visit for long that morning, I had observed several times while talking with Priscilla, an unusual flurry of activity around her in the spirit world. There were so many entities in close proximity to her that the air was literally buzzing with energy. It reminded me a little of the sound of bees. I couldn't understand what I was experiencing, or what the purpose was for so many spirits to be with her, and I soon put it to the back of my mind. It was intriguing, however, and I found myself trying to explain to Ray what I had felt the moment we got into the car. There was no explanation for it, but I felt that it was significant.

I had no way of knowing that this was the last time Ray and I would ever see Priscilla in the flesh again. I believe that this may be why there were so many spirits around Priscilla when last I saw her; I feel that they were aware of what was to take place and were very close to her, in large numbers. I also understand now the importance of Priscilla hearing about her fathers safe, happy existence in the spirit world. Maybe some of her own doubts and fears concerning death had been quelled before she, too, crossed over. I believe that she had found great relief and happiness knowing that Kelly was able to be with her in spirit.

It was a tragic accident, merely three weeks after we had gathered, that would take Priscilla from the ones who loved her. The circumstances were heartbreaking. Priscilla had just finished mowing her lawn and was riding the mower down the shoulder of a two-lane country road, headed back to her mother's house to return it, when she was struck from behind by a car speeding well past the limit. It turned out that the driver was unlicensed, and although some present at the scene suspected that she was also impaired, a roadside sobriety test was never administered.

Violet was able to be with her child almost immediately, for the incident happened right in front of her home, but it was too late. Priscilla was gone. She had died upon impact. It was August 23rd, 2020.

Not more than a few weeks had gone by before I had a brief, but impactful visit from Priscilla. I was outside doing yard chores when an image flashed before my eyes. It was Priscilla, looking sombre and wearing black clothing, standing before me. Her father, Kelly, stood closely behind her, also wearing dark clothing and looking very serious. I could understand why, for the situation surrounding Priscilla's death was very bleak, and the family was really suffering. I heard only one sentence, and that was from Priscilla. "Tell my mother I KNOW how hard she tried" echoed in my mind.

A short time later Priscilla returned, strongly urging me to pick up a pen and paper to record words she had to say to her son, Kirkland. It was a short paragraph:

"To my son, I am proud of the young man that you are, prouder still of the man you will become. Do not follow all of my examples, rather, go by your heart and the pull you feel in your soul. I am here with you, you are not alone, you have not been abandoned."

Priscilla is a very persistent individual, both while she was here on earth and now while she is in spirit. Despite my schedule being jam-packed with activity, making it quite difficult to immediately find the time to get to a phone to call Violet, Priscilla did not give up. More than once, I heard Priscilla repeating the words she had to say to her mom quite forcefully, and I knew that I had no choice but to try to contact her mother.

When Violet and I did finally have the chance to talk, she was able to share with me the personal details of her daughter's death. The whole entire scene had played out like a nightmare, as anyone can imagine. I will not relay confidential, private information concerning this incident, except to discuss one thing, with permission from Violet. The words that Priscilla had spoken had more significance than I realized.

Yes, as most mothers would do for their children, Violet had tried hard to be the best mom she could be to her daughter. Priscilla had struggled with many issues while she was here on earth, and Violet had tried, hard, to steer Priscilla down the right path. Now that she was in spirit, Priscilla would be very aware of all of the effort that Violet had made for her, that is true. She knows how hard her mother tried. But I think that Priscilla was referring to something else at the moment she spoke to me.

Priscilla *knew* just how hard her mother had tried on that fateful day to keep her alive, to will Priscilla's spirit back into her body, to keep her safe. She knows of the anguish her mother experienced. You see, Violet had stayed with Priscilla the second she had come upon the body of her daughter lying in a ditch. Violet held onto her daughter in the grass, cradled her daughter, and kept her safe for *four hours* until paramedics arrived and could take Priscilla away. Violet never left Priscilla's side. Priscilla KNOWS how hard she tried.

I was moved to tears when Violet also told me that God had blessed her with a vision as she sat with her daughter that day. A vision of Kelly, reaching out with strong arms to catch his child as she flew into the air from the force of the car hitting her. Priscilla never knew the pain of that collision, for her father had caught her, and gently laid her down. Violet knew, unwaveringly, that Priscilla was okay from that moment on.

Violet also told me that the message I had received for Kirkland echoed words that Priscilla had written to him in a letter from years prior, urging her son not to follow all of her examples. There were previous occasions that Priscilla had made poor choices and lived a hard life. She did not want to see Kirkland make the same mistakes by following her path.

The memory of seeing Priscilla and Kelly, looking so solemn and dressed so darkly, did not leave me for a long time. I prayed as often as I thought about them, and their family. I wished for nothing more than to see everyone involved strengthened, healed, and to be able to experience joy once again. I could not imagine the pain that the family must be going through. Priscilla's brothers, Rick and Clayton, had also been on the scene of the accident immediately, and were witnesses to the horrifying event. The entire family was traumatized.

The intense warmth of spring brought about great relief from the blustery winter winds of Southern Alberta in 2021. I was outside pulling weeds in my flower beds, although it was only the 9th of April and still very early in the season. Movement out of the corner of my eye caught my attention, as well as a blur of color, and I paused what I was doing momentarily to get a better view. Strolling towards me was the spirit of a woman wearing a beautiful, golden-yellow shirt. Completely surrounding her was a swath of sparkling, yellow color; it glimmered and shimmered in the soft light illuminating the scene. The woman was Priscilla. She stood alone, smiling as she looked down at me. I caught a brief flash of happiness from her, and then she was gone.

I have to say that I was very happy to have seen Priscilla, especially since she was looking so good. I personally found it odd to see her dressed in yellow and surrounded by the aura of yet another shade of yellow, although there was no reason to think that. I hardly knew her, and could not make that judgement on her choice to appear as she did. Still, yellow seemed so unusual to me. Perhaps it was such a stark contrast to the dark colors that she had appeared in previously, that made the yellow seem out of place. However, yellow was a wonderful indicator to me of Priscilla's overall spiritual health. It was such a bright, cheerful color to present to me that I understood immediately that she was doing well.

It was a couple of weeks later that I found myself chatting on the phone with Violet. I wanted to tell her of my visit from Priscilla, but felt foolish for doing so, all I had to share was a vision of her in yellow. I didn't find it all that significant, except, of course, for the fact that she was doing well. That was important. So, despite my hesitation, I found myself blurting out to Violet exactly what I had seen.

Violet listened carefully, then paused for a second before she spoke. “The yellow color, that is interesting,” she replied. I almost fell over when she said that. It turns out that Priscilla had an intense love of yellow sunflowers when she was here on earth. They were her favorite. They made her happy. She decorated her home with sunflowers, and lots of people associated yellow sunflowers with Priscilla. Violet also told me that she had very recently been on the phone with friends, requesting that they plant sunflowers in memory of her daughter. Violet had also planted some. The significance of the yellow color and sunflowers really hit home with me a week later, however, when Violet sent me a picture of the headstone that memorialized Priscilla’s final resting place. It was adorned with, of all things, sunflowers. How beautiful.

Spring passed swiftly into hot summer months, and soon I found that the middle of August had come. Seeking refuge from the heat of the day, I languished in my basement office, enjoying the cool air. Idly sifting through old photos on my computer, I discovered a file initially installed on the computer when we ported pictures from my husbands’ phone. Curiosity got the better of me, and upon inspection, I was delighted to find pictures and videos from the birthday celebration we had attended the previous year.

I scrolled through each, frame by frame, until one video, in particular, stopped me in my tracks. It was a short clip, only seconds long, but it was of Priscilla. She was wearing a white blouse, and silver hoop earrings. The only sound to be heard on the clip was her contagious laughter. She was slapping her leg, leaning back in her chair and laughing heartily. It made me laugh just listening to her, there was so much joy there. I mused to myself about whether or not I should share the video with other family members, but ultimately chose not to. I did not know if the video would be too painful for them to see; there were only three days left before the one-year anniversary of her loss.

August 23rd, 2021 started off like any other day for me. I had completed my chores for the morning and was sitting at the kitchen table enjoying a cup of coffee. The house was very quiet and still, and sunlight was streaming through the curtainless windows. I was feeling very peaceful in my surroundings. Without any warning at all, Priscilla's strong energy pattern suddenly manifested in the room, very close to where I was seated. I could feel such a powerful vibration coming from her it was almost overwhelming. Obviously, she had an important reason to be with me, one that could not be ignored. It was no coincidence that today was the anniversary of her death.

Wordless emotions impressed upon me the need to go downstairs, immediately, to find the video clip of Priscilla laughing. I had no idea why exactly, but that did not matter, for the moment I had jumped to my feet and headed to the stairs, I could feel, very intensely, Priscilla right behind me. Such was her urgency to have me go down to my office that I almost felt as though she would push me down those stairs herself were I to try to disagree. Please understand that Priscilla would never have hurt me, or literally pushed me, but she was trying to convey the importance of her mission. And I heard her loud and clear.

Once I got to my office and pulled up the video on my computer, I had another urge impressed upon me to send the video clip to Priscilla's sister, Candace. I felt a little uncomfortable contacting Candace out of the blue on a day such as this, but there was no way I was going to deny the request. Candace and I were familiar with each other on social media, but I had not ever spoken to her or met her. I took a deep breath and hit send on my message request, explaining that I had a short video clip of Priscilla and asking permission from Candace to send it.

Initially, my inquiry was met with silence. I could see that the message had not been read, although I patiently waited. Surely there had to be a reason that Priscilla was hounding me to send the video at that exact moment? The insistence I had felt was unmistakable. No answer came from Candace, however, and I began to shift in my seat, ready to depart for the comfort of my kitchen. Nonetheless, before I could manage to rise from my chair, I was once more overcome with urgency; this time to record onto paper a short dictation from Priscilla. She had words to say to Candace and she did not want me to forget them in the meantime as I was waiting for a response. I grabbed a pen and paper, recording the following words:

"Keep rejoicing in the love we share together, still. It is not gone. I am not gone. Be at peace, for the circumstances do not change, cannot change, and I have to move forward in support and love from those dearest to me. I need you to gather your strength and celebrate, as I shall celebrate with you, life, the good times, and the losses. Be at peace, for I am as well."

The words trailed off, and Priscilla disappeared. I was sure she would return when Candace contacted me, and that is exactly what happened.

It did not take long for Candace to return my text, affirming that she would love to have a copy of the video. I replied, indicating that I now needed to speak with her on the phone if she was agreeable to that, and sent her the clip. Candace responded with her number, and I called immediately. Understandably, Candace was very emotional on this day and she answered the phone in a tearful state. We chatted for only a few minutes as I took the time to explain as best I could how my abilities work, and to stress that this was a gift from the spirit world. Her gift to do with as she pleased.

Initially, Priscilla was seated right next to me as I read her words to Candace. My voice cracked and trembled with emotion while I did so, and my body vibrated with the intensity of the energy that was merely inches away from me. Priscilla departed from me before I was finished reading, however, and I was certain she was with her sister. Candace was listening intently to every word and was quietly sobbing by the time I was finished speaking.

Through her tears, she began to explain how desperately she had been trying to hang onto Priscilla's memory, daily. How she was reliving the circumstances of her death anew, over and over again. Candace was grieving heavily the loss of her sister, unable to release her strong emotions of despair, in part due to the fact that resolution had not ever come about for her. The woman who had taken Priscilla's life remained free to live her life, and indeed, at that time, no charges had ever been laid against her concerning this incident. Candace felt robbed of the life she should have been able to share with Priscilla, and, try as she might to stop it, a small vein of bitterness had grown and crept into her heart.

I was awed at the honesty of the words Candace shared with me. I felt honored that she would share her grief so openly with a person who, up until that moment, she had never spoken with before. I could perceive that the words Priscilla had spoken were resonating deeply with Candace, and I was grateful for that. But it was what Candace spoke of next that gave me a clearer understanding of just how beautifully this interaction with the spirit world had been planned.

As it turned out, the reason Candace was unable to respond immediately to my initial message about the video clip was because she was driving her son to work. But what was most interesting was the text that she had received just before she got in the car. It was from a close friend of hers, although she was unprepared for what he had to say. The message was simple, and it said: “Priscilla cannot heal and move forward if you do not heal”.

Candace told me that she did not respond to the message at all, for her reaction was not calm. She said that her initial response was to lash out in anger, indignant that the sender of the message would dare to say such a thing. That was *her* sister, *her* loss, he had no idea of what he was saying! She could not just “let go and heal.”

However, Candace is a wise woman, and she tries hard to listen to the inner pull that guides her. She told me that after her son had left the vehicle and she was returning home, alone, in her thoughts she began to mull the words that her friend had spoken. She told me that she felt Priscilla close to her in those moments, and that she felt Priscilla encouraging her to heed what had been said. Candace was still struggling with the thought of moving forward without Priscilla. I suspect that she might have felt that releasing the grief and pain of her loss would mean that she was releasing the honor and memory that she sought to carry for her sister. She did not understand that letting go of the pain *was* doing honor to the memory of her loved ones, and allowing their love to be celebrated.

Then, upon returning home, Candace discovered the message from me. The words I read to her from Priscilla only confirmed what had been spoken to her earlier. I actually wonder if Candace would have been so open to the message from Priscilla if she had not had time at first to process the idea that her grief was holding Priscilla back. Maybe her reaction to my message would have been similar to the message that she had from her friend. Denial. I think it is beautiful to see how lovingly God arranged this entire encounter from start to finish.

The urgency I had felt from Priscilla to contact her sister was due in part to the fact that everything needed to be so perfectly timed. I had to have the video ready to send to Candace when the time was right, I needed to have the words on paper so they could be read at the perfect moment. Priscilla left me immediately after those words were put to paper so that she could be with Candace on the drive home, after Candace got the text from her friend urging her to heal. Priscilla needed to be there to help her sister accept the truth of the messages she was receiving. Candace had to be prepared to hear the reality of Priscilla's words to her, and that was achieved with the first message.

Priscilla urging Candace to accept the circumstances as they were could not have rung truer. I had no idea how impossible it had been on a daily basis for Candace to do exactly that. Priscilla's explanation that she needed to move forward from those she loved only meant that she could no longer be held to her loved ones through their grief and their inability to accept. Priscilla was trying to explain that those bonds needed to be cut, with love and support, for her journey forward. It did not mean that Priscilla would never be there with her loved ones again.

When Candace and I were discussing the video clip of Priscilla laughing, and I told her what day I had discovered the video, she found that to be of significance as well. You see, the last time Candace and Priscilla had spoken on the phone it was August 20th, 2020. This also happened to be the birthday of Candace's son, Aidan. The following year turned out to be a difficult birthday to celebrate because the family's main focus was on the fact that this was the anniversary of the last day Priscilla had spoken with them. But it was also the same day that I found the clip of Priscilla laughing and looking so happy. I think she was trying to tell the family to celebrate the birthday, and hold onto the joy. It was a final gift to her nephew, and a reminder to try to be happy no matter what life hands you.

Candace started the process of acceptance right there on the phone that day, as her understanding grew. I believe her spirit felt lighter than it had in a year, maybe longer, for Candace has suffered much loss in her lifetime. I was so grateful to God for His love and healing touch. Candace contacted me the next day to tell me that she knew without a doubt that Priscilla had been with her the day before, and that she understood Priscilla would not want Candace to be falling apart like she has been. Candace let me know that she now felt peace, despite the loss of her sister. She explained that she has also lost a child, a brother, a father and her best friend at this point in her life. I was overjoyed to hear her explain that although she may grieve their loss for the rest of her life, she has now come to the understanding that she has to start living for the "living" and not hang onto what she cannot change. I was so grateful to see the healing process truly begin.

I have not had strong contact with Priscilla since that day. I plant sunflowers now, in memory of her. I suspect that she is doing just fine. Occasionally, I am reminded of her as a brief burst of energy announcing her presence flits through the room. But, just as quickly, that energy disappears, leaving me with a soft smile as I remember the love and energy that is Priscilla. The love that lives on.

Priscilla and son Kirkland.
(Picture supplied by Violet W.)

(Kelly and Violet (pictures supplied by Violet W.)

Author notes: I wanted to share that as we came into the end of 2022, Violet was finally able to find some closure in this tragic situation. She fought hard to see that charges were filed against the individual that was driving the car that day. Also, the RCMP admitted publicly their negligence in the initial investigation, and issued an apology to the family. Violet went on to file a claim against the insurance company that represented the owner of the vehicle involved in the incident. In so doing, Violet finally felt that justice was served, as far as she could take it. Her daughter was ultimately vindicated when the insurance company settled in Violet's favor.

I have watched Violet tolerate a seemingly endless amount of emotional suffering and pain through enduring the loss of her daughter, Priscilla. And I am in awe and admiration of the strength, determination, and sheer grit Violet possesses, to this day. She is a fighter. She is also a woman who inherently understood that in order to walk free, she needed to acquire acceptance of the situation and forgiveness for all who are responsible.

This in no way means that what happened to Priscilla is acceptable or right, only that Violet has to come to terms in her heart with the outcome of that tragic day. She does not walk with hatred and bitterness, Violet walks with peace. She will not let loathing consume her. She is also grateful beyond measure for the love and support of her children and their spouses as she has sought healing. Her love for God, and her faith in Him, is immense. Violet knows, without a shadow of a doubt, that she will be with Priscilla again one day, and she cherishes the fleeting moments when she can feel Priscilla's spirit nearby.

Thank you, Violet, for allowing me to walk with you, and share in your journey. It has been an honor.

A DOG NAMED PEACHES

June 27, 1999 – October 20, 2010

Peaches was a purebred AKC registered Bichon Frise that I met when she was just a young dog, less than a year old. For those of you that are not familiar with the breed, Bichons are supposed to be soft, fluffy, pure white dogs that are calm, friendly, outgoing, and love to be around people. Peaches, however, was not any of these things.

Raised outside in an old chicken coop with a heat lamp and some straw for warmth and bedding, Peaches was an attention starved pup who was badly in need of a bath. Her proud owners at the time saw Peaches as a money-making venture; and they treated her as such. Peaches was living outside with her sister of the same litter named Gretchen, and the mate to the girls, another registered Bichon, named Buddy. The girls were born in June of 1999.

My first visit with the dogs was a shocking one for me. Being on good terms with the owners of the dogs, as they lived near the same rural community as us, we were looking forward to meeting the puppies. I had 3 small children at the time, no dogs of our own, and I thought that this would be a great experience for the kids. Perhaps it was a good thing to have dogs close by for the kids to go play with them, once in a while. However, one visit with them told me that this was not going to be so.

Not only were the dogs in a chicken coop, as I have said, they became completely hysterical and unmanageable whenever they saw people coming to visit. Consequently, when we entered the “kennel” the dogs went crazy jumping over each other, and the boys, to try to get up into our arms for attention. They were clawing, barking, and yelping. They were pawing at the air, pawing at our legs and the boys’ chests and faces; anything to be the one to get the closest to us. It wasn’t a great experience for anyone. The dogs were dirty, noisy, and very misbehaved and untrained. All we wanted to do was get out of that coop and get away from those poor dogs. I was horrified.

I will say though that out of the three dogs, Peaches did stand out of the crowd for me. There was something about her that I fell in love with right away. She was a bit more reserved, she hung back a little more, she had big beautiful eyes, and I really can’t explain the connection that I felt with her. Of course, these were all just fleeting thoughts and feelings that I had, and I paid them no heed; this was not my dog, and she was not going to be, right?

I recall only one or two other visits with them not long after the first visit, but honestly, I just could not bear to see the conditions they lived in or the lack of emotional care they received. Each time I saw the dogs they were dirty and out of control in that chicken coop. Attention starved, yes, but a person was unable to get near them because the dogs just would not calm down. And each time I saw them, Peaches was my favorite; something about her tugged at my heartstrings. Unable to change their situation, I had to ignore it and turn a blind eye to it. Nothing I am proud of, but I still do not believe there is anything I could have done to change it.

By all standards, the dogs' basic needs were being met and no one was breaking any laws.

A couple of years went by, and my life and the lives of the people around me began to change drastically. I was no longer staying in touch with the owners of the dogs on a social level at all, and I often wondered how they were doing. Sadly, I had heard rumors about how many puppies were being generated by Peaches and Gretchen. In my opinion, I felt the number to be too large, for it was indicating that the owners were not even skipping breeding cycles for the girls. This I believed to be a correct assumption, for I had noticed that their living quarters in the chicken coop were not even segregated, which would allow the stud dog access to the females at all times. Judgmental or not, I strongly disapproved.

A friend called me one day to say that the owners of the dogs were moving out of the province and could not take the animals with them. I pondered what their fate was to be next. I did not have to wait long, for my girlfriend had decided to buy them, sight unseen, to try breeding them for some extra household cash. I was a little surprised that my friend was buying these particular dogs, surely she knew their situation?! But, as it turned out, she had not ever been to the property, and was not aware of the dogs' living conditions. She was buying them based only upon the owner's friendly reputation within the community. Also, it was too late to warn my friend about the condition of the dogs, money had already exchanged hands. Well, my friend was in for a surprise.

The day that my friend took possession of the dogs I arrived upon her doorstep. A social visit perhaps, but part of me was very curious about the condition they were in, and I wanted to reacquaint myself with them. I think that I was hoping deep inside that I was wrong about my former assumptions and observations. I think I was hoping to find that I had been harsh in my opinions. I found, to my horror, that I had not been wrong at all. In fact, I discovered my friend in what can only be described as a near state of shock. The conditions of the dogs were deplorable. All three were filthy dirty, with their fur no longer any semblance of white, but instead a dull and dingy grey. It was matted to the skin, and very, very long, having grown out almost to the floor. They were particularly terrified of people, all people, especially men.

Peaches was the worst of the three in her terror, although I would not discover this until much later. It was Gretchen that I held in my arms that day, trembling and shaking and trying desperately to hide her head in my lap while my friend carefully cut all of her hair off with scissors. Gretchen's fur was too matted and dirty for even the clippers to cut through it. Peaches and Buddy had already been banished outside to a makeshift kennel in a former barn; all hopes of these dogs being house dogs had been dashed. My friend was disappointed beyond belief. Neither of us could believe that anyone could be so cruel and neglectful to a little dog, and then turn around and sell the dog as good breeding stock. It was a situation that just made you want to cry.

Despite my friend's best intentions, the dogs were simply unable to be rehabilitated. At least this time they were blessed to be owned by a woman who was extremely diligent about cleanliness. Their kennel, although in a barn outside, was always spotless whenever I saw it. Their new owner was fastidious about keeping their fur clipped as short as possible, and they were always sparking white as snow.

Free to run about the yard sometimes, during the daytime when my girlfriend was outside, I had a chance to catch a glimpse of the dogs now and then. However, they were almost wild at this point, they never really recovered from their initial upbringing and having no trust of strangers. Because they had never developed a relationship with me, I also fell into the wary category of stranger. Peaches, who was still my favorite of the group, tugged at my heartstrings as she would slink by me, head down, tail between her legs, headed fast for the nearest, safe, out-of-the-way corner. During those rare sightings of Peaches, for some reason I would always be struck by the strange thought that Peaches really hated to have her hair cut so short, you could always see her pink skin under her fur. She would almost look like a big rat with her nearly naked tail. And somehow, I just knew how much she really truly hated to look that way. She really did. She was embarrassed.

I believe that my friend did not do badly for the dogs at all, and that she did the very best she could with them. They were always well cared for by means of food and shelter. Their shots were always up to date. The dogs were always clean, and treated with kindness. But I also understood that my friend did not comprehend the emotional needs that they had. She did not connect with the animals in the same manner that I would. She did not understand the great longing these animals would have had for attention and love, in order to begin to heal the wounds that were in their hearts. She was unable to give of herself the time that was required on so many levels, and so the paranoia and the abnormal behaviors of all three dogs remained. It hurt me to see this, but again, these were not my animals. All I could do was wince and turn away in my own heart. It was painful to observe as I am a healer of the soul for all things, be they human or not. Suffering is hard for me to watch and endure when the cure and the solution are so obvious.

A couple of years passed by. The year was 2004, and Peaches, Buddy, and Gretchen were now around 5 years old. I received an odd phone call from my friend; it turned out that she was no longer interested in owning the Bichons. I suspect that she had realized that perhaps other dogs, maybe *any* other dogs, would be easier to deal with than those three Bichons, with all of their issues. She wanted to know if I was willing to take them.

To be fair, my friend realized that the dogs needed a lot of care, and she also was aware that they were getting older. I had no place for them to come home to right away, as these were not inside dogs. With that understanding, it was decided that they would not be sold to me, but rather given to me, so that I could afford to construct new lodgings for them. I, in turn, also understood that if I did not take the dogs, my friend felt that she had no other option but to put the dogs down or sell them, and my friend did not want to do that. I could not turn them away!

Almost immediately plans were put into place, and accommodations were created for three little dogs, outside of our home. I felt this to be a tragic solution, but after so many years of outside living and no formal training, I had absolutely no choice if I was going to take those dogs at all. Buddy was the worst of the three, being a stud dog and still fully intact (never neutered) he did not hesitate to lift his leg and urinate on anything and everything he came into contact with. This was unacceptable for any kind of inside living, and I couldn't bear the thought of trying to house train a 5-year-old male dog. As well, we had Jake, our Mini-Schnauzer stud dog, who was very well trained and living in the house with my females. The likelihood of numerous dogfights between the two males was obvious. So, a new home in the garage right beside our house was created.

My husband, Ray, was very thorough in the creation of two new kennels, side by side, in the far corner of the building. With sidewalk blocks for the floors, and wood and wire constructed walls, the dogs had very large, comfortable living quarters. They had access to a segregated run behind the garage by means of two doggie doors cut into the garage wall. With this setup, I was able to separate the girls from Buddy in order to give them a much-needed rest. The dogs would be able to see the house easily from the garage door whenever it was open, being mere feet away from our main entrance to the house. I was hoping this would allow them to become a little more socialized with people in general. Time to bring them home!

It was July of 2004 when I drove with a small kennel in my truck to go gather up Buddy, Gretchen and Peaches. Their now former owner was away for the weekend camping, and the dogs had been left in an outside run in the main part of the yard. I had been told to gather them up at my leisure, that the dogs were being cared for by another person while my friend was away. I arrived in the yard with a plan to take the dogs, one at a time in the small kennel, back to our home, returning each time until I had all three. Easy plan, or so I thought, but I couldn't have been more wrong.

I was very alarmed to discover that although the dogs had been left in an outside run, they were in the hot sun with little shade. Their food and water had run out, and they were in obvious distress as a result of this, for they had been there two days already. Apparently, the individual responsible for the dogs had forgotten them. Even more upsetting was the sight of Peaches, who was not only cowering in the corner, but extremely pregnant. She would not come near me at all, for she was terrified. I was a stranger.

Buddy was a little braver than the girls were, so he was happy to approach me once I was inside the enclosure and it became apparent to him that I meant him no harm. He was familiar with my scent, and, after a few minutes of making his acquaintance, it was not too difficult to scoop him up under my arm and place him into the little kennel to make the journey to his new home. Aware of the situation the girls were in, I stuffed my pockets full of food for them before returning once again. Still, it took some time before a shy and trembling Gretchen came near enough to me to sneak a piece of food from my outstretched hand, longer still before my patience had won out and she felt secure enough to eat the whole offering. I was able to first pet her head, and then her back, then pick her up and take her to the kennel in the truck, headed once again for the house.

My return trip found Peaches still in the corner, shaking hard and panting, but refusing to come anywhere near me. She was terrified and now she was alone, without her constant companions. I was very aware of her confusion. Although I had put water into their bowl upon my first arrival, and I knew she had to be very thirsty, I could see that she had not moved from the safety of her corner. I did not want to force her: I knew that her trust in me was vital to our future together. So, I sat down on the ground, hand outstretched, food in my palm, and waited. And waited. And waited a very long time.

A total of forty-five minutes passed before Peaches finally decided that I could be trusted. She crawled toward me, tail between her legs, shaking so hard that I wanted to cry just watching her. I did not move. I was almost holding my breath I was so afraid that she would change her mind. She came up to me, and very carefully and cautiously took a piece of food from my hand. I must have looked at her funny though, because it was then that she tried to turn away. At that point I had lost interest in the waiting game. I swiftly and painfully jumped up onto my stiff, numb feet, grabbed the poor dog, placed her in the kennel, and we started on the ride home. I'm sure that it was the longest ride of Peaches' life. She was in so much agony over her strange surroundings, the kennel, the truck ride, new sounds and smells, that she was making little noises of distress and nothing I could say to her would comfort her. I drove as quickly as I dared and jumped out of the truck the second I had it parked, running around to the passenger side.

As I opened the door to the truck, I paused before I removed the kennel. A strong feeling was warning me not to let her out into the garage before first making friends with this scared little creature. But what was I to do to gain her trust in so short a time? Instinctively, the answer came to me as I opened the door to the kennel. Peaches was sitting there, backed up as far as she could go, staring at me with wide, wary eyes. Trust no one, that's what those eyes said to me. How well I understood her fears. Murmuring quietly and calmly to her, and with a smile on my lips, I reached in and very carefully and very firmly began to do something I am sure no other human had ever done for Peaches before. I reached between her front legs and scratched her tummy. The look of shock on her face was priceless. Her eyes got big, she tried to back up but could go nowhere. I kept scratching and rubbing. "Oh, rub tummy", I kept saying, over and over. Soon a look of calm came over my dog, her eyes began to droop, and her head hung down in relaxation. Peaches was mine, and she was Home.

Especially important to Peaches were her own puppies, the litter she bore shortly after she came to live with us. She loved them in a way that I felt was a little different than that of my other dogs. It was almost as though those little puppies were creatures that Peaches felt safe to lavish her love upon. She exhibited such deep contentment when she was curled up with them that it almost broke my heart. I have always deeply regretted not keeping one of those puppies in our home for Peaches to be able to love for all time. It still brings a crushing grief to my throat and tears to my eyes that I did not give her that security. Peaches was a beautiful mother. I know that at least three of her pups passed away before Peaches did, all three in unusual accidents, and their owners had let me know this. I always felt a strange sort of comfort in that knowledge; I knew in my heart those pups would be there waiting to greet Peaches when her time here on earth was finished and she crossed over to begin a new journey.

I wish that I could go on to tell you that everyone in this story lived happily ever after, but of course, that is not the circumstance. Although the dogs did not have a miserable existence, I would be lying if I said that they were impeccably groomed, bathed little dogs in perfectly clean surroundings. I did try, that I will say. They did get haircuts, although I let their hair get a little longer than it should have, but I preferred that anyway for warmth. I did cut and file their nails. I was not prepared for the likes of Buddy and his constant peeing on every surface he could find, however. Nor was I prepared for the basic filth of the dogs if they felt that it was too cold in the winter to go outside to the bathroom. It was then that they would mess on their blankets, which were provided to them for warmth so that they would not have to lie on concrete floors. This was a frustrating situation for me, and an impossible situation to rectify. So, the reality is that their home was not perfect at all. They were also alone in the garage a great deal of the time. However, I was greatly encouraged to see the dogs' personalities blossom, and they began to live a life that was joyful.

Their daily life included a mile-long walk with my children, and regular interaction with me and whoever else happened to be out in the garage. At first, their reaction was to be fearful of anyone who entered the building that was not family. They would run to the farthest corner of their kennels, or even dash outside. Gradually, with consistency and their safe surroundings, all three dogs began to change. They were always acknowledged and greeted with kindness and patience, especially by me and my children. We really understood their special needs and their background. Everyone who met the dogs had been explained their unique situation, so that they, too, were always kind and gentle in voice and manner. Trust was growing in the Bichons, and it was amazing to see.

It took quite some time, but eventually the dogs were clamoring for attention at the wire enclosure and happily pawing at the air and waiting for you to come and say hello. Some behavioral problems were evident with Gretchen and Peaches, but these were mostly mental health issues, an emotional fragility of sorts that they never did recover from. Their inability to handle new or strange situations was always evident.

As time went on, I noticed that Gretchen was obviously the alpha female of the pack. This disturbed me because she was a little mean to Peaches, and I did not like seeing that treatment of any creature, let alone the dog that I had a soft spot in my heart for. Finally, after much debate, the decision was made to bring

Peaches into the house and integrate her into the family. Permanently.

This was a tough decision as I was fully aware that I was bringing in a six-year-old dog that had never been house trained and had huge social issues. Throughout their lives, whenever Peaches or Gretchen were about to have a litter of pups, and right through until the pups were weaned, they were all living inside the house of their owner. But during most of that time the adults were in the kennel or closely watched due to those very issues. Consequently, proper inside behavior was not a skill any of those dogs had learned. However, I was going to try my hardest to make Peaches a part of our family. I also felt bad for leaving Gretchen outside in the garage, but I knew that I could not leave Buddy out there alone without any company at all. He would surely die of loneliness.

I am sure Peaches thought that Heaven had come her way when she was moved into the house to stay. A clean, warm, soft bed and a loving family. On the other hand, it had never become more apparent that Peaches was such a traumatized dog until she came into our home. Loud noises terrified her. Strange people terrified her. Lights and freedom were overwhelming for her and mostly she preferred to stay in her kennel, until the day she died. The kennel was safety for her. We kept it in the corner of the dining room, one of the busiest rooms in the house, in order to acclimatize her to human activity.

Meal time was painful for Peaches and it was painful for the family to watch. Although the food dish was a mere ten feet away from her kennel, Peaches would slink out of the kennel, sprint around the door of the kennel to the wall, then creep along the wall a foot or two until she could run under the nearest chair. From there she would race under the table, then she would run along the wall again, make a dash for it out into the open floor space to the food dish, and snatch a piece of food. She would then turn around and retrace her steps, back into the kennel to eat that piece of food; a process that was repeated for every single bite she ate. It may have seemed cruel, but I refused to move her food into the kennel, or any closer to it. I knew she may never come out of that kennel again if I made it convenient for her, and she *had* to learn that she was safe.

Just the same, it took years before she would walk right out across the floor and sit in the corner by the food dish to eat. And even when she did do that, seldom was her tail out from between her legs. But, very slowly, she did learn to willingly come out of her kennel. It also took years for Peaches to come out and greet strangers, but she finally conquered that fear as well, eventually even coming to greet the men who were her greatest fear.

Regardless, Peaches was always happiest if she could put a barrier between herself and the world. My favorite picture of her is the one that hangs on my wall to this day, portraying Peaches with her back against the wall, leaning against her kennel, with the boys' winter boots forming a protective wall in front of her. She had squished herself into the corner and couldn't have been any happier at that moment in time, judging from the look on her face.

Amazingly, Peaches would do almost anything for me despite her anxieties: exiting her kennel when I called, and going almost anywhere I asked her to go. Her faith and trust in me were awesome, for she had so little faith in herself and others. She had learned the hard way, and at a very early age, that life can be so tough. I think Peaches loved me for that tummy rub, I think she loved me because I never raised my voice to her. I never lost my patience with her, even when it took two and a half years to fully housetrain her. Two and a half years! Thankfully, her biggest messes were puddles on the kitchen floor. No matter where I was in the kitchen, any time I turned my gaze to the kennel, Peaches was there, big eyes watching me - always watching me, full of love.

Instinctively, children seemed to understand what Peaches had suffered through in her lifetime and that she needed extra patience and attention. My boys would never hesitate to crawl into the kennel to sit with her, especially Zachary and Adam. The open space in my kitchen would fill with the emotion of peace, love, and contentment when they would sit with her. Many children that would visit also crawled into the kennel with her. Peaches was very loved.

I think that Peaches really knew that she had become a part of our family when we took her camping with us to the mountains, one time in 2006. We took one of our other females, Belle, with us, also. At first, Peaches was terrified to even be in the vehicle and had her head stuffed behind one of the kids sitting in the back seat of the truck. Eventually, after cautiously poking her head out a time or two and observing that Belle was actually enjoying the truck ride, Peaches decided that the ride must be safe, she was with family after all. Therefore, she also relaxed and enjoyed the ride. It was awesome to observe.

Once we parked the truck and trailer, we were concerned that we might lose Peaches somewhere in the bushes or along the river's edge, but she was very happy to run and play with Belle, and she never let us out of her sight. Every night she sat in my lap or in Ray's lap, curled up warm and cozy, watching the fire and being petted. In the best way possible, she was never the same after that trip. Her love for us became more evident, her humor more obvious, her contentment deeper.

Peaches blessed my family with her presence for six years. But, 2010 was one of the most difficult years of my life, and not only did I suffer the loss of my dear Jake in May, it was also to be that in October I would suffer the loss of my dear Peaches. Sometime in the month previous I had noticed that Peaches had begun to swell unusually large in the abdomen. Although she seemed to be suffering no pain, I knew in my heart that it was only going to be a matter of time, and so began the quiet waiting, the painful noting of precious moments passing by. On October 20, 2010 I knew that day had come.

As I drove my beautiful, patient, wonderful dog to see the vet just one final time, I began to talk to her and tell her everything that she had meant to me. It was just her and I that day; the significance of which I was yet to understand.

Because of what I had previously experienced and learned with my dog Jake and his spiritual shepherd, I explained out loud to Peaches that she needed to walk with her own particular shepherd, and not be afraid to go with him when she met him. It was then that my spirit guide corrected me, and I heard her voice inside my head explaining to me that Peaches' shepherd was female. I relayed that message to my dog, still not understanding the importance of that comment, and uncertain if Peaches could even comprehend my words, but through my tears I told her anyway.

I told her how I loved her, and oh, how I loved her, how I had always loved her, so much. I thanked her for everything she had done for me, for how hard she had tried to please me, and how well she had succeeded. As I spoke these words to her, once again I felt as though my heart was breaking. But my emotional pain was irrelevant, and I could not leave Peaches to suffer any longer, so on I drove, calmly, lovingly reassuring her all the way.

Once we arrived at the vet office, a quick look at Peaches confirmed to the veterinarian that indeed, the swelling was Peaches' old body just shutting down and it was time for me to say goodbye. I held onto Peaches, held her close and whispered in her ear as the vet, a wonderful lady, gave her the injection that would ease all of her pain. When her eyes were closed, and her physical journey was over, I wrapped her body in a warm blanket and carried her out into the car to take that final journey back home to be buried beside her friend and companion, Jake.

I sat in my car in the parking lot of the veterinarian's office, composing myself for the drive, when suddenly my composure began to crack. For there, in front of me, a vision appeared, swift and clear. It was my Peaches; she had already beaten me in a race to get back home. It was evident to me that she was not aware that she was in spirit just yet, but I could tell by the way that she carried herself that she knew that something was just a little, well, *different*. She was trotting out front of the house, right alongside the caragana hedge, headed towards the garden shed. Her tail was up like always when she was outside and happy, she was fit and slender, her coat was sparkling white and.... she had a puppy running in front of her, a white one, and a few trailing behind her. The sun was still shining, and the sky was very blue that day. Peaches was so happy. Then my vision was gone. And tears blurred my eyes.

My drive home was slow and careful. I took time to savor the sun and the sky and enjoy Peaches' last day here on earth. I let the tears fall. After her remains were lovingly shown to her faithful remaining doggie family so that they too could say goodbye, Peaches was carefully placed and buried beside Jake, and her grave was marked with a rock. I went into the house and methodically began to prepare supper as Life somehow continued on. My remaining house dogs, Belle, Holly, and Mystique were all quiet and subdued and steadfastly avoiding going into the kennel for any reason at all. They seemed to understand that Peaches was not coming home, and we all knew that the kennel was her bed. No one wanted to go into that bed without her.

I also caught myself glancing at that empty kennel, and my gut had wrenched. I was avoiding looking in that direction again as hard as I could, but old habits are hard to break. Consequently, while I was standing at the kitchen sink peeling potatoes, I caught myself once more glancing over my shoulder at what was to be an empty kennel. My throat closed off with emotion and I stifled heavy sobs when I realized that the kennel was empty no longer, for there lay Peaches, a vision in spirit form, curled up into a contented circle. She was surrounded by those pups I saw earlier, and gazing up at me with shining eyes. It was a sight so unexpected, so beautiful, and therefore so unbearably painful that I found myself tearing my gaze away and turning my back on that precious image out of pure grief before I could even stop myself. As quickly as I could I turned back again, horrified by my actions and anxious to regain that connection, but I knew what I would find: a kennel as cold and empty as it had been before. Regret fills me to this day for allowing that pain to control me, and allowing myself to close my eyes and turn my back upon such a brief and wonderful visit.

It was some days later, as I was able to look back on the last hours of Peaches' life with me, that I saw how perfectly God had planned that day for a little, humble dog.

I had originally wanted to wait for Raymond to come home from working up north in Fort MacMurray so that he too could say goodbye to Peaches, and be with me at the vet office to support me in my grief. But I had then decided *not* to wait for him, so as not to make Peaches suffer any more physical discomfort. I had also chosen not to bring the boys with me to spare them from the pain of putting down their cherished pet. But in hindsight, perhaps I was merely listening to a choice that God was making for Peaches: choices made to ease her journey into the spirit world.

Peaches needed to cross over into the spirit world without fear, she needed to cross peacefully. As much as she may have learned to love my husband Ray and my children, they were male, and somewhere deep in the recesses of her memory, men caused Peaches to be uptight and fearful. Remember, an angel told me that Peaches had a female shepherd to walk with her. Also, it was just me and a female vet alone in the room with Peaches, who, for a second, had seemed anxious, and then at once had become calm when she realized that it was no one but us three alone in that room. No men.

I believe that God loved even the smallest of His creatures, a simple dog, enough to understand her pain, and spare her that last worry in her final walk from this earth so that she could go in peace and without fear. I am grateful and honored to have been present with Peaches at the end of one journey, and at the start of another. Thank you, God. Thank you for the insight and the gifts you grant to me. Thank you for the joy of having Peaches in our life, and for all that she was able to teach us. Thank you for the love of a little dog. Please keep my Peaches safe and walk with her forevermore, let her know how much she was loved and still is today, and how very worthy she is. Amen.

Peaches (Photo by Shannon Harwood)

Afterword to "Peaches"

BUDDY & GRETCHEN

Not a lot of mention is made of Buddy and Gretchen's fate after Peaches was moved into our home and became a permanent part of our family. As they stayed living in the garage, it was never easy to involve them in much of a life with our other dogs, and training was always an issue. I was always unhappy with their living conditions. I never did agree with having small dogs outside, and I was always strongly against the way they were raised to begin with. Of course, had they been mine from the beginning they would never have been put outside in the first place. I will always be sad about this. But I did the best that I could for them under my circumstances, and I provided for them as I did for my other dogs. I wouldn't have had it any other way. Daily walks continued to be a part of their schedule unless the weather was totally unbearable for the kids and dogs alike. Grooming was never a favorite thing for either the dogs or me, although they for sure got a bath, nail trims, and haircuts.

Buddy and Gretchen did continue to thrive emotionally, and they were always happy dogs in that respect, becoming eager to greet even strangers. They learned that they were in a safe environment. They understood that they were loved by me. They made the best of their situation and they were brave little dogs with strong spirits.

One promise I had always said I would make to Gretchen, was that if Buddy were to die first that I would move her inside the house to be with our family as well, no matter how many dogs were here with us at the time. Well, exactly one week after Peaches died, on October 27, 2010 that promise came true.

I had noticed, only days after Peaches was put to sleep, that Buddy had started to lose large patches of his fur all over his body. Even though he appeared to be healthy otherwise, I simply could not leave a dog out in the garage in the wintertime with no fur. That would be beyond cruel no matter how many heat lamps he had. And so, for the final time in the year 2010, another trip was made to see our veterinarian.

The vet confirmed for me that Buddy had an internal issue going on which would become part of a larger problem later. Buddy was not a young dog, and his life had been hard enough, so putting him down was not a difficult choice for me. Emotionally I grieve for Buddy because I know that he could have had so much more than he did in his life. He was so smart in so many ways, and he deserved so much more than he ever got. Of course, whether or not it is all mine to carry, the guilt and the pain inside of me is there. But still, I hope that somehow I was able to help Buddy to heal, if even just a little, and to move forward on his journey.

I pray that somewhere out in the spirit world Buddy has a great, big, green field filled with flowers and trees, lots of companionship, and not a fence or a gate or a door in sight. I hope he is free. I hope he is joyful and does not carry an ounce of pain or memory of pain within him. I pray that he has love.

Buddy, too, was laid to rest here at home, beside Peaches.

Gretchen was brought inside that very same night, and my promise to her was fulfilled. She also has had to suffer through a bit of an adjustment period, but time has been easier on her than it ever was on Peaches. Gretchen seems not to suffer the same extreme paranoias that Peaches did. Lights and sounds are tough for her as they would be for a dog her age that has lived so long out in a quiet garage, but men are no longer terrifying to her, nor are open spaces. Her tail has not ever been between her legs and she walks with little concern. She is 11 ½ years old now, but for the most part took less than three weeks to housetrain.

Gretchen loves to be part of the family, and another thing she loves is soft beds. Her worst trait is that she prefers to hide in dark quiet corners, so we are constantly shutting doors to thwart her latest escape plans. The morning routine in our household, when I come out of the bedroom and greet and pat all of the dogs and we frolic and get rowdy, is her favorite time. Gretchen stamps her little feet and makes sure she gets equal attention, jumping up on me and making noise just to be sure she does. I am content inside myself that I could give her a chance to have a family, and to experience this love, even if it is so late in her life. To have kept my promise. And life goes on.

September 18, 2011:

Just when I had thought that my story had ended concerning my little Bichons, I find myself here once again at my computer with my heart in my throat. Gretchen's time has come much sooner than I had ever thought that it would, and for that reason, I mourn.

Sadly, I have to say that Gretchen had behavioral issues that ran much deeper than I was able to repair. Although she rapidly adapted emotionally to joining our human family and her doggie family in the house, her toilet training only lasted as long as she decided it would last, and, at any time she chose, all efforts to maintain that training would be disregarded. She became a master at urinating between the kennel and the wall where it would remain undetected for long periods of time, or on dark throw rugs in front of the door where wet boots and shoes would mask the appearance and odor. Once I became aware of her antics and took steps to correct her behavior, she would not hesitate to urinate on her bed if she were kenneled, and even on the floor in front of you if she chose. This would be followed by long periods of positive behavior and dry floors until something would trigger yet another round of negativity. I could never quite figure it out, what those triggers could be, as Gretchen was always treated with kindness and never a harsh word or hand.

In June of this year, out of desperation, I finally booked an appointment with my vet once again. I could not take the messes anymore, nor could my family. It was pretty awful. To my amazement, four days before her appointment, Gretchen stopped all of her bad behaviors completely and I could not bear to carry out the deed. It was almost as if she understood that we had already dug her grave out back, which we had. I laughed and said that maybe Jake, Peaches and Buddy had paid her a warning visit, and happily I canceled her appointment. Although Gretchen still had an occasional accident on the floor, I was glad to look the other way.

Then, for reasons I will never understand, once or twice in July Gretchen started to defecate on the floor. I tried to pretend it was not going to be an issue.

In August I had to have surgery that required a four-day stay in the hospital and a lengthy recovery on the couch at home. Gretchen did not like to be in the living room much, so she rarely had contact with me, and that was the beginning of her worst behavior ever. To add to the stress, I was only home for a week after the surgery and then suddenly re-admitted to the hospital with complications for another two weeks, with no one home but my teenage children. That did it for Gretchen and she went on a urinating, defecating rampage in the house. That also did it for my husband, Ray, when he came home after working up North for ten days. I came to the miserable conclusion while still admitted to the hospital that Gretchen's time had come and phoned my veterinarian.

On Friday, September 2, 2011 Gretchen was laid to rest. She was 12 years old.

The only way that I could say goodbye to my dog was over a two-way radio while Ray was driving her into town in his truck, for I was still confined to the hospital. I prayed to God and begged that she would be able to understand and recognize my voice and comprehend my words. I had shed so many tears the night before that I had hardly slept. I was devastated that I could not be there with her. Her appointment was at 2:00, and it was not long after that time I experienced a vision of all three of my little Bichons, with sparkling white coats and raised, happy tails. They were greeting each other with joyous, loud barking while sprinting around the green meadow at home, running in circles, just having the best of fun. Sobs catch in my chest and tears run down my face even now at the memory of it. I pray they have such peace.

My discharge from the hospital was unexpected, happening late in the evening of the 4th of September. It was not until the next day that I was able to sit in the brightness of the morning by myself, in my living room, in peace and quiet and collect my thoughts. I had no sooner sat down for a mere minute, and had hardly settled into my chair, when outside the window across the living room in front of me, movement caught my eye. I glanced at the beautiful Mountain Ash tree ripe and heavy with red berries, perfectly framed in my window, and caught my breath.

Swirling gracefully in the air in small loops and circles and stopping to land on a tree branch in perfect sight of me was what I now call "Jake's butterfly". Only this butterfly was perfect. Brightly colored and almost shiny it was so vibrant. The sun danced off of its wings, and it was very large in size. I had not seen one since the day Jake came to say good-bye to me.

Once again, I knew that this butterfly had a message for me: Gretchen was okay, she was fine. She had been delivered to the other side, she had made her journey, she loved me, and she understood. All was well with Gretchen. I could feel it. Relief and self-forgiveness washed over me, and tears flooded my eyes. I was going to be okay, too.

Buddy, Gretchen, and the boys.
(Photo by Shannon Harwood)

NOW IT IS TIME

My personal life has been heavily influenced and shaped by my spiritual encounters in the best of ways. I find that I am blessed to receive guidance in many areas of my life, if I am willing to listen. However, it would be very difficult to exist in physical form upon this plane if I were to be in constant, unending communication with those in spirit. There is a purpose for us to be here in the flesh, and, just like you, I must also learn from my mistakes and find rewards in my efforts. I cannot, and do not, receive words of guidance on every single matter that is laid before me.

I am always grateful for the visits from the spirit world, although some days I can be slow to see what is obvious and right in front of me. Despite the fact that contact is made with me, I do not always immediately recognize the importance of some of the messages I get or some of the visions I see. Chalk it up to human error on my behalf.

I do not ever wish to seem nonchalant about my gifts, however, since the spirit world is an everyday part of my life on some level or another, it is not unusual for me to be accepting of their presence and continue about my day without giving it much more thought. I try hard to be obedient when I feel that God is trying to show me something, and my wish is always to serve, but when it comes to myself and personal messages, I can be a little slow on the uptake. Fortunately for me, when I appear to be having an episode of unintentional blindness, the spirit world is usually very patient with me. I am sure that there has been more than one time in my life when I have sorely tried their patience, just the same.

Humor is also prevalent in the spirit realms, and more than once in my lifetime I know full well that my guides and loved ones have been laughing at me, or perhaps I should say, laughing with me. I have often remarked that if there were cameras in my home, people would think I were crazy should they observe me wandering about an “empty” house, giggling uncontrollably. But it happens more often than I would care to admit.

For example, I am phobic of spiders in my home, not that we have many. I have no issues with a spider doing his job outside where he belongs and I would never disturb one out there, but I am always on the alert for those little eight-legged arachnids in my dwelling. And they are removed by any means possible when they are discovered. As a result of this, I find myself in the habit of quickly scanning the walls and ceilings in my house whenever I enter a new room. I do it so frequently that it has become automatic, I am hardly aware that I am doing it, to be quite honest.

At any rate, quite some time ago now, I found myself pausing at the entrance to my kitchen before entering, intently scanning for spiders on the ceiling. Much to my satisfaction, there were none to be seen, and my relief was evident in my thoughts: “No spiders here!” But just as quickly as I had formed the words in my mind, a very masculine voice retorted, “Except for the one over your head.”

I laughed out loud as I stepped into the room, and replied with some sarcasm just as swiftly in return, "Yah, right!" Then I stopped and turned to look over my shoulder at the ceiling behind me: right at the black spider that was, indeed, fixed to the ceiling above the exact spot in which I had just been standing. I had no choice but to laugh out loud, and I could hear the laughter being shared with me.

The spirit world has also been very prevalent throughout my relationship with my husband Ray. I believe that events were set into place long before we ever met, that ensured our paths would cross. And I will admit, right here and now, that I never recognized how important a role Ray would play in my life when I first met him. Despite my blindness, the spirit world could see our destiny far clearer than I was able to, and they have been instrumental in not only pairing us together, but also in helping us to succeed as a couple since 2002.

I had started a new job as a server in a very old, large bar in one of the small towns located about twenty kilometers away from my acreage. I was working weekend shifts, and my starting weekend was busy. I enjoyed my shift, and don't recall anything out of the ordinary happening.

My second weekend shift, beginning on a Friday night, started normally enough for me. It was busy in the bar when I walked into the building, and my focus was purely on my upcoming duties. I did not see Ray seated at a table in the center of the room with a group of his co-workers, enjoying a drink after a long, hot day working on a pipeline in Southern Alberta.

However, according to Ray, the second I had walked into the pub that night and he saw me, he was struck with the immediate understanding that I was the one thing in the world that he had been searching for all his life. He didn't know why he felt that way, he didn't know who I was or anything about me, but he just knew that I was for him. He saw inside of my soul somehow, and he just *knew*. Ray said that everywhere he has ever gone, his entire life, he always looked for something, or someone; he didn't know exactly what it was, but he knew he was constantly searching. And when he saw me, his restless search was over.

I still remember the first time I laid eyes on Ray Harwood, and I was *not* struck with the knowledge that he was anyone important to me. It is funny how that first sight of him is burned into my memory just the same, as I have met many people over the years that I do not remember meeting for the first time. But I remember Ray. I remember coming up to his table and before he even said a word, I took one look at the cut of his jaw and the harshness in his face, and I thought to myself that this was the *most* stubborn man I had ever seen in my entire life. It would turn out to be a most painfully true observation, in more ways than one.

From the first moment I approached his table, Ray was determined to get to know me on a personal level, and I was every bit as determined to not have that happen. He may have felt a strong inner pull, but I did not. I simply was not interested, despite all of his attempts to strike up a friendly conversation. I was professional and pleasant, but I made it apparent that I was not looking for a new friend. I knew nothing about him, but it was easy for me to see that this was a man who carried a lot of baggage from his past. I had enough to deal with, and I did not want more.

Although I only saw Ray in the bar on weekends, and he seldom stayed for more than a few hours, he was persistent in his efforts to charm me. I was always sociable but distant when I would approach him, and inevitably I would find myself being rather curt and rude if he tried to flirt. It didn't seem to matter; his tenacity was nothing short of amazing. Ray would even come up to the till and order his drinks from me if I was not working the floor, and strike up a conversation. I can clearly remember seeing Ray with his arms folded up on the polished wooden serving counter as he leaned against it, chatting with me. He almost always wore a blue and white denim shirt, with cowboy boots poking out from under his faded jeans. He was pleasant and funny and polite, and I enjoyed our conversations, but I did not reciprocate any mutual attraction.

Eight weeks after he had first laid eyes on me, Ray asked if I would like to go out for a drink after work. He also ended up with my response, a swift and sure "no, thanks" and a stony-eyed smile. I honestly could hardly believe it. Was he ever going to give up? I turned away from Ray and began walking across the large, open room towards the serving station to go and fill his order. Then suddenly, without warning, the strangest thing I had heard in quite some time flashed through my mind. Clearly, and loudly, I heard the loveliest voice, right in my ear. A woman declared to me, "Now... it is time." That is all that she said. It stopped me dead in my tracks.

This voice was utterly beautiful. Crystal tone, perfect in pitch, and it reminded me of a bell. There was no mistaking what had been said, although I must admit I had no idea who said it. I was absolutely confounded, and in a split second silently but vehemently replied, "*Now*, it is time?! Now? You want me to talk to *him*?! Now?!" Silence was all that followed my query, and I understood that this was my answer.

When I have been shown without a doubt that the guides who assist me in the spirit world have a path for me to follow, I go down that path. I might not always have much time to think about whether or not it is my loved ones assisting me, or my holy spirit guides, but I understand that the source of the message is "good" and has a purpose. So then, I guess that you should not be surprised to hear that I only stopped for mere seconds when I heard that voice, and wondered why on earth "now" was time for anything with this person that I wanted nothing to do with. Then I took a deep breath, turned on my heel and marched right back to Ray Harwood, standing in the corner by the pool table. I looked that man straight in the eye, and, acting like the previous two minutes when I had just shot him down had not even happened said, "Hey, do ya want to go for a drink after work?"

I know he was shocked. I could feel it rolling off of him in waves and it was hard not to smirk. But although I had just surprised the stuffing out of him, his face remained straight as an arrow. Cool as a cucumber he merely looked down at me and said, "Sure, I'll wait around for you to finish your shift." And that was that.

As it turns out, we sat up all night talking, and we covered every topic we could think of to discuss. I was very surprised to hear that Ray's mother had died just before I met him, her funeral had been only one week before the night he first saw me enter the bar. I wondered if this might have been the female spirit who was urging me that "now it is time."

Throughout the evening, despite my silent requests for answers on how I could help the individual seated before me, or why I was supposed to be there, no response came. It was obvious to me that Ray was a very intense, headstrong individual, who carried a lot of unresolved issues, and I was having a hard time seeing past that.

At one point in our discussion, I found myself blurting out that I am a psychic medium, which is something I rarely do. In fact, I think I surprised myself when I said it. I am not sure what I was expecting him to say, but I had to giggle when he replied, quite enthusiastically, "Cool! I've never met anybody like that before."

As the conversation continued into the early morning hours, much to my surprise, I began to feel a connection with Ray unlike anything I have ever felt before. We were able to understand each other on a level that no one else ever had. Although we were very different from each other, we were eerily similar at the same time. We spoke aloud words the other was thinking and it was almost as though we could hear each other's thoughts.

We were still chatting when the sun came up. I think we were both shocked to discover all of the similarities from our past, despite the fact that he was a cowboy and I was a former biker/medium for God. I could go on at length about all that we learned about each other that night, but instead, I will only say that we have been together ever since. It was as though a magnet was drawing us together and we could not stay away from each other, despite very complicated circumstances in our lives. True to observation, Ray could be every bit as harsh and stubborn as I had understood he would be when I first met him, but I was also surprised to discover that he was a very sensitive, loving individual underneath the attitude. What astounds me is how oblivious I was to understanding just who Ray would become to me, and how I almost needed a frying pan upside my head just to get me to talk to him. Thank goodness for the words, "now, it is time!"

Winter came quickly in 2002. It was a chilly November evening that Ray and I found ourselves watching television together, snuggled up on the couch. Suddenly I became very aware of the fact that we were no longer alone in the living room, and at that moment I also caught a small movement out of the corner of my eye. I looked down towards the direction of my feet and there, at the other end of the couch, was sitting a short, tiny little lady. If you haven't realized it yet, it was a spirit lady sitting on my couch, and a rather interesting one at that. I could see that she was petite by the way that her feet did not touch the ground, but rather hung in the air, like mine do when the couch is too tall. Her hair was short and curly and carrot orange-red, her fists were clenched in her lap, and her jaw was set. What was even more fascinating to me was how this woman appeared to be right in the middle of a full-fledged silent temper tantrum. She was absolutely fuming mad, and every inch of her posture screamed that it was so. What I did not understand was why. Although she was staring straight ahead and not looking at me, I felt as though she was perfectly well aware of my presence and was ignoring me. Yet, at the same time, I did not feel as though she were angry at me. I also felt as though she was somehow comforted to be near Ray. Then it dawned on me - this was Ray's mother, Olive. Just as suddenly as I began to come to this understanding, weak human that I am, the television caught my eye momentarily and when I returned my gaze to the end of the couch, Olive was gone.

I was almost stunned at the vividness of this encounter with Olive, and I was quite astounded to see a spirit with such an attitude. I chuckled aloud when I had the thought that I now knew where Ray got his famous temper from. When I told Ray about the lady that I saw and what she looked like, he confirmed for me that Olive looked like that when she was younger. When I mentioned the temper tantrum, he enthusiastically nodded his head in affirmation and seemed quite familiar with that part of her personality. I found it all kind of funny. I'm not sure if she was showing me the temper tantrum because she was actually having one at that particular time, or if she was showing me that behavior so that Ray could positively identify her. Years later one of Ray's sisters also confirmed for me that Olive would completely ignore you if she was mad at you, and not talk to you at all.

It was closer to Christmas 2002 before I saw Olive again. Although I had not seen her since that occasion on the couch, recently I had become very aware of a strong spiritual presence in my life; an energy pattern that was not familiar, although it was comfortable. I also felt as though there was a new and different voice that I was hearing, but I didn't know who it belonged to. The voice also sounded suspiciously like the voice I had heard in my ear that night in the bar telling me it was time to go and talk to Ray. I became sure who the new voice belonged to, however, on the night that Ray was decorating the Christmas tree.

I truly had no idea at that time how hard our first Christmas together might have been for Ray. It was the first Christmas that his mother was not on this earth, as she had only passed away eight months earlier. His old holiday traditions were gone, and his new love felt little joy when it came to celebrating an exuberant Christmas. I know that he carried a void in his heart and I am sure that his mother also knew this. Ray was trying to be cheerful just the same as he was putting up the lights and bows on the tree, and I sat on the couch observing him and waiting for my turn to dress the tree with ornaments.

I suddenly noticed movement in the air above his shoulder and looked up to see Olive hovering in the air behind Ray, but she looked totally different than she did the first time I saw her. This time she was looking down on her son with love and happiness and contentment. Her face was glowing with such pride and tenderness I could have wept. Her appearance was also vastly different this time around; her face was rounder, her hair was no longer orange but light in color and straighter, and I could see that she was heavier. I could only see her from the chest up. I marveled at what I was observing, for Olive truly was rosy of cheek and almost appeared to be glowing she was so radiantly happy. I noted with some surprise that her energy pattern was indeed that of the unfamiliar entity that had been nearby.

I remember that she did stay for a little while, not a very long time, but it almost seemed as though she was visiting with her son and enjoying our family. It was a lovely time for me too, because as weird as this might seem to you, I got to enjoy watching, and therefore learning, about Ray's mom. I meet many people for the first time after they have crossed. I told Ray that his mother was there with him, and I hoped it was of some comfort to him that she was near. It was then that Ray told me that Christmas was one of his absolute favorite times of the year and his mother's too, and how his big family used to gather together and there was lots of baking and music and laughter. Personally, I found Christmas rather difficult and almost painful at that time, and always had. Our Christmas was small and quiet, and suddenly I understood why Ray's mother had been there with her boy. What a lovely gift.

Olive remained a steady presence in our lives for the first few years we were together. It was amazing how involved she became in our relationship. She was not there to interfere, but to assist us with communication and achieving resolution with stressful and complicated family situations. Ray had some very ingrained, damaging opinions about himself and some of his past relationships. Olive was instrumental in helping me to understand the core issues, which, in turn, were helping me to deal with some of Ray's emotional reactions, helping him to find resolution and healing.

Although I am a medium, my beliefs are not anything that I have expected Ray to accept in his own life. I have never tried to force my opinions on him, my children, or anyone. I do not have any expectations that he should have to live up to concerning spirituality. I believe that Ray does have a strong belief in God, and I know that he believes me when I talk about my personal experiences with the spirit world. I know that he has had some very interesting occurrences of his own with spirits, both good and bad. I have always believed that God would show Ray proof of His existence and His spirit world when He saw fit to do so. I have no need or desire to provide proof of the spirit world; I am happy to leave that to God, in His control, and serve as His instrument when He sees fit. However, I certainly never expected God to show Himself to Ray as obviously as He did.

It was springtime in 2004 and our day began much like any other, although we had happily made plans to go up into the mountains for the day, quadding. Ray wanted to return to the site of an ancient landslide we had found on a previous trip on the quad, the rocks there fascinated him and he wanted to bring some more home for landscaping. I remembered the slide area well, there was an amazing, awesome, tremendous energy up there that I had not ever felt to such a degree before: I knew that this was a special place. Although I was eager to re-visit the area, I was dreading having to ride down the rough trail that led to the secluded landslide. The trail was a difficult, narrow pathway. It became so treacherous in some spots that I was required to ride on the right fender of the quad just to keep some weight over the rear tire that was most firmly on the ground, because to our left the trail had started to wash away down a steep mountainside. To keep myself calm and focused so that I could try to enjoy the ride I had begun to pray to God, asking Him to let my guides be near and to protect me and Ray. I began to switch my concentration inward as I became aware of the presence of higher spirits around me and I was curious to see who was there with me.

Almost immediately I saw Sharimia, who is my main guide, standing off to one side to allow a man that I did not recognize to come closer to me. He was a very handsome man, who had a beautiful glow to his features. His hair was a golden sandy brown color and it was cut short. I could see that he was smiling happily at me. I felt very reassured by his presence and that of Sharimia, and I was determined to keep my attention on them rather than the rough ride.

I don't remember any specifics concerning the conversation that I shared with these spirits, but I do know that it took me very little time to tune into the fact that the male spirit had an amazing sense of humor and he was quite entertaining. I was enjoying myself immensely when, very unexpectedly and right in front of my eyes, there appeared floating in the air a word that looked as though it had been written with white-hot electricity. The letters were large and jagged around the outer edges and they seemed to pulse and shift with energy. They spelled out the word EON and as soon as I had taken notice of the word, I heard the male voice in my head say, "My name is Eon: E-O-N".

Well, I can assure you that I found all of this to be quite remarkable. I had not ever experienced anything such as this, especially not floating, electric words. I wondered why this man's name was so important that he should show it to me in such a dramatic way, but suffice it to say I had received the message clearly, or so I thought. Obviously, this male spirit had a name and it was Eon. However, it soon became apparent to me that Eon still had something he was trying to communicate to me, because mere minutes later I heard his voice in my head again, "My name is Eon: E-O-N". Once again, I saw the floating electric letters hanging in the air. I communicated back to this entity with my thoughts that I understood and that I had gotten the message clearly; his name was Eon.

My wonder and amazement at the unique experience I was having was starting to wane as this spirit repeated once again the whole process from beginning to end, and then again. Clearly, I was missing something crucial, but I just did not comprehend what it could be. Upon hearing Eon repeat his name and show me the letters for the eighth time I was losing my patience, didn't this guy get it? Couldn't he understand that I could see and hear him clearly?

It became obvious that he could indeed understand me well, for Eon was displaying a large, friendly smirk on his face like he knew something I did not, and he appeared to be finding my frustration amusing. Seeing that smirk only added to my aggravation. I began to seethe a little when Eon once again repeated the sequence in my head.

"What-the-heck?" I thought to myself and to Eon, "I don't understand what else you are trying to say. I get it, I understand, you've introduced yourself to me. Your name is Eon. E-O-N. What else do you want me to understand?" For a tenth, and final time, I saw and heard Eon's name, and as I lifted my head heavenward and rolled my eyes to the sky in utter annoyance, comprehension suddenly flooded over me - and now I was the one looking utterly stupid.

For crying out loud, this spirit wanted *me* to introduce him to Ray! Really, truly, seriously?! How could I have been so sightless? How could I not have seen that? The humor of the situation did not escape me, how silly I must have looked, like a child kicking her heels. I saw Eon looking down at me, grinning openly and nodding his head. Silly, yes, but funny too, and we both laughed at the miscommunication.

One might wonder why Eon chose that way to make his request to me, but I believe that it was done in a manner that I could not deny or confuse since it was so simply and plainly shown to me. Hence, I would have no room for doubt as to what was needed - the introduction of Ray to Eon. Although I did not understand why, I knew that this introduction was important. I was also very grateful to have such certainty with this message; I have always been taught that it is up to each individual to seek out the names of their guides *themselves* and not to rely on another to do it for them. So, this contradiction of what I have been taught needed to be obvious and clear before I would have ever been obedient and done as I had been requested to do. Now that I understood what was required of me, I bided my time and waited patiently for the right opportunity to pass this information on to Ray. I knew that I would not have to wait long, and I focused my attention back on the trail.

It was not long before the trail opened up to a vast expanse of lichen-covered rocks and boulders that once had been the top of a mountain which stood in the background of the immense debris field at its feet. The air pulsed with an ancient, powerful energy that was awe-inspiring, almost breathtaking. This energy seeped through my body and into my spirit. I felt a deep calm inside of me and experienced a profound connection to the raw energy that surrounded me. Ray and I began to pick our way through an endless swath of dense, rough stones, stopping every now and then to examine the more interesting ones.

At one point I came walking up behind Ray as he was gazing at the mountain before him, and without hesitation I said to him, “Ray, your holy spirit guide is here with you and he wants me to introduce you to him. His name is Eon, E-O-N,” I said and I continued moving past Ray onto a flat spot of ground that lay before me. Ray and I have a telepathic connection that can be very strong and clear some days, so it was not surprising to me to hear his voice in my head, loud and sarcastic, saying “Yeah right, *prove it*.”

Well, God answered Ray’s challenge immediately. Without warning the bright blue, cloudless sky right above Ray reverberated with a resounding thunderclap, KA-BOOM! The ground beneath my feet shook, and I threw back my head and laughed into the air, not even pausing in my stride or looking back to see Ray's reaction. God proved it alright.

Ray is a firm believer in Eon now, I can assure you.

What I found amazing was how God answered Ray. I, myself, would have been curled up in a ball on the ground waiting for God to strike me with a lightning bolt for being so disrespectful. God decided instead to make the ground shake with His answer. I understood at that moment, as I believe now, that my husband has an important journey to undertake spiritually. I would love to know what his purpose ultimately is. I cannot say how many times I have felt as though a huge spiritual battle was raging around Ray, a battle between good and evil struggling over Ray's salvation. I think that Ray could be an amazing spiritual teacher, and evil knows this. Evil also knows that if Ray and I could come together and work in the manner that God intends, with complete trust and harmony, without the painful baggage from his past, we would be an unstoppable force for God and we could change many more lives. Evil does not want that, either.

As our afternoon at the landslide was coming to an end, we loaded up the quad with a heavy selection of rocks to take back home with us. We made it out of the worst part of the trail on our return trip with success, and the narrow path had widened into an easier track to travel. Rain started to fall and I was hoping it would not become a downpour. Periodically my mind would wander over the events of the day; it truly had been an awe-inspiring, life-changing moment in time for both of us. The ground was becoming slick with water as the rain became heavier and I was growing mildly uneasy about the remainder of the ride to the truck, worrying about the deteriorating conditions.

We approached a short steep hill, and I hung on for the climb, not too concerned about the ascent as it was not what we would consider a challenging hill. I was more miserable about the rain. We had almost crested the peak as Ray shifted gears, and in one split second that gear missed the shift, popped into neutral, and the quad began swiftly rolling backwards down the hill. We were unable to stop on the steep wet grade. I tucked my head down and pushed it into Ray's back, the terrified thought racing through my mind that we were loaded down heavy with rock and would probably flip over the quad. I hung on for dear life as Ray was trying urgently to regain control of the machine, when it abruptly stopped its descent only three-quarters of the way down the hill. I jerked my head up, curious to see what could have caused us to halt so suddenly, and jumped off the quad to have a better look.

At first, it appeared that the quad had been high-centered on a log. As Ray drove the quad up the hill and off of the "log", we realized that somehow we had rocketed backwards down the hill in perfect line with a hard, dead spruce tree lying on the ground that still had its sharp, pointed top. As we rolled backwards over it, the trunk of the tree had gotten wider as we approached its base. Soon it was so wide that it had forced the quad to stop in mid-roll with the axles hung up on this dried-out length of spruce wood. This is what saved us from landing at the bottom of the hill and possibly flipping over with the jolting force of that abrupt stop. But what also became sickening to realize was that had this spruce tree with its sharp, hardened tip been pointed up off the ground instead of lying flat on the earth, it most certainly would have impaled me as we raced backwards into it. It was a chilling prospect to consider. I was giving thanks to my Creator once again for His protection, and my life, as I climbed up to the top of that hill and waited for Ray to drive the quad fully off of the tree and up the hill once more. I wasn't interested in riding that part of the trail any longer.

Looking back on the last twenty-one years of my life with Ray, it has been more than obvious to see the effort that has been made by the spirit world to assist us in our spiritual development, and our growth together as a couple. Not only do our holy spirit guides walk with us, our loved ones do as well, and they have the best of intentions for us. They try their hardest to aid us in even the smallest of endeavors if it will be of benefit to us. I am truly grateful for their support and assistance, and most especially for their persistence, especially on the days that I am oblivious to some of their messages!

Shannon on the quad loaded down with rocks, grateful to be alive, and headed home. (Photo by Ray Harwood)

THE BRIEFEST OF ENCOUNTERS 2

There have been many instances that I have experienced encounters with the spirit world that were brief and sudden; fleeting moments in time that have taught me a great deal very swiftly. I might be overwhelmingly aware of an entity for mere seconds, yet the information that is imparted to me in those moments can be substantial. Many of these occasions leave me in awe of the lessons I am blessed to receive. Because these visits are so short it is impossible to relay them in a lengthy manuscript, therefore I compile them together as one, in no particular order, so that you might also partake of my experiences.

≈

March 23, 2021. Rosie H. died today, early in the morning, after a lengthy battle with many health issues. Rosie was a very strong woman who had lived a hard life. Although her body was frail, and her speech was slurred and hard to understand, her mind was sharp right up to the end. The lines on her face told the story of a life that had been difficult and sometimes harsh, but Rosie was beautiful.

Rosie's husband, Lyle, called to tell us just after 9AM of her crossing. While he was speaking on the phone with me, I had a sudden vision appear in front of my eyes. It was of Rosie. Her features were very refined, and her skin was clear and practically glowing. Rosie's hair was appearing to be shoulder length, straight, and shiny; very different from the short and curled hair that

I was accustomed to. She was almost unrecognizable to me, as I had met her much later in her life when she was considerably older. Rosie was looking upwards, with her neck stretched out and her head flung back as she was zipping along through the air, literally flying around with her arms stretched out behind her. Yes, much to my astonishment, Rosie was *flying*. I could see the joy in her features. I could feel her ecstasy at her new found freedom. I could feel the deep peace and contentment that radiated from her as she surveyed the beautiful, scenic, earthly sights below her. I felt a powerful emotion which translated to words, that Rosie was having fun flying. Literally just that. Fun flying. I was amazed at what I was seeing, but reluctant to share this sight with Lyle, who was so fresh in his grief and shock that he might not be able to process what I was saying. Indeed, I must also admit to feeling a bit foolish to have to describe to anyone that I had just seen a spirit flying through the atmosphere, looking somewhat like the fictional character Peter Pan. I even questioned my sanity for a mere moment because the vision I had seen was so unusual. However, it had also been an undeniably clear and remarkably vivid sight. I decided to keep silent about what I had witnessed, for the moment.

Later in the afternoon, I was chatting on the phone with one of Ray's sisters, Bonny Lou. She had been one of Rosie's closest friends and confidants. I had no qualms about sharing with Bonny Lou the vision I had received of Rosie, for Bonny is very comfortable with the fact that I am a medium and I have shared many experiences with her. I was describing to Bonny how Rosie had looked, and explaining how I knew by her appearance that she had been very ready and prepared to cross over. Rosie had come to terms with, or resolved, a lot of her issues and she was ready to meet God. Bonny Lou was very interested in what I had to say about Rosie, so I took a chance and hesitantly relayed to Bonny the rest of the vision, about Rosie having fun flying. I was not prepared for the emotional, incredulous, and joyful reaction that I got from Bonny Lou when I shared that vision with her. She was absolutely shocked at the words coming from my mouth, but overwhelmingly happy to hear them.

You see, unbeknownst to me, one month prior to Rosie's crossing, she had shared with Bonny the most beautiful of dreams she had just experienced. She dreamt that she was flying. Flying over all of the places that had once been important to her. Flying. Having the time of her life just soaring around. The dream was important enough to her that she had told Lyle and Bonny Lou about it. She felt as though God was showing her not to be afraid of the death of her physical body. She had no way of knowing that the dream was a prophecy, and today that prophecy was fulfilled.

Rosie is flying and looking down on us all. Ready to move forward with freedom and joy, safe in her surroundings and no longer held to the constraints of her ailing physical body. This confirmation from Rosie to her loved ones gave her the ability to share the message that she is happy, free, and at peace. Thank you, God.

Bonny Lou volunteered to tell Lyle of the vision I had seen, I felt too awkward to try to explain it to him. I understood that because of the dream Rosie had shared with Bonny and Lyle, hearing of this vision from Bonny Lou would only enhance the importance of that dream for Rosie's husband. I knew that I had been correct with my decision when I read the public statement that Lyle had posted on social media the following day, a letter to his sweetheart:

"What does one do when the love of your life gets her wings and flies away? My angel has earned her wings and left me in this ungodly place. Fly on my love, for we both know we will fly together one day. I will never replace our love, for there is no one else like you. You've touched the hearts and souls of everyone you knew. I couldn't count the people. You thought to say those magic words, I need to say to you that I love you honey. Yes, fly on my darling angel but know that we will meet again. A stronger love will never be, as you're also my best friend. I love you my Rosie. P.S., fly slow, I'm getting old."

What a touching, heartfelt confirmation that Lyle posted that day. The message from Rosie had been heard. I rejoice for receiving such an unusual, visual gift that verified the truth of God's promise to Rosie; that her physical death would not be painful and that indeed, she would be free to fly, just as her dream had shown her. It has been a valuable lesson to me as well, to not be fearful of passing along a message that to all accounts seems strange and difficult to explain, regardless of my hesitation. Had I stayed silent, so much would have been lost. God bless your journey, Rosie.

≈

For over twenty-three years now I have had a great relationship with another couple, Bill and Becki M., who also welcomed Ray with open arms when he came into my life a few years later. Although we do not see them as often as we should, which is so often the case in today's busy lifestyle, Bill and Becki are important people in our lives and we cherish our friendship. They will do anything to help another in their time of need, no matter the situation. They have also suffered some huge losses in their lifetime, which only adds to their compassion and empathy for others. They are a unique couple with a very large family, and their house is seldom quiet or empty.

Bill's health began to rapidly deteriorate at some point in the summer of 2020, and after returning home from a lengthy hospital stay, he was not ever physically as strong or energetic as he used to be. I only saw Bill a few times after that, all the way into 2022, for so many complicated reasons, including my own health issues and surgery. Because I had not seen him for so long, I had no idea that Bill had been declining as much as he had been.

On Wednesday, November 16, 2022, I was surprised to received a phone call from Becki telling me that her beloved had been whisked away that morning by ambulance to Calgary, where he was waiting for medical attention. It was determined that Bill was experiencing multiple organ failure.

All of Bill's family that lived nearby raced up to the hospital as quickly as they could to sit with him and keep vigil at his bedside. Fortunately, the remainder of his large family were able to speak with him by phone before he passed away on the morning of Friday, November 18th. The suddenness of his crossing was shocking and very overwhelming for everyone.

Bill was a man of deep faith who loved God and tried hard to abide by His word. Because of this, Bill was not afraid of death. He understood that not only would he meet his Maker once again, he welcomed the fact that he would once more be reunited with those he loved who had crossed over before him. Bill likewise knew, without a doubt, that he would continue to see his loved ones left behind on the physical realm. He understood that although his spiritual body would embark upon a new path, it would also include his family. His wife, Becki, also shares the same faith, and this gave her the ability to remain exceptionally calm and accepting of all of the events and changes that were now taking place in her life.

Saturday afternoons in my household can be a time when we enjoy mindless hours watching nothing in particular on television, especially if the weather is cold and we are not able to go for a ride on our motorcycle or do yard work. Such was the case on the afternoon following Bill's death. Home improvement shows were playing, and the wind outside was blowing with gusto. My mind was relaxed and unfocused, idly wandering upon a multitude of subjects, only to be suddenly replaced by a sharp, clear vision of Bill M. standing before me.

Bill looked simply amazing. I could hardly contain my delight to see him looking so trim and physically fit. He even cast a slight glow, appearing to be a very pale blue-white translucent aura around him. Although his hair appeared to be silver with age, his physique was not that of an elderly man, nor were there lines on his clean-shaven face. He was positively beaming, with a grin that spread ear to ear, as he stood behind Becki with his right hand upon her left shoulder. He appeared to be engaged in very animated conversation, for he was openly laughing and gesturing with his right hand stretched out in front of him. I could not hear what was being said, but I did not need to know. It was more than obvious to me that Bill was just fine, he was with his family, he was overjoyed to be with them, and he had shed his earthly troubles. He had obviously been freed of any past transgressions and was eager to continue forward.

I saw Bill for what seemed like a fraction of a second before my sight cleared and the television was once again my main focus. I became aware of the time on the clock, and I realized that there would be little time for me to contact Becki and relay to her the news of Bill's visit, as we had made plans to head to the city late that afternoon and it was almost time to get ready to go. I patiently waited the next day for the right moment to talk to Becki in private, and I did not have to wait long.

The timing of Bill's visit could not have been more perfect, as it turned out. When I told Becki what I had seen, and that it had been in the afternoon of the previous day, she replied with a small chuckle that indeed, the family had been having a very lively conversation at that time. She said that there was plenty of light-hearted discussion about which personal items should be left in the casket with Bill, who had been somewhat of a jovial prankster himself whenever he got the chance. Jokes were being made about leaving Bill with a cheeseburger, a bag of nails, and some cartoon-character pyjama bottoms. (All of which did make it inside the casket.) Without a doubt, Bill would have been present for *that* particular conversation if he had any say in the matter at all. The gesturing and the laughing were something Bill would have definitely been participating in: "bring it all on!" Lovely, indeed.

Then it was Becki's turn to make me cry. She shared with me a beautiful story about the morning that Bill had passed. She was at home, sleeping in her recliner chair, when suddenly she heard Bill's voice, loudly exclaiming, "Honey, honey!!".

"What?" she cried out, momentarily thinking him to be in the room with her, but he was not.

"I'm gonna go now," he said, his voice ringing in her ears.

"It's okay, Bill, you go," said Becki. "Go be with God, free from all of the pain. You go, it's okay." And with that, he was gone, and deafening silence was all that remained.

Next to be awakened by Bill's voice was his son, Mackenzie, who was sleeping in a motel near the hospital where Bill lay. His brother, William, and his wife Melissa, were with their dad while Mackenzie rested. "Son, son!" called Bill, "Wake up now, it's time to go to Mom. Go to Mom now. She needs you. Don't stay here any longer," he said. And once those words were spoken, he departed.

Minutes later both Becki and Mackenzie received a call from William. Bill was gone. As Becki spoke, I shed silent tears for them all. What a beautiful, bittersweet gift to hold on to.

The day of Bill's funeral was cold and blustery, but inside the funeral home it was warm and comforting, and Becki and her family were holding up well. Bill's casket was the most unusual I have ever seen, as it was designed as a graffiti casket. Everyone was invited to write their final words to Bill in colorful markers, all over the casket. Many people did so, including me. I found it a fitting tribute to such a colorful character of a man.

During the memorial, Becki was sitting in a chair beside her husband's casket, with the congregation in the pews behind her. Without a doubt, Bill was standing behind his wife, his hand on her shoulder once more; that scene flashed briefly in front of me. The service was simple, without a lot of pomp and ceremony, but it was very beautiful in its simplicity. At one point there was a slide show of pictures on a large screen at the front of the room. I could see that Bill was partaking with us, enjoying the memories.

What happened next was shocking to me, only because it was such a raw, emotional, unexpected moment. I observed Bill turn away from the screen, towards his beloved family and friends, and although I could not hear his thoughts, I could feel his emotions. He was overcome with a sudden understanding, and very deep insight into the fact that everyone at his memorial was there because they really truly loved him; far greater than he had ever comprehended before.

It was not that Bill didn't understand he was loved, he did. But Bill is a very humble man, and he did not think too hard about whether or not he was loved. He accepted that he was loved, but he did not credit himself with the fact that he made people fall in love with him because of who he was and how he treated others. He did not think of himself as particularly cherished and now he could truly see that indeed, he was. Very cherished. Very loved. Very missed. This reality moved that man beyond words, and as I watched him, he briefly lowered his head and wept. Tears were falling from his eyes onto the floor as he bent slightly at the waist, with his hands on his knees as if to support himself, and embraced the love directed at him by an unseeing crowd. It did not take him long to regain his composure however, and the last time I saw Bill he was wiping the tears from his eyes and standing strong and straight once more. Rejoicing.

I was so grateful to be able to share such comfort with Becki, after the ceremony. Grateful for the strength that was granted to her with this news. Grateful for the gift that was granted to me, a gift that facilitates healing. Grateful to see such love.

Thank you, God, once more.

Bill M. (photo supplied by Becki M.)

≈

One of the things that I love about working with the spirit world is the fact that no two messages are ever the same. Of course, there are always instances in which those who have crossed over simply wish to express their love and good wishes to those left behind; a reminder that they are not gone and that their loved ones are not alone. But quite often those messages of love, although simple, can lead to something much more substantial for the recipient of their messages.

Such was the case for a young lady named Hailey C. Hailey is a close relative of my husband, Ray, and I have known her since she was just two years old. At the time of this writing, she is twenty-one. Unfortunately, due to complicated relationships within the family, my relationship with Hailey is merely on a casual basis. I can go many years without seeing her or speaking to her, even though our relationship is quite comfortable and not strained.

Hailey's father passed away quite suddenly and unexpectedly in February of 2022. I did not know her father, Michael, very well, and I hadn't spoken to Hailey in quite a long time, so other than sending prayers for both of them I remained silent. I was not connected to Hailey in any way, not social media or any other means, so had little option in the matter.

Months passed by quite swiftly after Mike's crossing. Life on an acreage with animals and gardens is never boring, and I often find myself pulled in ten different directions all at once, leaving me with little time to focus on one thing for very long. I have found that quite often, when my attention is split between several tasks, the spirit world likes to announce its presence at those very inopportune moments. I believe that this element of surprise and shock during the times I am least expecting contact is quite beneficial. I can have little doubt as to what I am currently experiencing, because two seconds previously I was just peeling potatoes and thinking of little else besides feeding chickens, or whatever was next on the list.

Such was the case late one August morning, as I was washing fresh eggs out of the coop, methodically checking off the daily tasks that had been completed and those that were yet to come. I swiveled on my heel to turn and grab a towel off of a nearby chair, when to my surprise, I almost collided with the spirit of Hailey's dad, Michael. He stood before me in blue jeans and a T-shirt, looking down at the floor and shuffling his feet. I was so unprepared for that vision I felt my eyes growing wide with shock. Indeed, I suspect my appearance was rather comical in that split-second, mouth hanging open, saucer-shaped eyes, and wet, dripping hands. However, my mood quickly grew sombre as I realised that Mike appeared to be quite serious and solemn looking. I knew his visit was very important.

Understanding the significance of Mike's visit, I was a little surprised to hear him simply say to me, "Please tell Hailey how much I love her." That was the beginning and the end of the message, there was nothing more. Just as quickly as he appeared, Mike disappeared from my line of sight and I was left standing alone in my kitchen trying to digest what I had just seen and heard.

I now also had a little bit of a situation on my hands, for as I have stated before, I had not been in touch with Hailey in years. I did not feel comfortable having my husband reach out to Hailey on my behalf, for I did not want her to feel obligated to talk to me. This was the same reason I did not connect with her on social media. I figured that she would accept any invitation I sent out to her, but I would never know if it was because she was interested in having a relationship with me or if it was out of family duty. I had no way of knowing how she would react to what I had to say, although truthfully, I have not ever had a bad experience with anyone who has received a message. Deeply troubled by the circumstances but unsure of what to do in regard to the message from Mike, I did the only thing that I could, and that was to pray about it.

I explained to God from the depths of my heart the issues I felt were hindering my ability to reach out to

Hailey. I told Him of my willingness to pass the message along, but that I was unsure how to go about doing that. I asked Him to please show me the direction to travel in this instance, and then I let the matter go. I knew, if it was important, this matter would be resolved.

It did not take long for my answer to come.

No more than three weeks after my visit from Mike, without warning, I received a request from Hailey to connect with me on social media. I almost fell over I was so incredulous. Of course, I responded to that invitation immediately, with a joyful heart and grateful prayers to God for answering me in this situation. The path I needed to take was now clearly laid out for me. It was almost impossible for me to remain patient and not immediately reach out to Hailey with news of her father, but I did not want to overwhelm her mere minutes after connecting. I tried stoically to bide my time.

Mike was not willing to be so patient, however, and the same day Hailey and I made contact, Mike was near me once more, making his presence obvious and being very insistent that I call his daughter. I understood completely his urgency, he knew quite well that I had heard him and received his message, and Hailey was so important to him that he could hardly wait for her to know that he was truly nearby. I let him know that my intent was to reach out on the upcoming weekend, not to fear. I am not so sure that he believed me, however, because Michael returned time and time again in the following days to urge me to call, repeating Hailey's name more than once. I had to admire his persistence; he almost drove me crazy, but I bided my time.

Later that week I was once again aware of Mike's energy pattern in the room with me. Once I acknowledged him, he showed me a vision of Hailey sitting together with Mike on their living room sofa when she was just a young girl, they were facing each other and laughing and laughing. It was a moment of pure joy between a father and daughter, and I stifled an emotional sob for Hailey's loss. Next, Mike let me feel very strongly the fact that Hailey was quite concerned for her father's well-being since he had crossed over. She was very worried, and this was another reason that Mike had appeared. He wanted to relieve those concerns.

The weekend came quickly enough, and I reached out by text to Hailey, who seemed quite happy to have heard from me. I laughed when she told me that she had just seen my profile for the first time online, and that she had felt compelled to reach out to me. In no time at all she had relayed her number to me and we were chatting on the phone. Gradually, after catching up on current events together, I began to ask Hailey if she was aware that I had published a book. As she has seen my husband's posts online, she answered in the affirmative. I asked her if she was aware of what the book was about and if she knew that I was a medium, and her response was also yes. I then, as gently as I could, said simply, "You're really worried about your dad, aren't you?" Hailey was quiet for a moment, then, unsure of where my line of questioning was going, responded with "Aaaaahhh, yes?"

"I know," I responded, "because he told me you are."

Experience told me that the silent response from Hailey was most likely shock at hearing this news. Before anything else could be said, I continued on with relaying how I had seen Mike standing in my kitchen, how he had looked, and the words that Mike had given me. I explained his strong desire to have Hailey know just how much he loved her, how very persistent he had been in having me relay the message to her, and that he desperately needed her to know that he was okay. When I told her of the vision that Mike had shown me, the precious, intimate moment between father and daughter sharing their joy in laughter, Hailey began to quietly cry. I knew that all of this was very important for her to hear.

Throughout my conversation with Hailey, I was also very aware that Mike was in the room with me, listening intently to everything that was being said. After I explained the vision that had been shown to me, I began to hear very strongly the word "regret" from Michael, and I have to say that this caught me by surprise. We all have regrets; most mortal beings do. But this has not ever been overwhelmingly important for those in the spirit world to relay to those of us left behind. They would rather spend the precious moments allotted to them with their beloved focusing on the positive messages and affirmations they can bring, not regrets of the past. I instantly realized that this must be a very imperative issue for Mike to even say such a thing, and I mentioned this to Hailey immediately.

Now, it is here that I have to say that when I first saw Mike in my kitchen, I understood instantly that he had some issues that he was dealing with in the spirit world. I knew Mike had some unresolved matters that were extremely important for him to work through. His very appearance spoke of that, and I have dealt with this before. Upon hearing of his deep regrets, Hailey and I had a personal conversation about the fact that her dad was okay, that he said he was okay, but that there were some things he needed to work on while he was growing and learning. Hailey understood immediately what I was speaking of. Then Mike really, truly astounded me by asking Hailey for forgiveness. I heard him clear as a bell. This, also, is not something I have encountered so blatantly. To have an entity express regret and ask for forgiveness tells me that the message was far beyond any importance I might have originally placed on this communication from Michael.

Not only was he asking for forgiveness, Mike also began to apologize profusely to his daughter, repeating more than once how truly sorry he was. Hailey was emotional, letting her father know that she loved him, and that she had forgiven him long ago. She was feeling truly empathetic to his emotional pain, and she did not want to see him suffer. Mike reinforced to Hailey that he was there for her now, that he would be there for her in the future, through weddings and babies and all of life's celebrations and challenges. It was so important for him to let her know that he was always going to support her. Mike's message ended on a positive note, emphasizing once more his sentiments of love, and then he was gone.

As I have stated before, I had not seen or talked to Hailey for many years before this day. I was not involved with her as she grew into a teenager. I knew that when she was little her dad had fought hard to win custody of her, and that he won that fight. I knew they were close when she was young, which was reinforced by the vision he showed me. I did not have news of her upbringing later on in life, and Hailey began to describe to me how she had developed a very tumultuous relationship with her dad as she grew older. I did not know about the bitter arguments or the traumatizing events that began with the breakdown of Mike's mental health, and ended in their estrangement when Hailey left home. Worse still, as Hailey explained, was that although they made amends a few years later, the relationship had remained strained and Hailey and Mike seldom even spoke together on the phone. The last time they had contact with each other was in September 2021, and Mike died in February 2022 without speaking to her for five months.

I could now completely understand why Mike, as a father, had such an overwhelming need to let his daughter know how much he really does love her, how very important she truly is to him, how he has such strong regrets, and why he needed to apologize. He has a strong desire to form a new bond with his daughter and move forward with their relationship, despite the ethereal veil that separates them. I believe that their new journey has started together, and I thank God for such a healing moment to have taken place. I am forever grateful to have been a part of it.

Mike and Hailey (supplied by Hailey C.)

≈

My life has been, to put it mildly, very interesting. I have met a wide variety of people from all walks of life and I have befriended many of them. If you have read my memoir, Journeys into the Realm of the Spirit World, you may recall a story about my Auntie Carole, and the slightly rough-around-the-edges group of biker friends of mine that she entertained and fed hot chocolate to when we showed up unexpectedly on her doorstep back in the 1980's. That group of individuals meant a lot to me, and I had become particularly good friends with one of them, a man named Lee W. Perhaps, had life taken a slightly different path, Lee and I could have become more than friends, but our relationship never developed past friendship, and never could have. Lee had no idea that I had grown to love him genuinely as a friend, however, and I had sincere concern for his well-being in general. I never told him. We lost touch after 1994, and I did not ever have a chance to speak with him again.

Sometime early into 2023, I could not say when exactly, I began to feel quite intensely an energy pattern which felt strongly to be that of Lee. No words were ever exchanged, however, and I had no idea for sure what the meaning behind his visits could be. A while later I discovered that Lee had indeed crossed over quite recently, in March.

Lee's presence continued to silently announce itself from time to time, until one day in the fall. I was sitting quietly at my desk, preparing for the upcoming events of the day, when once again I felt the strong energy pattern that announced the arrival of my old friend. But this visit was to be a little different, for without warning I began to hear Lee's voice in my head.

"You were a friend to me." It was a simple statement.

My only reply was, "Yes."

"You love me," said Lee.

His words made me pause momentarily in surprise before I responded. “Yes,” I said, “How did you know?”

“I feel love every time you think of me.”

His words echoed loudly in my mind, and then he was gone.

I cannot begin to explain how truly profound this moment was for me. I have always understood that we are each energetically connected, spiritually and emotionally, to all other living beings in our universe. However, not once have I considered that absolutely every single thought I might have for another could, quite literally, be felt, if that thought and emotion is sent with purpose and intensity, such as prayers are. Every. Single. Thought.

≈

True love crosses all boundaries, race, religion, and gender. It is not for me to judge those who choose to travel a path that is unique to what society considers to be acceptable. All of my life I have been an unusual character who dances to the beat of my own drum. More than one person has considered me to be far out of their range of what “normal” should be, and I embrace that. I also try hard to embrace the unique and exceptional qualities I observe in every person I meet. I appreciate those who share their true selves with me.

It was during a visit with one of my girlfriends in 2009, that I happened to make the acquaintance of a very dear family member of hers, his name was David. He had arrived in town the previous evening and was only planning to stay for a few short days. My timing was perfect, or I might not have ever met him.

My girlfriend, Samantha, had spoken of David several times, and she thought quite highly of him. Because of this, I found myself immediately relaxed and receptive to his presence, even though I knew very little about him. David was an extremely pleasant, mild-mannered man. He was over the age of fifty, slender in build, with greying hair and glasses. Nothing unusual seemed to jump out at me during conversation. After a short time, the men in the house retreated to the kitchen for coffee, and Samantha and I remained in the office, chatting.

Samantha and I were having a great visit, and discussing a wide variety of topics. I had almost forgotten that David was in the house when I exited the office to head to the washroom. Unbeknownst to me, David was just about to leave that room as I was about to enter, and we swerved sharply to avoid a collision. We made fleeting contact, arm to arm, hip to hip, and laughed apologetically as we did so.

Perhaps I should interject at this point my struggle with being around people I don't know well. I do not like to be vulnerable and open to the energies of "strangers." Only because I have discovered, over the years, that if my guard is down and I touch them, I have the ability to accidentally pick up on some very personal details about them. This only happens occasionally, and it is not something I enjoy. I do not have the desire to interpret your energy pattern and be susceptible to a strong belief or memory you hold, without warning and without a cause to do so. These unexpected encounters have left me somewhat disturbed and a little rattled, and I avoid them at all costs. If I am prepared to be in a social setting and my spiritual and energetic guard is up, so to speak, I have no problems.

Of course, because I had been in a comfortable and relaxed conversation with my girlfriend, my guard was down and my energy was somewhat extended when I almost ran into David. I didn't give it much thought when we had brushed against each other, and the laughter was already spilling from my lips as my brain began to register a very sharp and clear vision.

Honestly, I can only describe what I experienced.

Without any warning at all, I was absolutely overcome with what I instantly understood to be a memory that David carried. There was a very young man with blonde hair, appearing to be on his hands and knees before me, although I could see only his upper body. He was looking back over his bare shoulder, and his face was soft and gentle, with a hint of a smile playing about his lips. I could see that this young man was in a playful mood. At the same time my eyes beheld such a sight, I began to feel a deep longing, brought on by an intense loneliness, and a love so strong I could have burst from the intensity of emotion. It was so beautiful a moment that I could have cried. But, let me tell you, I was completely stunned by what I saw. Absolutely *shocked* would be another good way to describe my reaction. I was swallowing hard as I shut the bathroom door, trying hard to make sense of what I had just witnessed.

I have to admit, after the shock came panic. My past is riddled with awful experiences at the hands of sexual predators (not ever my father), and for one terrible moment I overlooked what I had just experienced emotionally, focused only on the nakedness and the youthfulness of the man I saw, and related it to my personal horrors. I almost began to panic, thinking this man David was also a predator. Thankfully, rationality took over my mind very swiftly as I began to relive the powerful sensations of love and sadness that I had simultaneously experienced with the vision. David obviously loved this man very much. I was confused.

Any questions I might have had for Samantha after my encounter with David were left unanswered, there was not enough privacy at that moment for that kind of chat.

When I was finally able to discuss my vision with Samantha, I was a little hesitant about how to approach it. I am not usually keen to disclose private details about other people, however, in this instance I desperately wanted information so that I could complete the puzzle before me.

As I began to explain that I had made physical contact with David when we crossed paths, Samantha raised a questioning eyebrow at me. She is keenly aware of the reasons behind my reluctance to be in public or with strangers. As I began to carefully describe the very young, blonde-haired man I had seen, I was surprised to note that Samantha began to smile with familiarity and not astonishment. When I began to describe the unbelievably powerful emotions that I had experienced, the love, the loneliness, and the longing, tears began to sting my eyes from the sheer, genuine beauty of what I shared. It was overwhelming. Samantha also had tears in her eyes, and it seemed as though she was sad for David.

When my words fell silent, Samantha merely sat there, seeming lost in her thoughts for a moment. I could see the memories flitting behind her eyes. After a brief pause, Samantha spoke, explaining to me that indeed, the young man in the vision was David's spouse, an individual much younger than David himself. They had been together in a committed relationship for many years until the blonde-haired man had fallen ill with cancer and crossed over. David had remained alone ever since. It was heartbreaking for everyone involved.

I have to admit, I was amazed to hear this information. My entire interaction had been very impactful, it left a permanent mark upon my heart. I was sad to hear of such a tragic loss, and I could feel the huge void that was left in David's life. However, I was also grateful for the confirmation I received from Samantha with her explanation.

Unfortunately, despite what I had learned through my interaction with David and Samantha, I had no comforting words or message to pass on to David about his partner. My encounter had merely been an exchange of information, similar to that of reading a book. The young man had not been present in spirit when I saw the vision. Just the same, I am truly grateful to have had an accidental exchange expand my understanding of the power of love; grateful for the opportunity to learn.

≈

"You are not alone" is a message often repeated by those visitors from the spiritual realms to their beloved left behind on the physical realm. It is a quote I have recited many times over, for I have had countless experiences that prove it to be so, and it is a comfort that I wish to share. One of the most reassuring sights I have ever witnessed, which enforces my belief, happened many years ago. I believe it was in 2002.

Ray and I were very early into our relationship when news arrived concerning an elderly uncle of Ray's, named Carl D. He was terminally ill, and family members had already started to gather together to be with him in his final days. Ray had hoped to be able to see Carl before he passed, and in no time at all we had thrown a change of clothing into a bag and were on our way to our neighboring province of British Columbia, and the hospital where Carl lay.

Upon our arrival, once introductions had been made, I tactfully removed myself from the gathering at Carl's bedside and seated myself at the farthest end of a sofa that was situated in the corner of the room. I did not wish to intrude on such a private moment, and there were several family members holding vigil at Carl's bedside when Ray joined them.

Time passed swiftly for me as I observed the activity in the room. Nurses were occasionally entering to check on Carl, and the family was quietly conversing. What I was finding utterly fascinating, however, was all of the *spirit* activity in the room. The room was absolutely bustling with energy. I could feel the pure, refined energy of Carl's holy spirit guides, I could sense the energies of family members and loved ones who had crossed over many years before. I understood that they were present in support of Carl.

However, the spirit world was also in attendance for the people that had gathered in the room with Carl, especially his immediate family. This was a very important moment in every aspect, and no one would be left unattended and alone. There were so many spirit entities in the room that I could not count them all if I tried.

At some point in the day, Ray and his family had moved their group conversation off to the side, away from Carl's bed. I had a perfect view of him. He appeared to be resting peacefully, but it did not take long before I noticed Carl's eyes begin to flutter. I called Ray's name and nodded my head in the direction of the bed when Ray glanced my way. It took mere seconds for Ray to shepherd the group around the bed, and my view of Carl was obscured.

I did not need to see Carl to know when his spirit was released from his body and his new journey had started, however. I only had to see what was happening before me. The entire time we were in the hospital room, right up to that very moment, I had been aware of the vast number of spirits that were in the room with us. It was impossible to ignore them. Imagine my surprise when, in the blink of an eye, most of those spirits just disappeared! They were gone in an instant, without warning. I could see quite clearly that the room was not entirely empty of spiritual beings, but for the most part, we were suddenly alone. And I understood almost immediately the reason why: Carl had also gone.

Without a doubt, Carl had crossed over. The multitude of spirits that had suddenly disappeared were accompanying him, escorting him on the next phase of his journey. Carl was not alone, not for a second. He was surrounded by Love.

Although the moment was sombre, my heart filled with joy. It was an honor to be witness to such an overwhelmingly beautiful scene. I was humbled to be granted understanding. I was deeply comforted to observe that Carl did not travel alone.

I find myself struggling to find the appropriate words to describe the massive importance of this lesson, not just for myself, but for everyone. *We are not alone.* Ever. Not in our darkest days, or our happiest ones. No matter our struggles or our successes, God does not abandon us. He is able to support and guide us through the tireless effort of His holy spirit envoys, and our cherished loved ones. No matter what you may be going through right now, please know that you are not on your own, no matter how lonely you may feel. Take heart and gather your strength, your faith, and your love. You can walk the path that is set before you. You are *not* alone.

≈

As you have read by now, I have had some extremely humorous events take place because of my inability to always understand what I am being shown. There are days when my human assumptions can truly cause me to miss the point of the message, despite what may be obvious to someone else. I do try hard, but can really miss the mark on occasion. Such was the case with my very dear friend, Kaye.

Kaye had travelled to my house in Alberta, from her home in British Columbia, in September, 2007. She was there to attend my wedding which was only a few short days away. We have been very close friends for many years, since the '90s, and we feel a bond as though we are sisters. But despite that fact, I had not ever met any of Kaye's family, or even seen pictures of them up to that point in time. Nor had I ever had a spiritual message, or an encounter with any of Kaye's loved ones who had previously crossed over, even though her mother and father had passed many years prior. I did, however, have a mental picture formed in my head of what I thought her parents would look like, based largely upon the short stature and nationality of my friend.

At any rate, Kaye had arrived just in time to experience the crisp air and gorgeous colors of fall. The persistent and frequent winds which often scathed the prairie landscape surrounding my acreage were still and quiet on this beautiful day. We were seated outside near the koi pond in my backyard, chatting animatedly about every subject we could think about. I had turned my gaze away from Kaye and towards the waterfall spilling into my pond as we chatted, and found a surprise waiting for me when I turned back to focus once more on my friend: we had company.

Standing directly behind Kaye, with her hand on Kaye's shoulder, was a beautiful woman who looked like a character out of an old television show from the 1950s called "Leave it to Beaver." This woman was slender, and she appeared to be of average height. She wore a shirt-waist dress which was common back in the day, consisting of a button-up front and a slightly accented waistline that flowed into a full skirt. Her hair was styled in a similar, outdated manner and I could see that it was about shoulder-length. She had very lovely facial features, beautiful skin, and a calm, pleasant demeanor. I was intrigued.

I immediately relayed this information to Kaye, explaining in detail everything that I could see, and asked if this woman was familiar. "I think that's my mother!" exclaimed Kaye.

Puzzled by her response, my brow furled and I shook my head negatively. "That's not your mother," I stated, and proceeded to explain once more what the woman standing with Kaye looked like.

"Shannon," said Kaye, "I am sure that is my mother."

"That can't be your mother!" I exclaimed, all while giving my friend a strange look of disbelief.

Now it was Kaye's turn to give me a puzzled glance as she began to laugh out loud at my absurdity. "*Why* can't it be my mother?" she chuckled in good humor.

"Well, because!" I spluttered, "Isn't your mother super short and heavy, with red, rosy cheeks and short, curly hair?!"

Laughter exploded from Kaye's lips, and she could hardly contain herself as she responded, "No! Where did you get that idea from?! My mother is my height, slender, and looks like she was in "Leave it to Beaver!"

Now it was my turn to laugh out loud. I could not believe my mental picture was so backwards in comparison to the actual facts, just where did I come up with such an idea? I did not have time to ponder long, of course, as there was a purpose for this spiritual visit and there was a very personal message that was about to be relayed to Kaye.

After the message was delivered and her mother had departed, Kaye and I reviewed the events of the day. Kaye was overjoyed to have heard from her mother and to have received such an important message. However, we were still laughing. It was hysterically funny for both of us that Kaye had to convince *me* who the entity was that I saw, and to this day it has remained somewhat of a private joke between us.

≈

I cherish the fact that we are each unique, distinguishable entities within the unfathomable structure that contains God's Creation. No two are perfectly identical, mirror images in both heart, mind and deed, even if they seem to be a twin in appearance. For those very same reasons, I have not ever experienced two identical interactions within the spirit world. One could not begin to describe the infinity of distinctions that exist within all of us, that separate us and make us easily identifiable. Some are far more obvious than others.

I have to share with you the story of one of the most unbelievable individuals I have ever seen.

It was June of 2021, and a very dear friend of mine, named Tina W., had been staying at my house for a couple of days helping out around the acreage. Tina and I have only been friends since August 2020, but we hit it off immediately when we first met, and formed a bond as though we had known each other for years.

On the second day of Tina's visit, as we sat at the kitchen table drinking our morning coffee, the conversation turned to the subject of Tina's dad, who had passed away in 2016. Tina had been discussing with me her relationship with her father, how she had become quite close with him in the years before he crossed over, and how much she still missed him. She was grateful to have had the chance to bond with him, as they were not close when she was younger.

Engaged as we were in conversation, my focus had remained entirely upon Tina, and rarely did I glance away from her. I was not aware of the fact that there was a spirit entity present in the room with us, until movement caught the corner of my eye, and my gaze casually shifted away from Tina's face to examine what the cause would be. I was momentarily taken by surprise as I observed one of the most *fascinating* individuals I have ever seen. Because I was seated, my head tipped back slightly so that I could better assess the apparition in front of me. I was having a hard time keeping my face straight simply because I truly could not believe what I was seeing.

Standing slightly behind Tina, yet off to the side, was a man of average build who appeared to be rather tall. He was calmly observing my reaction to his presence, looking down at me from his vantage point. He did not have much of an expression on his face, yet I felt that he was slightly amused at my obvious effort to remain nonchalant. It was a genuine struggle for me to do so, I must say.

The very first thing that grabbed my attention was the large hat the man was wearing. The hat appeared to have a very wide, round, flat brim, and as I peered up at him the unusual shape reminded me somewhat of a small Mexican sombrero. However, the color of the hat was also astounding to me, for it was a beautiful, rich, dark shade of red. And then, as my eyes began to take in the rest of his appearance, I noted that this man was completely dressed in a full, well-fitted, outdated suit. That was only the second time I have had a visit from a spirit dressed in a suit. But here was the icing on the cake: that suit looked like it was cut from the finest red-colored, *velvet* cloth, a sharp contrast to his sparking white shirt. Literally, this man looked to be from the 1970s.

My first, instinctive impression was to make a comparison between him and the flamboyant, eccentric men that would flaunt “ladies of the night” on their arms, and drive them in full view with the tops down on their convertible cars, hoping to drum up business. I couldn’t help myself, his image was perfect for the time period. I also had the strong impression that his name started with an F.

By this time, Tina was beginning to look a little puzzled, for my eyes kept darting to the “empty” air next to her, and I am sure the look on my face must have been priceless. I gathered my composure and joined the conversation once more, unsure of how I was going to announce the arrival of our visitor.

I am not sure exactly what statement Tina made in reference to her father, but I do remember making the comment "You never know, your dad could be sitting here right now in his cowboy hat, visiting with us at the table."

Cowboy hat, you might ask? I agree, it was no cowboy hat that I saw, but I was truly at a loss trying to find the right words.

Her face lit up as I said that, and Tina quickly replied, "Funny you should mention that, my dad was buried with his favorite cowboy hat."

Now was my chance. "Can I tell you what I really saw?"

As Tina nodded her head, I began to speak. I relayed to her every detail I could think of, starting with the odd, flat-brimmed hat that was definitely not a cowboy hat. I have to admit, I was almost expecting disbelief from Tina, for the vision I had was no less than astounding to me. Receiving confirmation was the furthest thing from my mind. Imagine my shock when Tina did exactly that.

I may have struggled with identifying the hat, but Tina recognized it immediately. "That's my dad's favorite hat!" she declared.

Continuing on, Tina relayed to me that her dad had an extensive collection of hats. Not only was he very fond of his cowboy hat, he truly loved his sun hat. His sun hat was very unusual for one specific reason: it was an old hat with a very wide, flat brim. An antique RCMP hat, otherwise known as a Stetson. I understood immediately why the shape of the hat had reminded me of a miniature sombrero, because in my vision the man wore a crisp, new hat to go along with his striking new suit, not his normal, worn-out favorite. And proper, well-cared-for RCMP Stetson's have a very distinct, perfectly flat, large, round brim.

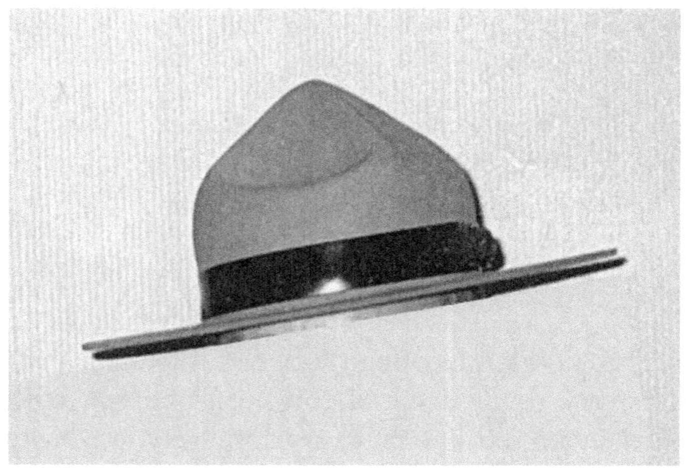

The shape of this hat was so unusual that it was perfect for Tina to identify her father with. However, before I could begin to ask why on earth the hat looked deep red in color, and not tan as it would be in the physical realm if it were vintage RCMP, Tina went on to further explain.

Her father's name was Floyd, and not only did he love hats, Floyd also had a passion for dressing very well, in the manner of a true gentleman. His style was flamboyant, with ruffled shirts and cuffs occasionally peeking out from under his formal suit jackets. Whenever the occasion would allow, Floyd was dressed to perfection. Floyd also loved trains, woodworking and the color candy-apple red. It was his absolute favorite.

Red. This color also happened to be a family favorite, enjoyed by Tina, her son, and her grandson.

I couldn't believe what I was hearing. Floyd had shown me a strange, red hat, with a flashy red suit to match. Exactly what he loved when he was alive. Hats and suits, and a flair that was instantly recognizable; especially when he showed me his favorite hat paired with such a color, and the fabric of the suit. Wow. Although in reality, Floyd never owned a candy-apple red velvet suit or hat, his daughter informed me with a grin that he sure would have if he could have! Tina was ecstatic to have received such a confirmation with his choice of attire. Her heart felt at peace in the undeniable knowledge that Floyd was with her.

Even now, I chuckle to myself as I recall that vision. It was one of the strangest, most delightful things I ever saw. Nice to meet you, Floyd!

Picture of Floyd W., supplied by Tina W.

HOLLY BERRY

December 12, 2006 – April 4, 2012

At this moment I am overcome with sadness and tears just trying to remember the beginning of my memories with my pet, Holly Berry. Although it has already been eleven months since her passing, I have discovered that it is still very difficult to face my memories, finding it easier to look away from those times and bury them in my mind than to subject myself to yet another bout of stabbing emotion in my heart and renewed weeping. I miss you so much, little Holly-doggie, I wish with all of my heart that you were still here with me and the rest of your family.

Holly came into our life with the rest of her litter-mates on December 12, 2006. Her birth was uneventful with the successful arrival of a litter of 7 pups. Her Dame was my Mini-Schnauzer, Belle, and her Sire was my Bichon Frise, Buddy. Because of the odd combination of breeding, the result of an accidental encounter, I had dubbed all of the puppies as a cross-breed called Schnaubies. Schnaubies are the most wonderful dogs I have ever had. I would have kept several if I could have found the room in our already full house. Schnaubies are energetic, fun-loving, loyal, intelligent dogs. They also are very calm and make great lap dogs. I had decided to keep one of the pups from this litter of Schnaubies because it was Belle's last litter before retirement. I had always made a promise to her in my heart that I would let her keep one of her babies instead of selling all of them away and leaving her to suffer the loss.

Out of all of the pups in the litter I had planned to keep one of the four females, but I was not yet positive which one. I had been leaning towards a beautiful, light tan-colored puppy that I had nicknamed Angel, but I was waiting until the puppies were older before I made my choice as I wanted to be sure of their size and temperament. I was leaning towards keeping Angel because of her coloring. She was the only female of the litter with that color of fur, the rest were various colors of dark grey and off-white.

As the days went by and the puppies began to develop more strength and energy, I noticed that one puppy in particular seemed always to be the noisiest. She cried and whined quite loudly as she attempted to crawl over the writhing forms of her brothers and sisters. It seemed as though she was always trying to crawl out of the kennel towards the kitchen table where we often sat. The puppy was soothed immediately when one of us would pick her up and cuddle her. I remember commenting that she seemed to be a very intelligent puppy, motivated on having her needs met and spending time bonding with humans. She could get quite demanding about being picked up frequently and was often slightly annoying because of her vocal protests at being left in the kennel.

As this puppy grew older and was able to walk out of the kennel into the kitchen area, I found that she became a very quiet dog. I realized that all of her noise had just been frustration at not being able to move freely on her young, unsteady legs. However, now she was often underfoot, patiently waiting beside my feet, waiting for attention. I noticed that when I picked her up and held her to my chest to cuddle her, she would snuggle right up under my chin with her head draped over my shoulder and become as limp and comfortable as a rag doll. It felt awesome, you could feel any stress you might have just melt away when she did that.

As the puppies grew in size and I began to consider selling the litter I found myself questioning my choice to keep the pup named Angel. She was a beautiful color, true, but I noticed that Angel did not seem to be too emotionally connected to any of us humans in the family, and I really wanted to keep a dog we could bond with. What was also very apparent was the fact that the little puppy that was always so whiny seemed to be very much attached to me in particular, shadowing me around the kitchen regularly. She also greeted everyone else with a constantly wagging tail and a pleasant disposition. I began to realize that truly, this puppy had selected me and my family to be her family, not the other way around. The choice was made then to keep her.

I did not have to think long about a name for our newest family member. She was born in December, so an obvious choice for me was Holly Berry. I really loved the pun on words as her name called to mind the beautiful actress Halle Berry, and Holly was just as gorgeous inside of her soul as the actress was in appearance. Holly was always an amazing dog right from the start, extremely intelligent and always patient, loving and considerate to humans and dogs alike.

We had four other adult dogs in the house when we brought Holly into our family: Jake, Belle, Mystique and Peaches. With three Mini-Schnauzers and a Bichon in the house, we found that a Schnaubie fit right in and soon everyone was fast friends. Being the two youngest, most playful dogs in the pack, Mysti and Holly soon became inseparable; one was never far from the other on most occasions.

I don't have many specific memories of Holly that I wish to write about. Holly was born in our home and she never left except for a rare visit to the vet. She was a secure, well-loved animal that had no neurotic tendencies like most of the other members of her dog family had. What I wish to convey most is just how special and wonderful Holly truly was, she was unique in most everything she did because of her odd, almost human outlook on life. Holly had a special way of reaching out to every person she met with her gentle style and her patient way of hanging back until she was noticed and acknowledged. She seemed to have wisdom beyond her years and was very accepting and calm. Just like her mother, Belle, Holly had impeccable manners and I often called her my "little lady."

One of Holly's favorite things to do was to sit patiently in the corner of the kitchen, watching me cook and waiting for me to notice her and pick her up. The second she was in my arms and snuggled up to my chest she would flop over my shoulder. I would close my eyes and hold her, and feel my body relax and my blood pressure go down while we stood there in silence. In many instances I would also refer to her as "my blood-pressure dog" and snuggling with Holly was one of my favorite things to do. Ray and the boys all loved Holly dearly, and she connected with each of them in her own amazing way.

Holly enjoyed life to the fullest, having fun seemed to be a mission in her life. She was always excited and interested to play and interact, especially with Mysti.

One of my favorite pictures of Holly shows her and Zachary in a close-up headshot, cheek to cheek, with purple-colored stains on Holly's fur on both sides of her face. It looked like make-up, but it was juice from beets she had been snacking on. She reminded me of a little girl playing dress-up. I really love that picture.

Holly had short legs and a long body with a constantly wagging tail. Her hair was curly and coarse, and she had developed the same beautiful coloring as Belle, silver, cream and grey. Her eyes were very expressive and gentle, and there were many times that you would see her with her lips stretched back into a lopsided grin. Holly was never an ounce of trouble in her life. Many times, I can recall watching Holly and Mysti chum around together and thinking then that being the two youngest of the pack they would be the last of our pack to depart from us, friends forever. Although, on more than one occasion I can remember saying to Ray that with our luck we would be stuck last with the yappiest dog of all, Mystique, who drives us crazy with her high-pitched, excitable barking no matter how much we love her. I had no idea then how painfully accurate this statement would be.

I have mentioned before that the year 2010 was a very stressful year for our family. Along with the terrible loss of my brother, Trevor, and also a few friends and extended family, we lost our beloved dogs Jake in May, Peaches in October, and Buddy in October as well. I was devastated with emotion for the entire year it seemed, and I felt horrible for my three remaining dogs that had lost so many of their family members. Their deaths had affected Holly, Mysti and Belle hard. For almost a week following each loss they were silent when they were outside instead of the happy barking one often heard each time they went out, and for the most part, they all had little appetite. Sympathetic to their pain, we each made sure to lavish the dogs with as much attention and love as we could so that they could heal, too. The kennel in the kitchen looked empty without all of the dogs piled in a heap inside. No matter how many pillows we had lying around in the house, they all liked to commune together on one bed. Even more, I envisioned a future of watching Holly and Mysti grow old together, for surely my aging Belle would be next to go. This is what I told myself, this is what I prepared myself for.

Nonetheless, 2011 passed by swiftly and 2012 began uneventfully enough. Looking back on the next events, however, I can see why hindsight vision is so perfectly clear. How I wish now that I had been more inquisitive and more obedient when I saw and heard the things I did back at the very end of March 2012. Had I done so my beautiful Holly may still be here. However, human that I am, I failed to put the pieces of the puzzle together and in my opinion, I failed miserably. Forgiving myself has been difficult to do.

My first clue should have been when I became very aware of the presence of a fourth dog in the house, one there in spirit. I could feel the energy plain as day. I did not question it for I understood that sometimes our cherished pets are allowed to come back for a visit with their loved ones, and I am comforted by their company. The next afternoon as I stood in the doorway to call the girls inside, I clearly saw Jake bounding up onto the deck with the rest of the dogs, and I recall even holding the door open for him so that he could enter, too.

Next, what caught me a little by surprise was the sudden awareness of the energies of *all* of my dog family that had crossed over into the spirit world, and they were running into the house and up the stairs with Jake. I could feel the activity around me and see a blur of color and fur as a joyful reunion was had by all present. I did note that it seemed odd that all of the dogs were together again, but I shrugged the quick flicker of uneasiness away.

My next clue should have been a couple of days later when I noticed Holly give a quick yelp as she jumped up onto the chair in my office. I heard her, and I wondered about it, but as I watched she piled herself onto the other two dogs already stretched out on the seat and immediately settled herself down to sleep. She did not appear to be hurting in any way and I assumed, mistakenly, that she had stepped on something sharp, or twisted something when she jumped, and that she was fine.

It was later that morning as I took a break from the computer and looked over at Holly, still quietly resting in her chair with the girls, that I heard a strong voice in my head tell me that I should take her to the vet. I also clearly remember my retort, for I assumed that all was well with Holly. "Why?" I had replied without pausing to think. She looked healthy and I did not think that a vet would find anything wrong with Holly. Why take her in? The voice said nothing more, and I am sorry to say that I went on with my day, unaware.

I continued to notice the energies of my deceased dogs about the house for the next few days, but remained clueless as to why they persisted there. So much time had gone by since they had first departed from this world, it was puzzling to constantly be aware of them. Almost always, the ones around me who have crossed over pop in from time to time, some to say hello, some to learn from me, some to teach me, but rarely do they stay around for extended periods. Although I was well aware of all of my dogs being present in spirit, I did not question, nor did I understand, the significance of their visit.

What turned out to be the last day that Holly was alive was not an overly unusual day. I had noticed that Holly seemed a little more subdued than usual, but that was all, and later that afternoon Holly and Belle were cuddled up together on the chair in my office as I worked at my desk. When I got up to leave, I thought it strange that the dogs didn't follow me upstairs as they normally did, but soon I forgot about it. Later that night I observed Belle and Holly still laying together on the chair and thought it a little weird and out of the ordinary, but that was all. I did not let the dogs outside for their final time before bed, one of my children did. I wonder if I would have noticed then that there was something dreadfully wrong, although I doubt it. But how could I have been so blind?

The following morning, April 4th, upon awakening I knew I had cause for concern regarding Holly. I could hear my son Zach coaxing Holly to come out of the kennel where she slept at night. I could tell by his continuous encouragement that Holly was not able to do so. I jumped out of bed and began putting on my clothes just as Zach was knocking on the bedroom door to voice his concerns over Holly, who could hardly stand on her own without falling over. I took one look at Holly and became alarmed; her head was hanging, her tail was drooping, and she wobbled back and forth unsteadily on her feet. Still, she attempted to wag her tail when we asked her if she would like to go outside, so I gently picked her up and carried her out of the house to the grass and set her down. After only a few moments I picked her up again and took her back inside to lay her on the dog pillow in the kitchen. Her head fell over to one side as she stretched out and her eyes seemed glazed over.

I ran to the bedroom in alarm, calling out to Ray in panic as I told him how much she looked like Jake had the day he died. I was still in denial though, determined that Holly was only sick with some unknown ailment, not wanting to consider that she was going to pass away.

When I finally reached the vet by phone, I was told to bring Holly in immediately. I carried her in my arms out to the car and Ray drove us to the vet's office. Holly was hardly conscious by this time.

On the drive in I had a sudden, clear vision in my mind of Buddy, Holly's sire, and the day he was sitting in my lap in the car as we drove him to town to be euthanized because of a terrible, terminal health condition. He looked very clean and white and healthy in my vision. I knew he was showing me that this was how he looked in the spirit world, and that he was with us now at this important time. I didn't understand that Buddy was most likely there to prepare me, and to be with Holly, because she was dying.

We arrived at the vet clinic and they rushed Holly into the operating room so that they could insert an intravenous line into her leg and get some fluids into her. Another vet remained behind to tell me what she believed was wrong with Holly. I was horrified to hear her explain that because Holly was not spayed, even though she had never been bred, her uterus had most likely gotten infected inside and it could not drain. This was called pyometra. Holly was now septic and in shock. I felt appalled, I did not know that this could be the outcome of leaving Holly with all of her parts intact. The vet mentioned years earlier the possibility of rare complications if she was not spayed, but that was as far as the conversation had gone. Had I asked more questions and fully understood that it could be so serious I would have done something about it. Nonetheless, I was stunned beyond belief when only minutes after taking Holly away, another vet came out to tell me that Holly had just died on the table before they could even get the intravenous needle into her leg. The vet was so sorry. I went numb.

I am not always quiet when I grieve. I am so full of emotion sometimes that if I do not let it out, I feel that I will explode. When Ray and I were ushered into an exam room and Holly was brought to us I began to sob quite loudly. Our baby was gone, just like that. I could hardly wrap my head around it. Last night she seemed healthy and this morning she was gone. I cradled her in my arms, crooning to her and running my hands over her furry body. Gently I carried her out to the car and sat with her on my lap as Ray began to drive us home.

On that trip back to the acreage I suddenly realized, with painful clarity, all of the clues I had missed. The really obvious reason that the spirit dogs had been present for the last week in our house: they were there to be with Holly. They were there to comfort and greet her when she crossed over. They were there to try to comfort us all with their presence and prepare us for Holly's death.

I thought to myself that maybe if I had understood better when I first saw all of the dogs in spirit, if I had listened to the voice telling me to take her to the vet, Holly could still have been here. The vet tried to console me earlier by telling me that even they might have missed seeing any issues if she was not showing symptoms, but in my heart, I believe that Holly could have been saved if I had just taken her in a week beforehand. I am grateful beyond words that Holly was not alone when she left this world, but was surrounded by and greeted with love at the start of her new journey, welcomed by the joyful barks of those she cherished.

Upon arriving at home, Ray set about to digging Holly's final resting place beside the other dogs in the small pet cemetery in our yard. I took Holly inside to let Belle and Mysti sniff her and say goodbye. As I laid Holly on the floor on her burial blanket, I became overcome with remorse, guilt and loss. I began to cry even harder, soon I had thrown my head back and I was howling my pain out to the universe over and over again, unable to stop. It took some time for me to compose myself and wrap up little Holly to take her outside to Ray's waiting arms.

Once Holly had been properly buried and I had picked out her headstone for Ray to place at the head of her grave, I went back indoors. Ray continued with his memorial to our beloved pets by painting each of their names on their stones, which up to that point had stayed unmarked. It was a lovely tribute, not to mention the fact that with five graves now in the little cemetery it was getting confusing for some people to remember who was who.

It was later that afternoon that I found myself working in the kitchen, still dazed by the events of the morning and very, very sad. I was unable to bring myself to even glance in the direction of the dog pillow where Holly had last laid her head. The house was very quiet, and I was feeling tremendously alone when suddenly, out of the stillness, I heard the most beautiful female voice that simply said, "I love you, Mama."

I remember thinking how lovely her tone was and that she sounded like a young woman. I knew that this woman spoke *for* Holly. I collapsed against the stove and began weeping anew. I love you, too, Holly Berry.

Holly stayed with us that day; her spirit was plainly visible to me from the moment she had come into the kitchen to tell me she loved me. She ran with Belle and Mysti when I let them outside, and I held the door open for three dogs when they came back inside. She was there when I sat on the floor to be with my dogs, and she also got petted and hugged. Anybody watching me talking to Holly and patting the empty air would have thought me insane. When I got up off of the floor, Holly followed Mysti to the pillow, and I could see her cuddling up next to Mysti. It was a heartbreaking comfort to observe all of this.

I cannot begin to describe the amazing wonder my abilities can be, especially in instances that apply to me personally, for I am able to learn and to heal through the use of these gifts. I do also get to experience the elation of being reunited with those who have departed from me, something few people ever do. But equally hard to explain is the crushing, overwhelming sense of loss I can experience when the energy of my loved one must leave me once more, returning to the spiritual realm in which they now reside.

I do not ever ask of God to conjure up these spirits to visit me. I am of the strong belief that it is with God's will and approval that these visits are permitted, and therefore it is in God's time that the visits will take place. I accept that. I also make the greatest of efforts to ensure that I do not hold these spirits back with my wanting and my need of them, but rather encourage them to leave and move on when they must. I love them too much to keep them bound here. But, human that I am, these experiences can be painful, and my heart was still aching when I went to bed that night.

I awoke the following morning without Ray, who had to return to work shortly after he had marked the headstones on the graves, and without Holly. Poor Mysti was also feeling very alone and we had kenneled Belle with her at bedtime for company. Once the boys left for school the house was depressing and quiet. I turned on the television just for noise and company, not really paying much attention to the content of a morning talk show, and wandered into the kitchen for another coffee. As I prepared my steaming drink, I gradually became aware of another presence behind me and turned to see little Holly Berry at my feet, patiently waiting like she always did. I bent down and scooped an invisible dog into my arms and held her, just like old times, with her head under my chin. Although I felt tears stinging my eyes, I could feel my blood pressure dropping as I relaxed, eyes closed, and held my little girl one last time, swaying gently from side to side, unaware of anything else around us.

Through my fog of oblivion, I had barely been aware of the sounds of the television in the other room. I was only slightly conscious of the fact that Lionel Richie was beginning to sing one of his trademark songs, Three Times a Lady, for the audience on the talk show. At that moment I truly did not care about the show or the song, but unexpectedly and with piercing clarity I was suddenly hearing the words echoing across the airwaves, as though they were being sung to me alone. The words resonated loudly in my mind and I knew they were meant for me when the words I heard began describing a beautiful relationship coming to its inevitable ending, and of the love that had been exchanged when these individuals had been together.

I began sobbing anew, aching at the words that I knew Holly Berry, my little lady, was saying to me through the lyrics of the song. Hearing her love through Lionel Ritchie's words was breaking my heart, because I also understood that this was Holly saying goodbye. Goodbye to our earthly connection. I held her in my arms for as long as I could, but eventually I knew in my soul that I had to let her go. I walked over to the dog pillow where Mysti was lying and gently laid my little dog down beside her, whispering my love and my goodbyes. As I straightened up and began to turn away, I noticed Belle pick herself up off of the floor and walk over to the pillow where Mysti and Holly were. I thought that Holly was not visible to anyone but me, but I watched in amazement as Belle stretched out on the pillow. She was directly in line beside Mysti head to toe, but with one perfect, empty-looking dog-sized space between them where I could see that Holly lay. I knew that all three dogs were having their family cuddle time and I walked away into the living room, not wanting my dogs to have to witness my sorrow once again. Holly's visit was a beautiful, heavenly gift that I did not want to spoil with tears. I am so humbly grateful for that wonderful time I was able to share with her. I wouldn't have traded it for anything.

Even though I knew without a doubt that Holly was doing fine in the spirit world, it was still very difficult for the next few days. The house had never seemed so empty, and Mysti was completely lost without her constant companion. She was wandering aimlessly from room to room, sitting in silence outside while she scanned the yard for any sign of Holly. I knew that she needed to visit the gravesite and detect with her sense of smell where Holly's body actually was. After a thorough investigation of the freshly turned earth, Mysti was returned to the yard where she continued to sniff around, detecting the stale, fading scents that Holly had left behind. I knew for certain only a short time later that she had processed what we had tried to make her understand, for Mystique came over to where I sat, put her head on my knees and looked up at me with the saddest eyes I have ever seen.

I watched in agony as a large tear formed in her right eye and trickled out of the corner, rolling down her cheek. I completely lost my composure then, as heartbroken for Mysti as I was for myself. We sat there for a long time with her head cradled in my hands, exchanging very real emotions, each trying to comfort the other through our pain. I hope I never see a dog cry again.

If you haven't figured it out by now, my world completely crashed when Holly died. I carry a large burden of responsibility for her death and have struggled tremendously to let go of that pain, which I have been unable to fully accomplish. I understand that my grief has been intense because of the guilt I carry for not listening to the spirit voice that advised me to take Holly to the vet. My blind assumption that the voice was incorrect only silenced it from advising me further. A harsh lesson to learn but one I take accountability for.

Belle and Mysti have once again adjusted to their circumstances, although I can feel that Mysti has never really forgotten Holly and looks for her still. Sometimes I experience fleeting moments where I see Holly curled up beside Mysti, and occasionally I see Holly coming to greet me, stretching luxuriously as though she has just woken up from a nap, content and happy with her tail wagging. It is a bittersweet moment every time.

To this day I am emotional whenever I think of Holly and I get a waver in my voice and a tear in my eye. The pain of her loss is no less gut-wrenching. I think I am still in shock that I lost her at all, especially when she was so young and I had my dreams of a long-lived life for her. But dreams don't always come true.

My guides have tried long and hard to get me to see reason in this matter, explaining that Holly does not wish to see me suffering so terribly and it makes her sad to see me that way. She does not understand why I cry every time I see her. My spirit guides also ache with sadness to see me grieving so hard, and I have come to realize that even though I cry less than before, the dark spot of emptiness inside of me does not go away; it is clearly visible to those in the spirit world. This emotional pain and guilt are heavy on my soul, and it holds me down. I have to find a way to forgive myself for my fatal error in not listening to the spirit that had urged me to take Holly for help.

God knows my heart, and I believe that He is trying to heal me by giving me the strength to finally look back on my time with Holly and write about it. It took almost a year for me to be able to work up the courage to write about this part of my life. I knew that I would have to re-live all of my emotions and I didn't know if I could bear to. I know God wants me to truly forgive myself. I am hoping that through the torrent of tears I have cried all through the writing of this story that I have at least shed some more of the weight I carry. I hope to walk with the unconditional love that I feel from Holly Berry and surround myself with the peaceful knowledge that she exists today, healthy and happy and cared for. I know I am not alone.

Author notes: It is now 2023, and it has been ten years since the story of Holly Berry was written. I would like to report to you that I was finally able to move forward with acceptance of the circumstances of Holly's death, and forgiveness of myself for my part. It was not an easy task. I shall always yearn, to some degree, for this to have not ever happened, but of course, that cannot be so.

I pray, that if you struggle with similar issues of guilt and forgiveness, you may also find peace.

Holly Berry (Photo by Shannon Harwood)

OF ANGELS AND DEMONS

A very dear friend of mine, Bill M., the same man who I write about in The Briefest of Encounters 2, looked me square in the eye one day and matter-of-factly said: "If you see angels, then you must also see demons."

This statement could not have been truer, for indeed, I do. Although it is not something I talk about often.

When Bill announced his belief to me, my eyebrows raised in mild surprise and contemplation. I became thoughtful for a moment, pondering just how much information I should share with him. Memories flashed before my eyes, and a small, wry smile played upon my lips. I have had my fair share of battles with those creatures that do not walk with God. I have yet to change the path that I am on because of them.

In the end, I decided merely to confirm the words that Bill spoke to me, choosing not to elaborate at great length, although I was very open to any questions he may have had. Bill was satisfied with my response, and I felt as though it was because he implicitly understood my relationship with God and the work I do for Him. Bill knew, without further explanation, that demons, or any other kind of lower spirits, would not be tolerated in my quest to serve. I very much appreciated Bill's acceptance of me, especially from a man so devout.

Please know that I do not see demons because I encourage communication with them. I see them because they exist. I do not seek them out, I do not invite them into my space, and above all, I do not "consult the dead." I will only ask questions and advice from my own holy spirit guides; those that are *not* spiritually dead, or, in other words, not separated from God. This is very, very important to me. Any other interactions that I have with the spirit world do not cross that invisible line of discipline that has been set. I merely observe and learn from the spirit world. I do not ever inquire of the future, or try to manifest in any way, and demons are not ever engaged in such a manner. Period.

Now, having said that, as an adult and a psychic medium, I have had my fair share of interactions with those that do not walk with God. Their intent is always to intimidate me and sway me from my intended path. I have learned, from quite painful experience, that the harder they fight to stop me, the more important it is for me to forge ahead. I have never regretted the decision to do just that.

As a young girl, I was always aware of the spirit world to some degree. It did not take me long to figure out that other people were not the same, however, and I usually remained quiet about such things. It was hard for me to grasp the reasons why I was so different, and I was very sensitive to the energies around me, both human and spirit. From as early as I can remember I have tried to "heal" any energetic imbalances I felt in the people near me. I was very empathetic to their emotional needs, and although I was only a child, I would try hard to tailor my behaviors to suit those needs.

As an adolescent, I felt very much alone, despite the fact that I had a wide circle of acquaintances and a few trusted friends. I understood that most would question my sanity were I to speak of hearing and seeing "invisible" creatures. Even worse, as an out-of-control teenager dealing with substance abuse and adult situations, my abilities became just as unmanageable, for my behaviors were attracting the worst kind of entities; those that love to feed off of such strife. Because I did not understand how my choices were affecting my spiritual interactions, the chaos around me continued.

Many of the entities that I was seeing during that time in my life were dark, shadowy creatures, often emanating a deeply unsettling vibration of malice, which left me feeling very uncomfortable and vulnerable. There was also a strong presence of energetic disarray which frequently followed me, like that of an uncontrolled daycare with young children running around and screaming. There were occasional mornings that I would discover upon awakening, my room having the appearance of being thoroughly turned upside down, with clothing and footwear scattered everywhere, as though a whirlwind had been set loose in my sleep. My energy seemed to have no limits as to how far it would extend from my body some days, leaving me open and susceptible to picking up on the energies and emotions of others in a very intense manner. It was overwhelming trying to deal with all of it.

And yet, while I was very much uncertain of what was happening at the time, I also understood that these things were occurring only around me. No one else I knew was experiencing such interaction with the spirit world. So, the fear factor was definitely flavored with a little bit of ego and pride.

I did not understand that my fearful, egotistical, fascination with these spirits was exactly the energy they needed to consume, which in turn enabled them to stay with me. Because I released my energy so readily, they were able to employ that energy for the purposes of performing meaningless signs, or, perhaps I should say, parlor tricks. I did not understand how to control such activity, let alone remove it from me completely. Quite honestly, I am not sure if I would have let it go at that time. In a strange way, it was validation for me. Proof that I was important, somehow.

Imagine for a moment, being alone in an environment such as I was in at that time. I had no one around me to guide me regarding spiritual matters and how to control my abilities. I did not understand that good and evil were so prevalent, or that I could choose which spirits to allow around me. Drugs and alcohol heavily influenced me, which left me exposed to whatever presence was around me, good or not. My psychic abilities were manifesting at an alarming rate, and unchecked communication without the benefit of discernment is very dangerous indeed. I was not in a good situation.

Do I believe that God was with me during those troubled times? Absolutely. Do I know without a shadow of a doubt that my holy spirit guides were also with me? Yes. There were many times that I was aware of them, without understanding who they were, or their significance in my life. Most often they communicated with words and emotions, and only when it was of the utmost importance to do so. Did I understand that I had a "voice of reason" guiding me on occasion? Yes, but despite my awareness, I seemed unable to realize that many of the other entities that were around me were actually harmful. And their influence on me was strong.

It was not that I made a practice of engaging in any kind of conscious communication with harmful spirits, I simply did not understand what was really going on behind the scenes, so to speak. I did not realize that whenever I was able to tune in to the different energies around me, I was also, in part, releasing some of my own energy to do so. All mediums must have this ability in order to engage any form of spirit communication. However, in my youth I had no understanding of this concept. I also had no way of understanding that every time I released my energy to a spirit that was not of God, my energy was spent and never returned to me. A higher spirit will not only use your energy, it is returned to you in a more purified form than it was when it was originally released to them.

You may question why a high spirit would even need an energy source that is not straight from God Himself. I can tell you that energy in all forms is precious. If there is a source that is readily available to be used, a higher spirit will use it just as a lower or evil spirit will use it. The huge difference is that a higher spirit will only use your energy for the purpose that God intended it to be used. A holy spirit has the ability to purify the energy required so that it is better suited to their needs, and then use that energy before returning it to the original source. The medium in use is not ever left tired or feeling ill. An entity that does not serve God's purpose acts more as a parasite, stealing and contaminating your energy and most certainly not returning it. Over long periods of time, this can have serious effects on the medium who is using their gifts for less than desirable purposes.

Communication with one of God's envoys which goes beyond day-to-day interactions and guidance, messages that are of extreme importance, are able to be imparted without the need of outside sources of energy. God can and does allow His servants to employ the use of a pure energy source whenever it is deemed necessary to do so. And these messages arrive with a force that is undeniable for their intended recipient. Have you ever been in a dangerous, or life-threatening situation? And did you ever feel strongly that you were protected, or guided, out of that situation? Did you simply "know" you would survive, despite not foreseeing the outcome? Have you ever considered that it was because your own holy spirit guide was extremely close to you at that time? Can you see, in hindsight, that God did not abandon you?

I can say with absolute certainty, that although my teenage choices in life were not always well-thought-out decisions, and despite the fact that the consequences of my actions were often harsh, I have not ever felt as though God abandoned me. Looking back on my life, I can clearly see that I have always been protected despite my situation. I also take full responsibility for any hazards inflicted upon me by my own complicity. In those circumstances, I believe that my guides could only stand by and watch, for they will not force me to change or bend to their wishes. They cannot implore me to take action if I choose not to hear. Free will is a gift granted to all mortal beings, and the consequences of our actions become our teacher.

I have the same outlook on any trauma that I have experienced through no fault of my own. I do not feel that God deserted me, nor do I feel that He inflicted such pain upon me. God did not ever "do" anything to me. Unfortunately, free will for one must mean free will for all, God cannot be selective in who receives such rights. I have always had that understanding and acceptance of that.

It is the same with my gifts. Even though, as a teenager, I had no genuine understanding of their true purpose, and even though I struggled terribly with the influences of the evil and lower spirit world, I do not feel as though God abandoned me at that time. On the contrary, it has been during the traumatic times in my life that I believe my holy spirit guides have been closest to me. Could they intervene and stop all "bad" things from happening to me? No, and I say this for countless reasons that I cannot begin to list.

I do sincerely believe that we are subject to the influences of good and evil throughout our lifetime, whether we understand it to be such or not. During those moments, how we react and the choices we make determine the outcome of what are essentially opportunities for us to learn. We endure and prevail, despite adversity. The holy spirit world is there to encourage us and support us throughout our life journey, constantly working to inspire us to gather our strength and courage and to strive for success.

Ultimately it is their strongest desire to see all of God's children leave this mortal realm and return, as ethereal beings, to the higher spiritual realms which await us all.

This earth was created as a stepping stone, in order to achieve the knowledge needed to attain a much higher spiritual vibration, so that we can, indeed, move forward. Holy spirits wish to see us succeed in our search for truth, and to ultimately guide us in our journey home to our Creator. They endeavor to the utmost of their abilities to assist us in any situation that furthers our spiritual progression, and this encompasses almost every aspect of our lives.

Such was the case with the burgeoning explosion of my psychic abilities as a young teenager. I believe that my guides tried as hard as they could to be of assistance to me. I also believe that the evil side of the spirit world wanted me to become enthralled with the unusual skills I was developing, and overlook the discipline and effort it takes to serve a Higher Power. Or, perhaps they wanted me to be so frightened of them that I would run away from all forms of spiritism, never having the opportunity to discover the true purpose of such abilities.

I think it was obvious, even at my young age, to see the path I would ultimately choose and they were trying to stop me from taking it. Not that I am anyone special in particular, but my love for God has always been strong, even though I had little understanding of spirituality. Once I discovered the path I would walk as a medium, my desire to serve Him has resulted in many life-changing events, quite often for those most desperately in need of healing. Nothing that serves darkness would wish to see such freedoms granted to those imprisoned individuals, suffering under the restrictive weight of their own burdens. Therefore, I believe that every attempt was made to stop me from ever discovering the beauty and strength of God's spirit world.

By the time I was eighteen, I found that I had an interesting conflict of sorts taking place. I was now experiencing a few bumps and loud crashes late at night, and hearing audible prayers in my mind during the day. Prayers of thanks, and praise. Prayers of gratitude for the protection of my loved ones upon their safe arrival home. Prayers requesting guidance be granted to me. I found it particularly unusual, for I had never before been blessed with such powerful words, and I had never heard such a multitude of voices. I had not ever experienced such clarity. Each different prayer was marked with the arrival of a different voice, sometimes masculine and at other times feminine. And all spoke of their love of God. Their visits were regular, often daily, although brief. I have to admit, I was very intrigued. I began to question what more was out there, and what more could be learned. I also took comfort in what I felt was undeniable proof that there were moments when I was walking in the presence of angels.

It may come as no surprise to hear that as quickly as my interactions with what appeared to be angels were developing, so too was the presence of evil growing stronger. Again, I really did not understand my situation to be quite so black and white in regard to evil versus good at that time in my life. Spirit communication with me was "normal" and somewhat common, and I could not see the dangers in what I was playing with. I could, however, understand that the entities praying were far different beings than those that were not.

Quite honestly, the chaotic spirits were starting to alarm me. I spent many nights alone in the mobile home I shared with my first husband, as he was quite often working away from home at his job on oil drilling rigs. Being as young as I was, and still heavily involved in substance abuse, it was not uncommon for me to stay up quite late and finally pass out into sleep as deeply as though I were in a coma. However, no matter how much alcohol or drugs I could consume, or how inebriated I was when I went to bed, there were times I would find myself suddenly jolted into consciousness during the dead of night, as though a cattle prod had connected with my skin. I would lay in silence, confused as to why I was awake, only to hear the loud sounds of crashing and banging noises throughout the small home moments later. It did not matter if I was brave enough to inspect the house or not, the outcome was always the same. Nothing ever appeared to be out of the ordinary.

Slowly, the night time disruptions became more frequent and more intense. The noises were louder, and I began to find evidence once more of mischievous spirits, apparent by the disarray that would greet me some mornings. Foot-wear that had been neatly lined up by the door the previous evening would be scattered about upon awakening. Books and magazines precisely stacked on tables would appear as though they were unceremoniously emptied from a box at great heights, strewn across the entire surface of the table. These events did not take place every day, but they did occur regularly. And, as ever, it was frightening, but it was fascinating.

Not only was I experiencing great changes around me spiritually, I was also preparing for a new adventure physically. My husband had decided to pursue a career in motorcycle mechanics, and his school of choice was in Phoenix, Arizona. We were going to leave Canada and move to the United States in less than six months! At the time I had no idea just how radically my life was going to change, I had no way of knowing that I would be given the opportunity to meet an individual who would be able to answer every single question I would have about the purpose of my gifts, and how they related to God. And I could not see that evil was about to make a serious effort to stop me.

The correlation between my upcoming move, and the increased activity in the encounters I was having with the spirit world is undeniable now, in hindsight. But all I understood at the time was that as plans were being made to put our home up for sale and move into a rental property in a nearby town, the prayers in my head were becoming louder and more frequent, and the activity at night increased in frequency. My husband was seldom at home for more than a week at a time because of his work schedule, and usually gone for three weeks. Much to my frustration he saw and heard very little of what was happening, although I had been trying to explain what was going on after I went to bed. And of course, he was not home for the most interesting night I experienced before we moved, either.

The mobile home that we lived in was situated on a plot of land out in the country, on a farm owned by my husband's family. It was an older model, somewhat narrower and shorter in length than those you would purchase today. An addition was built on that served as an entryway and a porch, with a master bedroom in the back. The only entryway into the bedroom was at the end of a hallway inside the mobile. To enter the home there was a doorway leading into the kitchen from the porch. You could also view between the porch and the kitchen through a window that used to open to the outdoors before the addition was constructed. Inside the porch was a freezer, a multitude of tools, and an old Norton motorcycle. The bike was stripped down to its frame, handlebars, and a few other parts, standing solidly upon a couple of big cinder blocks. I knew it was safe to walk beside it, for I had bumped into it on more than one occasion and it did not budge. It had been waiting for a very long time to be reconstructed, but it was a project going nowhere fast.

There was an evening in which I must admit to having consumed more than my usual fair share of substances, and I had literally crawled into bed because I was so intoxicated. My head barely hit the pillow before I passed out, oblivious to my surroundings. Just the same, I found myself gasping for air as I reluctantly regained consciousness only a few hours later. My brain was foggy, and in my confusion, I was not able to comprehend why I was rousing.

Suddenly I heard the most awful crashing noise, the worst ever, and it sounded as though a small collision had just occurred. It was extremely loud and very terrifying, especially because I was alone and it was pitch black inside my bedroom. I had no idea what the noise was or where it came from, and I couldn't see a thing. Fear forced the air from my lungs, and my breath was raggedly sucked back down as I struggled to breathe.

Quiet and stillness began to settle upon the room once again, and I forced my trembling legs out of bed and put my feet onto the floor. No way was I going back to sleep after what I had just heard. I had to investigate, no matter how terrified I was. I turned on a small lamp and quickly scanned the room, verifying that I was indeed, alone. I grabbed my trusted baseball bat from its position in the corner beside my bed and reached for the door knob.

Remember, this was in the 1980s, out in rural Alberta. Not only were there no cell phones back then, there were no bedside telephones, either. In the country at that time in life, your telephone hung on the wall in the kitchen, on a "party line" shared by two or three other households: anyone on that line could pick up their phone and listen in on a call. If the call was for your home, it rang in such a way that you knew the call was yours. For example, your call to answer might have two rings in quick succession, your neighbor might have three rings, or one. At any rate, there was no calling for help from my bedroom. I had to locate the source of the disturbance on my own, no matter who, or what, had caused it.

Very tentatively, I reached my hand around the door frame of my bedroom into the hallway to switch on an overhead light. Brightness flooded the length of the hall, and I observed that it was empty. There was a small bedroom to my left, a laundry room directly in front of me, and the bathroom and kitchen to my right. Beyond the kitchen was the living room.

I carefully reached my free hand into each room, starting with the spare bedroom, and flicked on the wall switch from the safety of the lit-up corridor I stood in. I found each room to be in order, one by one. I cautiously entered the kitchen at the end of the hall but found that it, too, remained undisturbed. I shifted the bat in my hand as I slunk into the living room, preparing myself for an intruder or some kind of strange disaster, and was greeted with stillness and silence. I was dumbfounded. My house was lit up like a blazing star, every light in the house was on, and nothing was amiss.

I turned off the light in the living room and walked back into the kitchen, preparing to return to my bed. To say that I was disgruntled with the situation would be putting it mildly. I knew without a shadow of a doubt that my imagination did not wake me up, but, what had?

As I was passing by the kitchen window which looked into the adjoining porch, it was merely force of habit that caused me to glance into the dark room, now dimly illuminated by the light from the kitchen. I hadn't thought to look in there for the source of my disruption, but expected the outcome to be uneventful. I was walking by so quickly that I had already moved past the window before my brain registered an anomaly, and I stopped dead in my tracks.

I walked backwards three steps before stopping to peer intently through the window, certain I was mistaken with what I was seeing. My brow furled in surprise as I realized my eyes had not failed me. My hands gripped the bat tightly and I took a deep breath as I spun around, took two strides, and burst through the doorway, ready for whatever awaited me. I had no time to be afraid.

As it turned out, I had nothing to be fearful of. Much to my huge relief, I found myself completely alone and unharmed. My baseball bat was not needed, and there was no attacker to attempt to fend off. I did have a strange problem, however. The old Norton motorcycle, the one sitting solidly on cinder blocks, was no longer in its designated spot. On the contrary, the bike was laying on its side on the floor, a short distance from where it had stood. It had been flung off of the blocks so violently that when the handlebars made contact with the wall, they left grooves in the thin wood paneling, all the way down to the floor. This was no accidental upset, and I knew that the heavy Norton frame had not been unstable in its former position.

I approached the Norton and bent down to give it a cursory tug, but it was obvious that I would not be lifting the heavy metal frame on my own. Not only that, the bike was wedged so firmly against the wall that it would have to be dragged backwards before it could be lifted. I have to admit, I was somewhat in awe of the sheer force that had been exerted in order to achieve such damage to the wall. However, I can only imagine that had I been able to actually see the entity that was powerful enough to wreak such havoc, "in awe" would not have been my choice of words. "Terrified" might have been more apt.

Fully aware that there was little I could do about the situation at that moment, and certain that I was no longer in imminent danger, I returned to my bed. I would get help from a neighbor in the morning.

I was nonchalant the next day as the neighbor helped me hoist the frame back onto the cinder blocks, I claimed to have no understanding of why the bike had been positioned as it was. I was not interested in trying to explain. I did try to tell my husband what had happened, but he shrugged it off pretty quickly, and I take no offense to the fact that he most likely did not believe me.

I don't remember having many more issues in the mobile home before we moved out. It sold quickly, and we moved into town soon after. I thought my troubles were over once we had changed our place of residence, but it did not take me long to realize I was mistaken.

The house we moved into was a typical bungalow with a basement. It had two bedrooms and a large kitchen and living room, all on one floor. Back in the eighties the house was already rather old, and it was built in a manner that reminded me of farmhouses built long ago. I say this not only because of the solid construction and the simple wooden cabinets and baseboards throughout, but because of the very typical, rudimentary basement the house was standing on. I detested that basement the second I saw it.

I don't usually find basements creepy or unsettling, but this basement was both of those things. I found the stairwell to be dimly lit and narrow. An old, wooden door with worn and chipped paint greeted you at the bottom. Before one dared to grab and turn the rattling metal doorknob to enter the room before you, your attention would be immediately taken up with the ominous, black hole, dug out of exposed earth that was to your immediate right. It was an old-fashioned root cellar of sorts, although it did not have a door on it. It appeared to be totally empty, but I wasn't about to enter into it to verify that. The dirt had a damp, musty smell to it, and the darkness seemed to consume any light that was cast upon it. I had never seen anything quite like it before. It was deeply unnerving having to stand next to it while I fiddled with the antique knob in front of me. It felt like a setting for a horror film.

The old door was mounted on squeaking hinges, and it swung inwards as it was opened. Much to my surprise, the concrete structure was completely empty, devoid of any improvements. No walls, rooms, doors, or items left in storage. Nothing. The basement was a large, open room, with old-style wood-framed windows that one had to slide up to open, if that was even possible. The window panes were grimy and hard to see through. The paint on the frames was peeling and flaking off. Spider webs clung tenaciously to the corners, despite years of thick dust piling upon them.

Weak light filtered through the smudged glass, and it took me a moment to adjust to the gloom before I noticed that there was no light switch anywhere to be found. There was a bare bulb mounted to the ceiling in the middle of the room, and the only way to turn it on was to reach way up and grab a short pull-chain. I had no desire to remain there any longer, however, and there was no need to turn on the light. I spun on my heel and made my way very quickly back up the stairs and into the kitchen, breathing a sigh of relief as I did so. I hated everything about that lower level. I had no intention of returning to the basement if I had my way.

Our tenancy was on a short-term basis. It was only a matter of three months before we would be headed south, which would be very soon after my nineteenth birthday. My husband continued to work away from home in the meantime. I was alone a great deal, and my bad habits had not really changed much. I did not see the need for change. I was responsible, I cared for the home we lived in, and I was trustworthy when my husband was away. I had no problem with the way I lived otherwise.

It may come as no surprise to you to hear that the adverse spirit activity started up almost immediately after we had settled into our new abode. The bangs and crashes had begun again, but this time, much to my dismay, the noises came from the basement.

The scenario played out the same as it always had before the tirade of disruptive noises would begin. I was in my bedroom, deeply asleep, when I found myself swiftly awakening as though someone had spoken my name. My heart was pounding, and my breathing was heavy. The silence prevailed for several moments before the crashing noises ensued. But now, the sounds were different, louder than I had heard before in our old home, and they came from directly below my bed, in the basement. The best way to describe the noise would be to compare it to a table full of glassware being picked up and smashed against the wall. I could literally hear the tinkling sounds of glass falling to the floor, then silence.

Not a hope in heck was I getting out of my bed in the dark and going to the basement to check out the situation. Although it most certainly could have been an intruder, I would rather take that chance, because I knew deep in my heart that there would be nothing there were I to look. Somehow, I drifted back into an uneasy sleep and awoke in the early morning with the basement on my mind. I gathered my courage and made my way down the stairs to the basement door, tried my best to ignore the scent of moist earth beside me, and pushed the door open. Silence was all that greeted me. The dusty floor was barren, there was nothing destroyed laying in a heap on the floor. I shook my head in annoyance and made my way back up the stairs.

The noises continued to awaken me without any particular pattern, occurring randomly and without cause or provocation. What I was finding most interesting was that my husband was also beginning to complain of having his sleep disturbed when he was home. He was hearing the same sounds I was: glass breaking and wood splintering, as well as all kinds of crashing and banging. Upon inspection, he would find nothing. I was actually quite happy that he could hear it, even if there was no explanation for it. At least I was not alone.

I honestly do not remember if the spirits that were praying were around at that time or not. It could be that I had gotten so familiar with hearing their voices that I hardly gave it a second thought. It could also be that the memory of the final event to take place in that house wiped all other notable events from my mind. Terror has a way of doing that to a person.

It was close to the time when we were to leave for Phoenix, which was sometime during the month of January, 1987. Nothing was amiss in my life and out of the scope of "normal" for me, both physically and spiritually. I was happy and excited to be moving to the U.S., and had been very busy socializing with my friends and saying goodbye to those I wouldn't have a chance to see right before I left. My husband was away on one of his last shifts at work. All was well.

I had gone to bed as always, in the same condition as usual. True to habit, the hour was quite late, and I was in a deep, unconscious state almost immediately. It must have been around 3:30 in the morning when I was awakened once again by the sounds of breaking glass and splintering wood in the basement. But, even more unusual than normal, the noise was so loud that the floor beneath my bed actually vibrated and shook from the percussion. The echoing shockwaves throughout the house were unnerving to listen to. This was something I had not ever experienced, and I was more than slightly alarmed. There *had* to be something or someone in that basement. I was going to find out.

I briefly considered calling for help, but brushed that thought quickly away as I threw on the shirt and jeans I had been wearing only hours before. I wasn't waiting for help. Once again, my weapon of choice was the old baseball bat leaning up against my bedroom wall. And just as before, I checked every single room on the top floor, carefully turning the lights on and scanning the room for any irregularities, but finding none. I knew where I needed to go.

The lights in the kitchen were not bright enough to illuminate the stairs leading to the basement in any kind of manner that would be comforting. Standing at the top of the stairs looking down at the gloomy, narrow incline was a terrifying prospect to consider. I was very aware that I was alone.

I began my descent slowly. With each cautious step I took, my jaw clenched tighter and my heart beat faster. My hands began to shake as I took a firm grip on the bat.

I got to the bottom of the stairs, with the closed door in front of me, and the open root cellar to my right. Air wafted onto my face as though there was a light breeze coming from the cellar, and the strong scent of freshly turned dirt invaded my nostrils. I felt the hair on the back of my neck and arms begin to rise. I was too terrified to look over my shoulder, and I absolutely did not want to open that door.

The door knob rattled in my hand as I fumbled unsteadily to twist it. The hinges squealed in protest as I pushed the door open, but I hardly heard them. I was too busy listening to the air escape from my lungs and the pounding of my heart in my head. And then, suddenly, silence. I wonder if, for just a moment, my heart stopped beating.

My next move should have been to enter the basement and reach for the pull-chain which would be high above my head, in order to turn on the light. But instead, I was standing still, unable to move, and in complete disbelief. I found I could not comprehend what I was seeing. And no way was I going to walk into that basement.

Although we were living in town and street lights lined the streets, no light filtered through the old slider windows. The basement was a pitch-black cavern. And exactly where I would have had to reach for the pull-chain there was, suspended high in the air above, an ominous, glowing set of eyes. They were heavily slanted, yet reminded me a bit of teardrops, and they were *huge.* Bright, off-white, empty glowing eyes that stared down at me. Literally. My jaw went slack and hung open as I gaped incredulously. I felt as though I were drowning as I stared into nothingness, and it stared back at me. Before any thought of denial could begin to take hold in my brain, before I could question what I was seeing, those huge, luminous eyes slowly, and very deliberately, closed. For a moment all I could see was blackness. And then, just as slowly and just as deliberately, those giant eyes opened and continued to stare down at me. It reminded me of a big, lazy cat, basking in the hot sunlight, staring down at his dinner, deciding if it should pounce. And dinner was me.

That did it. I didn't need to see another thing. I was convinced, thoroughly and completely convinced that before me stood pure evil. I knew in every fiber of my being that I did not want to mess with *that.* I was not going to stick around and find out what was going to happen next, I was not going to try to engage this entity, I needed to get out, fast, NOW!

I am not ashamed to say that I turned on my heel and I ran, sprinting up those stairs and into the kitchen.

The bat went flying out of my fingers and skidded onto the floor as I spun around at the top of the stairs, racing through the house to grab my purse, my car keys, and my jacket, before bolting to the door; pausing only long enough to lock it before I dove into my car and drove as though the hordes of hell were after me.

The only place that I could think to escape to at such an early hour was my mother's home in Calgary. That was normally a two-hour drive for me, but I made it in half of that time, arriving near 5:00 AM, still scared out of my wits. Now, anyone that knows my mother knows that she is not ever out of bed before the sun comes up. She has always been late to bed, late to rise, and not too pleased if you wake her up early. However, on this day that fact did not deter me in the slightest, and soon I was banging on the door and calling out her name to grab her attention.

My mother was quite astonished to see me at the door, and she opened it as quickly as she could. She could tell by my demeanor that this was no time to be cranky about the extremely early hour. This was something I had not ever done before. I burst into the house in a bit of a frenzy, I was still feeling very alarmed about the events that had started my day. I knew that my mom might not fully understand what had happened to me, but I knew that she would listen, and I knew that she would believe me. She was not a stranger to hearing about some of my spiritual encounters.

It took me quite some time before I felt calm and strong enough to return to my home in Rocky Mountain House. The return drive was considerably slower than the initial journey had been, and it was dark outside by the time I pulled into town. I cruised the streets in my car for a short time until I saw one of my buddies on foot, headed for a nearby café. I pulled over and waved him to my open window, simply explaining that I was afraid that there had been an intruder in my house and I had fled. I shared with him that I was afraid to enter the house until it had been thoroughly searched. He was more than willing to accompany me, and he diligently explored every room, including the basement, before he announced that all was well, and we were alone. I never did try to explain to him the real reason behind my fear, he would surely have thought me to be bonkers.

That was the end of the bumps in the night in the rental house in town. I can only surmise that although I was fearful, evil had not succeeded in stopping me from trying to understand my gifts, and for now they had given up. I had not turned away. It would have been very apparent to all of those in the spirit world who were near me, that my resolve was set. I can be incredibly stubborn when I need to be, and although I was young, I was determined to walk my path wherever it led me. Evil knew that this battle was won, but not the war. They could see, far clearer than I could at that time, my search for spiritual enlightenment was just beginning. I know for certain that they anticipated many more battles to come, in my effort to be spiritually free of all hindrances. Some battles would be epic, indeed.

Our arrival in Phoenix was the catalyst for radical changes to take place in my life.

In the first few months that we were there, my life was the same as it always was in the sense that it did not change. I was a young woman who loved to have a good time. I loved to drink alcohol, I loved to indulge in all kinds of narcotics, and I especially loved motorcycles. I would ride anywhere, in any kind of weather, and I had a passion for Harley-Davidsons and all manner of British motorcycles, such as Triumphs and BSA's. Although I was physically unable to pilot my own machine due to physical issues, I was never long without a ride. I also thoroughly enjoyed watching bikes get repaired, I loved listening to the sounds of the motors and hanging out in the shops and backyards with the guys. My world revolved around that lifestyle in a big way. It had been so for many, many years of my short life. Seldom was I seen without my leather jacket, or my knife strapped to my belt. Even my wedding dress had been buckskin leather, head to foot, because I simply was not comfortable trying to step into a role I could not play. I was a biker, heart and soul, not a princess. I had vowed many times in my life that I was not ever going to change. No one would control me, or slow me down.

Had you told me that I would willingly give it all up in less than five months I would have laughed you right out of the room.

It was by no coincidence that I had the opportunity to meet a young man only a few years older than me, who was a medium. His sister was a friend of mine from Canada who happened to be living in Phoenix at the same time I was. My friend had told me about her brother and his abilities, and I was very interested in meeting with him. For the sake of his privacy, and all others involved, I will not say his name, but I will say that this man changed my life.

I could not believe all of the abilities this man possessed. He was absolutely in communication with the spirit world in a manner that I had not ever seen before. He could hear, see, and feel in much the same manner that I could, but he could gather far more information than I had ever been able to do, and he did so with ease. He did not appear to struggle in any manner to tune in to the entities that were with us. He could also read energy patterns as though he were reading a book, describing events of particular significance that had happened in my life, by merely holding my wrist watch in his hands. He described events my girlfriend had no way of knowing, either.

This man explained how he was able to receive important messages from the spirit world through the use of automatic writing, and how, over time he had developed his skills further to become a deep-trance speaking medium. A method with which the spirit world makes full use of the medium's physical body to impart its messages through speech. And then, to top it all off, he imparted to me that he was strictly employed for communication with spirits of God. Those that serve only Him, those sent to guide and teach and assist us in our journeys back to God, back to the higher realms from whence we were first called into existence. They were literal angels. Holy angels of God, or, holy spirits. Holy spirits that guide us daily through the Power and Wisdom that is our God. Holy spirit guides. Creatures in communion with God; those that were spiritually alive.

I will tell you right now, this conversation struck a chord deep within me. I felt as though I had just heard the words I had been waiting to hear my entire life. I was absolutely enthralled. The words he spoke were logical, and I felt the ring of truth stirring profoundly within my very soul. It was as though I could see clearly for the first time, ever.

Imagine my joy when the conversation expanded to include the subject of good and evil, and how there were many that served a master who did not love God. Those who obeyed a ruler who was spiritually dead - death meaning the separation of the spirit from God. These followers were also not spiritually alive. It was of the utmost importance to differentiate between those spirits that walked in Truth and Light, and those that did not. It was a concept that I grasped immediately, for I certainly had been having my own fair share of spirit interactions that were far from holy, for a very long time. But now I also realized that my holy spirit guides had been walking with me for as far back as I could remember, and I knew that they were the source of the prayers I had been hearing.

Before we parted that day, I was handed a book that would change my life. It was a book about a man who was a devout Catholic priest, in Germany, in the 1920s. This man was introduced to God's spirit world in such a way that was undeniable for him, and that spiritualistic encounter changed his life. Thereafter he went on an intense search for truth in regard to communication with the world of spirits, and its purpose in God's ultimate plan for mankind.

The purpose for writing his book was to share his experiences with all who desire to be closer to God, and to teach the reader how to achieve that ability for themselves in the purest form possible, through God's holy spirit world. He explains how those who are truly searching for their own personal relationship with God could achieve that, on their own, if they so desire. He goes into great detail about all of the various types of spirits that exist, and how to tell them apart. He researched at length different kinds of mediums; how their gifts worked, and what their purposes were for. He explains the differences between mediums who work for God, and those who do not, and the importance of strict spiritual discipline. This was a man who strongly believed he was guided by holy spirits of the highest order. Once I read his book, I had no doubt in my mind that this was so.

I can tell you that the same day I received this book, the evil spirit world tried its last night of trickery. I believe the only purpose for this small show of intimidation was a last-ditch effort to get me to disregard the book, and return it unread, out of fear.

I lived with my husband in a small studio apartment. It was a large, single, open room with only a tiny bathroom off to the side. A fold-out couch shared double duty as our bed, and we had created a makeshift divider for the room with an old, short dresser that only came up to my hip. It created the illusion of having a living room and a separate kitchen area.

My husband and I had been reading in bed that night for only a short time, before turning out the light and closing our eyes. We were both still quite awake and alert, however, when we heard the strangest sound come from the area where our kitchen table stood. *Ting!* It was a sound reminiscent of a crystal glass being tapped with a piece of cutlery. Odd, I thought to myself, but remained silent in the darkness.

I doubt that it was even thirty seconds later when I heard a second noise, identical to the first. But this time, I could have sworn it sounded closer to the bed. *Ting!* Had it really moved?

By now, my ears were keenly attentive to the faintest of sounds. I was on high alert. But the sound repeated a third time, louder still, and closer yet again than it had been before. It sounded as though it were at the dresser. *Ting!* This time my husband spoke up, and whispered to me, "What was that?"

I had no answers for him, but I had my suspicions. I was pretty sure that this was somehow related to my newfound understanding of the spirit world and God, the lengthy conversation I had that afternoon, plus the fact that I had the new book. I was more than certain that what was in our room was not holy. I began to do the only thing which I felt that I could do. Silently, I began to pray.

My prayers were for God to allow my newly-discovered holy spirit guides to remove this unholy entity from the room. My prayers were for protection, and even as I prayed, I heard a fourth tone, now undeniably closer to the foot of the bed. We were both sitting up at this point. The hair was standing up on my arms and the back of my neck, and I was almost squirming because I so badly wanted to switch on a light. I stood my ground and continued with my prayer, however, remaining firm in my conviction that this being would be removed and no harm would come to me. It seemed the most natural thing to do in this instance, to pray.

Once I ended my prayer, I sent a silent rebuke to the spirit in question. "Go! You are not wanted here!" And just as suddenly as the sounds had started, they stopped and came no closer. I was relieved, but I also felt a small sense of victory. Evil had not won, it had fled! Thank you, God, for protecting me! I have not ever again experienced such activity from the evil spirit world in my home since that night.

I soaked up information from the book like a sponge, and was eager to learn as much as possible from the young man who was swiftly becoming my spiritual mentor. Not only was he a medium who served God, he was able to introduce me to many others who were also searching. He hosted prayer meetings in a private home so that those of us who were interested could learn to develop our mediumistic abilities by following the guidelines laid out in the book. We were guided with wisdom and advice through my mentors' abilities to allow the holy spirit world to purposefully employ his skills, in order to more clearly communicate with us. These spirits were eager to identify themselves as servants of God, working together under the guidance and direction of their Lord and Savior, Jesus Christ. They were very strict teachers, and their motivation was to serve the will of God alone.

I devoted a large amount of time and effort to the practice of meditation and prayer, not only in weekly prayer meetings, but at home on a daily basis. And I began to experience contact with the spirit world in a manner that I had not ever anticipated. During my personal mediations at home one morning, while I sat quietly with pen and paper and waited for direction, I was suddenly blessed with a short, clear message that repeated itself in my ears, over and over. The voice said: "Only a spirit of God may enter me, for I want no other."

Once I wrote the message down, the voice was quiet. It was the first time that I had felt inspired by thoughts that were not my own during meditation, and I found it very interesting that I had been compelled to write those words on paper. Thus began my training as a medium for God.

One might question how I could follow God and still maintain my hard-core lifestyle. The answer is, I could not. I found with each passing day and every weekly meeting my resolve to live in the manner that I had up to that point was wavering. The more my spiritual education grew, the greater the conflict was within me to transform myself. I had already begun to moderate my behaviors somewhat, especially once I began to understand the importance of being a pure energy source for the purposes of spirit communication with my holy spirit guides. God was not forcing me to change, I understood that. But He was asking me to bring about huge changes in my life that would directly impact my greater ability to serve Him, if that was the path I would choose to take. I knew that I could not walk that fine line between two worlds forever. I had to make a choice.

There were many things I had to consider at the crossroads of my path. For me, serving God as a medium was of the utmost importance to me. However, in order to do that, I understood completely that there were many things I needed to give up to gain the spiritual freedom I sought. I could no longer tie myself down with the weight of addictions, no matter what form they were in. I needed to rid myself of any baggage that stood in the way of me achieving that goal. And this meant removing anything that would stand in the way of my progression to God. I felt that my entire lifestyle was an impediment at this point, and it needed a massive overhaul. Understand, once again, this was my choice. Had these decisions been enforced upon me, against my will, they would not have held true, and I would have not had the determination to succeed.

Living a life that includes motorcycles is not a problem. Enjoying the open road, seeing the sights, experiencing the wind in your face, and everything else that goes along with riding, is a gift, in my opinion. I still ride to this day. But, at that point in my life, the motorcycle lifestyle had become my *identity*. It influenced everything about me. How I dressed, how I behaved, how I lived, how my home was decorated, and who my friends were. My lifestyle consumed me, willingly. I loved the way I lived. I was a biker chick, through and through. This was the person the outside world saw, and this was the person my friends saw. However, I now understood that there was not much room for God inside my heart when I had placed so much importance on these things. I was ready to move forward.

I was about to take a monumental step in my journey. I started by making the decision to kick the drugs and alcohol together, at the same time. I was going to go clean all at once and commit to an extreme change. I decided that the upcoming Saturday would be the day. I didn't look at a calendar, so I was unaware of exactly what the date would be, but I didn't think that would matter. I was very wrong.

The day I just so happened to have picked was in actuality, Saturday, July 4th. In the United States, this was Independence Day. A day that meant very little to me as a Canadian, but it meant a whole lot to Americans in general. It was a huge day of celebration, or, in other words, a giant, country-wide party. Not the day to pick to get straight.

We lived in a small apartment complex which consisted of only two or three buildings, in the city of Phoenix. It was home to many of the men who were attending the same motorcycle mechanics school that my husband attended. Quite a few of these guys had become friends with us, and we all rode together. It goes without saying that we shared many good times, and, on July 4th my friends were eager to show me how they liked to celebrate their national holiday.

Much to my dismay, most of the guys brought their favorite substances to share with me, as I would have shared with them. Over and over again I had to take a deep breath and explain that I had decided to kick some habits, and refuse all that I was offered. And, of course, as with every test or challenge in life, I was not able to take the easy way out. It should have been no surprise to me that everything I could possibly think of that I loved to indulge in, was presented to me in some form or another throughout the day. Everything.

No matter, I had made a commitment and I was going to keep it. I had to turn all offers away. My silent prayers for strength were becoming more frequent as I felt my resolve wavering. The temptation to indulge was almost overwhelming for me. I felt sick to my stomach and I was feeling anxious. Still, I dug in my heels and braced myself for whatever was to come.

More than once I found myself under the painful scrutiny of a suspicious gaze from a member of my peer group. Any street credibility I had was rapidly eroding, and it was a painful, humbling situation for my ego to be in. I was the chick with the penchant for drinking most anyone right under the table, even the biggest of men. I could hold my own with the best of the best when it came to indulging in most of the eighties party drugs, and I would smoke anything I could get my hands on. Now, without warning, I was not only refusing to partake, I was openly admitting that the changes in my life were brought about by my new relationship with God. *God.* The initial look of shock on their face was almost always followed by an uncomfortable silence, and it did not take long for the party to move elsewhere, every single time I made that announcement. Understandably, I might add. I am sure everyone thought that I had lost my mind.

By nightfall, I was also certain I was losing my mind.

All day long, over and over again, I had encountered people from my community who were in a happy, relaxed mood. It didn't matter if I was outside in the courtyard, or hiding inside our tiny bachelor suite, the offers would come for me to share, and the knocks on the door seemed endless. Whenever I turned those offers down the reactions were always the same, why not have a beer? Why not smoke a joint? Why not snort a line? What on earth was wrong with something harmless like that? I could not find the words to explain.

I will tell you right now, this was one of the hardest things I have ever done.

As early evening commenced, my body was screaming for a drink, a toke, *anything* to quell the cravings I had been having all day. My friends thought I had gone insane, my husband thought I was nuts, and I had to stand firm in my convictions. It was hard to hold my head high when I would see the scorn, or the sneers, or hear the sarcasm when mention of God was made. He wasn't a very popular subject in my world. A world that was rapidly being lost to me the further I walked into my new commitment.

Darkness was setting in, and I honestly felt, at that exact moment in my life, that I could not bear the weight of one more temptation. I had done my best. I had tried, over and over again, to refuse to succumb to weakness. I had not turned away from God, I had not denied Him, and I had held fast to my vow. But I was breaking now, and I could sense the danger I was in. Danger in the sense that I was ready to chew my arm off just to get high.

I knew that I had to get out of the situation I was in. I had to get away from the party atmosphere that was so prevalent throughout the complex. But, where to go?

In total desperation to escape the torment I felt, and unable to steel myself against any more battles, either spiritually or physically within my own body, I did the only think that I could think of. I ran away. And, literally, the only place to run was up; so that is what I did. I raced up a simple, metal ladder which led to the rooftop of the three-level, cinder-block apartment building we lived in. Once I could go no further, I stumbled off the ladder and across the roof for mere feet, before collapsing in a crumpled heap on the cold concrete. Alone.

A huge, shuddering sigh of relief escaped my lips as my eyes closed, briefly, against the murky gloom of my dimly lit surroundings. And then the cravings hit me like a freight truck once again. This was soon followed by feelings of frustration, anguish, and humiliation. A tortured cry escaped my lips, as the fireworks display began to light up the night sky above me. "NO MORE!!!"

"NO MORE!!!" Now I was screaming in rage at the top of my lungs, screams that were drowned out by the reverberating echoes of the colorful explosions above me. My emotions ran unchecked as I hauled myself to my knees, with my fist extended up to the sky. My back arched as my head swung back, lifting my chin into the air.

"I CAN'T TAKE ANY MORE!!!" It was a statement, it was a plea, it was a demand, from the bottom of my lungs and the depths of my soul. I was begging God. I was telling God as loudly as possible what I was feeling and how I was struggling. My agonized screams and my sobs were uncontrollable. I swore to Him that I would not stop, could not stop any longer: if one more person offered me one more thing, I would take it! I was weak. I had tried my best, but please God, please, don't let anyone follow me up those stairs! I had lost the will to fight any longer.

Much to my huge relief, no one came.

I don't remember much more about that night. I hardly recall making my way back down the stairs and into our apartment. I do know that the next three days were a live version of my own personal hell as I suffered an endless stream of cravings, some body aches, and sweats. I shed a lot of tears. But I survived.

I walked through that battle stronger and more determined than ever to embrace what I felt was the truth. I would not look back from then on. Kicking substance abuse was merely the first challenge. I knew, however, that I could not stop there. In order to achieve a permanent change, I had to overcome many more battles and remove a lot more obstacles from my path. There is a saying: you lose to gain. This could not be truer. Everything I gave up in order to better serve God was rewarded ten-fold, in more ways than I can count. Starting with my newfound relationship with my holy spirit guides, and an increase in my spiritual understanding, abilities, and strength.

Take heart when I tell you that sometimes evil is allowed to set foot upon the path we walk, but that does not mean it will conquer us. Evil exists, yes, but so does good. Demons walk among us, but so do angels. At the end of the day, God is bigger and more powerful than anything out there. I am not afraid to depend on Him for guidance and protection, and He has always been there for me.

We must either rise to the challenges set before us, and become even more determined when we meet with adversity, or we can lay down our spiritual weapons and surrender. Surrender until the day comes when once more, we call upon our resolve, and upon our Creator to aid us. May you be blessed with strength and guidance as you wage battle in your own war. I pray you will be triumphant in your endeavors.

A LEGACY OF FORGIVENESS

Forgiveness. Such a simple word. Such a huge process.

Very often I have encountered entities in the spirit realms that have been unable to let go of their earthly grievances. Many hold fast to the traumas incurred during their time here on this earth. Some stubbornly cling to their former habits or attitudes, refusing to let go of grudges or painful issues. An inability to see beyond their own situations can leave them stuck in that reality and it can be a lengthy process to bring about change.

Forgiveness can be a challenge no matter where an entity resides, be that on the physical realm or in the spiritual realms. Our Creator does not abandon anyone, no matter where we are in the universe, but He will not force a single soul to change a thing if they do not want to transform by letting go. He waits patiently, with love.

Forgiveness can be taught by example; learning from those who have walked that trail before you. Forgiveness can be taught through faith and love; it nurtures the ability within us to forgive. Forgiveness can be taught in the mere act of receiving compassion from another, and experiencing the freedom of spiritual release. Forgiveness can change your life.

Hatred and fears can rule your world. Grudge-holding can dominate your life and weigh you down with the heaviness of hostile energy. But you can choose to free yourself from all of this self-destruction and release the burden from your heart and your spirit, gaining so much in return. You might ask what those gains could be? I would say that it is Healing, in almost every form.

Spiritual, emotional, and sometimes even physical improvements can be gained with the act of true forgiveness. It is almost shocking to see the long-term effects of refusing to forgive. The best example I have ever heard about what unforgiveness and hatred does to you is this: refusing to forgive and choosing hate is like drinking a glass of poison and expecting it to kill your enemy. Get it? The only one you are harming is you by your refusal to change and let go.

For some individuals, forgiveness is not a simple thing to achieve. Being able to move past the rage or the fear that could be consuming you can be very difficult. Accepting circumstances as they are and recognizing the loss, but moving forward with a willingness to step out of your situation, can be painful. Releasing the past and letting go of the hurt and the harm that was inflicted upon you, while leaving all of the old baggage behind and stepping into a new light, a new freedom, and a new thought pattern, can be challenging. Giving up the grudge or the need for revenge might seem impossible. However, all of these goals can be attained.

One must look closely at the many reasons and instances that forgiveness could be pertinent in. The most obvious example would be forgiving another individual for an act they might have committed to you or against you, or someone that you love. It can be hard to comprehend how granting forgiveness to that person can be most important for your self and your own growth, as much as it can be for theirs.

The emotional weight of holding bitterness or hatred, and the burden of carrying around such weight, can be crippling and affect so many areas of your life. Once forgiveness is granted it does not mean that we allow the harm previously inflicted upon us to be repeated again. God does not expect us to become a carpet to be walked on just because we carry forgiveness in our hearts. Forgiveness, in itself, is a strength. It should not become a weakness by allowing us to be taken advantage of once more. Forgiveness is about learning, understanding, and acceptance, for yourself and the people in your life. But it is also about having the courage to go forward and declare that you shall no longer allow the pain to continue and wrongs to be committed.

Now, how about taking the concept of forgiveness a step further and examining the possibility that you may be in need of forgiveness for *yourself* from within your own heart?

In the past, I have struggled with my own inner feelings of condemnation for acts that, at the time, I felt would be unforgivable. In my opinion, maybe I could have been better, done better, changed the path I chose and survived my life differently. I could have made better choices than I did in those particular moments. My actions and reactions created consequences for myself, but may also have had hurtful impacts on others. Unintentional impacts. In these instances, forgiveness of my self was crucial for my growth and my ability to move forward.

Many times, I have been unable to examine my own self-hate or loathing, and my inability to forgive myself, because I could not recognize the need to do so. I have found my vision clouded by the fog of these emotions, and this leaves me carrying added weight which can leave me buckling before I recognize it and free myself of it. Freedom is obtained by examining my perceived transgressions in detail, clearly and honestly understanding why I made the choices I did, and taking responsibility for what I can. I must forgive myself for what I cannot change, all while making every effort to implement any remaining corrections that need to be achieved. Leaving my spiritual baggage on the trail behind me and remaining determined not to pick it up again. Moving forward in forgiveness and love, for myself and anyone else involved. This is not an easy path to walk, but it is the best one.

All too often I have encountered individuals who have hated themselves as much, if not more than the adverse circumstances or people in their lives. Combine this inner grief with the burden of ill will towards those above-mentioned circumstances or persons, and you have a ticking time bomb that will explode, or maybe worse, implode, sooner or later. The resulting shrapnel of unchecked emotions can be devastating to everyone involved, most especially the person bearing the harmful emotions that needed purging.

What I find especially surprising, shocking even, is how seldom we, as human beings, allow ourselves to hear our inner voice of truth. This inner voice, our guidance, is so often shunned out of fear. Fear that the voice will condemn and shame, fearing that it shall do more harm, fearing that hidden misdeeds shall come to light and be even more painful to examine in the brightness. But how can one truly heal if we do not examine ourselves as closely as we might examine another? And when we listen closely to truth and do not deny it any longer, ultimately we will find the ability to see our issue with clarity and forgive ourselves. It is not as painful as we imagine it to be, most of the time. Trust me when I say that your own angels will not guide you with a voice that condemns, shames, or causes harm. We do that well enough on our own.

My favorite method of self-examination, at least initially, is to tell yourself a story. Not just any story. Your story. Listen to the journey you describe of your own life.

Try to keep any emotions or personal feelings about your story removed. Just tell the story of a person you once knew, not the person you are now. Start with the parents you were born to. For example, my own story might start like this: "There once was a young girl named Shannon. She was born to teenage parents who ran away from home to start their new family. Despite the love her parents had for each other, their personal differences got in the way far too often. There was a lot of alcohol consumed and a lot of disagreements between them. Shannon was exposed to many situations that left her feeling vulnerable and unsafe. (I would also describe those situations in my story, without a lot of emotional detail) As a result, she grew up very quicky and started to experiment with drugs and alcohol at an extremely young age. She made the decision to permanently leave home very early, at 14 years old. Shannon endured homelessness, hunger, drug and alcohol abuse, and lived a precarious life. She met a man much older than herself while she was living outside, and moved into his home as his partner a week after her 16th birthday." That might be the start of the story of Shannon. Told to myself as though I was a spectator, not a player in the story. I would continue with the story right up to the present day.

How would your own story start? Who were you born to? Were you cared for, or loved? Were you in harm's way, or danger? Did you grow up feeling safe and significant, or were you alone and struggling? What happened after you got older? What choices did you make? Tell yourself the story of your own life, strictly as an observer. See where the story leads to, see the events that shaped the main character, which is you.

When you hear your own story, do you not understand the actions that have shaped your life and caused you to react in the manner that you have? Do you see why you have made the choices you made? Could you forgive the person in the story if that person were not yourself? Most likely. You could forgive because you could *understand* why that person made the choices they did, you just read their story, after all.

Allow yourself to experience love for the person you were then and the person you are now. Be joyful in the freedom to forgive yourself of all of your inequities and mistakes, and move forward. Let go. Nothing in your past can be changed, only the way you perceive the past can be changed. Look at your life with fresh eyes and begin anew on your journey.

Change needs to come about freely and willingly for every individual, no matter how long that period of time may be in order for that to happen. It is also important to note that God forgives us *all* for our transgressions and He loves us equally, for we are all His children. It might be a hard concept to grasp that God loves you or me as much as He loves a serial killer or any other kind of evil-doer. But it is the terrible deeds that mankind commits that God does not love. It is the commencement of such acts that result in the need for not only forgiveness, but for transformation. A change of actions and deeds, and a change of heart, which then reflects upon our spirit. Going forward with a willingness for that transformation. As it is said, when we know better, we can do better.

My maternal grandmother, Leatrice (known as Lea), was one who also struggled with issues of forgiveness throughout her lifetime and into the spiritual realms.

Lea was an amazing woman, beautiful, intelligent, and hard-working. She was a wife, a mother to five children, and a dedicated homemaker and gardener. She loved to entertain family and friends and there was always room at her dinner table for anyone who happened to stop in. She was a very warm, caring woman, with many friends and close family members. However, there was another side of Lea that made her a formidable opponent if you should happen to cross her and incur her wrath. Lea was stubborn beyond belief and very set in her ways. Not much would change her mind if she had reached a decision. You might win a battle with Lea, but she would never forget it. And I suspect in some instances that she would never forgive it, either. It might be here that I should add that Lea and Carole, my Auntie Carole who I have written about in my memoir Journeys into the Realm of the Spirit World, were sisters.

I am the oldest grandchild in my immediate family. The announcement of my upcoming arrival into the world was probably somewhat of a shock to Lea, my grandmother, as my mother was just a teenager herself when I was born. Despite any reservations Lea might have had about the situation her daughter was in, she was as proud of me as she could be when I was born. I know that I was very loved.

I have fond memories of many visits out to Saskatchewan to spend time at the family farm as a child, and my grandmother played a huge role in my life during those visits. Most definitely her love of gardening has been passed down to me, a skill I first learned while helping in the large vegetable garden on the farm from a young age. I will always hold true to the values and lessons that were taught to me from all of the weeks of living on the farm during the months of summer. My grandmother was a very strong influence in my early years, very supportive and present whenever she could be, along with my grandfather and my mother's younger siblings. Quite often they were driving from the province of Saskatchewan where they resided, to the neighboring province of Alberta where we lived. They came to visit and celebrate special occasions such as my first communion, (I was raised Catholic), and major holidays such as Easter and Thanksgiving.

I am sad to say that as I grew older and had barely started my adolescent years, my relationship with Grandma Lea became very strained. There wasn't a person in my life that could comprehend why I had begun acting out in the manner in which I was; running away from home, consuming large amounts of alcohol and drugs whenever I could, seeing older men in intimate relationships, the list went on and on. My grandmother, although unaware of a large number of my transgressions, was puzzled by my defiance and the actions she was aware of, and had strong opinions on the subject.

Lea was also largely unaware of the circumstances in my home which were triggering much of my behavior. I could not understand at that time what the heck her problem with me was, nor did I care. There were many in my life who had issues and concerns with my lifestyle choices, especially at such a young age, but I would not reverse the path I had chosen to walk. I was also quick to avoid any one that I felt disapproved of my actions, and my grandmother was one of those people. It did not matter if she spoke a word to me or not, displeasure rolled off of her in waves during those moments we were together, something I could hardly ignore or be unaware of. Looking back through the lens of an adult I can also surmise that Lea, in addition to her frustrations, would have been very disappointed, confused, and saddened by my choices. This was something I would not have understood so well in my youth.

Despite the wedge that had caused such a great divide between us, Lea fought to hold on to the relationship that we did have. Our conflicts were most often verbally silent ones, although rife with emotions, but we still shared a strong bond of love. I had respect for my grandmother regardless of any situation. I believe that she tried as hard as she could to understand me, coming from her perspective.

I think that the whole family was somewhat relieved when I met the man who I would later marry. I say "somewhat" only because the age difference between us was fairly horrifying to most people since I was so young at the time, being the age of fifteen whereas he was thirty. However, the relief was in large part because there was now strong hope for all involved that I would settle down, leave street life, and perhaps, with a safer style of living, survive to be older than a teenager. Which is what eventually happened. Most of my loved ones, grandparents included, were present at my wedding, held a mere three weeks after my eighteenth birthday.

Grandma Lea may have had hopes that my life would change and that I would settle into married life and stability without any further issues, but not much changed for me at all. I was still determined to live my life as I chose. If that included a few beers, cigarettes and marijuana, then my new husband was welcome to join me but I was not about to change the road I was travelling. Or so I thought.

Fast forward to a year later and I found myself moving to Arizona, USA with my husband, who was going to attend a motorcycle mechanics training centre. My life was kicking into high gear with all of the fun I was having meeting new people and riding all over the desert state on our Harley-Davidson motorcycle with friends. I had no idea that my life was going to swiftly, radically change when I met the man who was to become my spiritual mentor. He introduced me to God in a whole new way that I could never have imagined. I committed myself to an entirely revised style of living, pursuing my dream to become a medium for God and to serve Him, never dreaming of the opposition that was to greet me.

Change does not come easily to many people. However, my transformation for God was almost instantaneous. I chose to remove all drugs and alcohol from my life, got rid of my weapons, and made the choice to shed my hard-core motorcycle lifestyle. All of this was my decision, freely made, and I was happy with my choice. I felt certain that my family would also support my decision to change with joy. I was positive that they would rejoice in my newly found sobriety and my relationship with God.

I was wrong.

The changes I brought about in my life were as extreme as they could get, and my family thought that I had lost my mind entirely. Instead of reacting with happiness to my new life and my new commitments, my family was confused and suspicious about my purpose to commit to God. They were even more horrified that I was speaking of mediums and a spirit world that served Him. My grandmother was a practising Catholic all of her life and she was *adamantly* opposed to spiritism in any form. Therefore, what I was experiencing was just plain evil in her mind, and she made her views known to me. Although I tried on more than one occasion over the years to alleviate her fears, my grandmother could never find it in her heart to change her opinion on my choice to serve in the manner that I did. This was just one more block in the growing wall that was separating us.

I would like to say that my relationship with Lea grew stronger with time but that was not so. The older Lea got the more set in her ways I found her to be. We had both stubbornly dug our heels into the ground on certain issues, more or less agreeing to disagree. Although I will not speak on her relationship with other members of the family, I am aware that I was not the only individual to run afoul of Lea's strong will and wrath. She could be quite formidable. Having said that, I must say my grandmother could not have been prouder when my three sons were born and blessed her with the title of Great-Grandma. She was absolutely glowing with the news of each arrival. And she always went out of her way to try to show her love to us all with many greeting cards, letters, and handcrafted treasures which still grace my home to this day.

My youngest child, Zach, was four years old when my grandmother was diagnosed with lung cancer. Although she fought bravely, the disease was advancing rapidly, and I drove to Saskatchewan early in the spring of 2002 to see her. I will always be grateful for that visit and the chance I had to connect with my grandmother as I read out loud to her a chapter from the book, "Chicken Soup for the Soul". She always loved listening to me read as a child, and took great pleasure in hearing me read once again.

2002 was also a very tumultuous year for me, and not only had I endured the breakdown of my marriage, I met my sweetheart, Ray, in June. We had a whirlwind romance and began living with each other very shortly after our first meeting. Although I had mentioned my grandparents to Ray, I had not had an opportunity to go into great detail about them, except to mention my grandma's illness.

Fall arrived, and September was a beautiful month. The weather was warm during the day, the air crisp and cool at night, and the fall colors were spectacular. Ray and I decided to escape our hectic lifestyle and head for the majestic mountain ranges to the west of our home, choosing to go completely off-grid with only a tent and supplies. We were well out of cell phone service and away from most of humanity, deep into the woods. I can still picture our serene little campsite, with our tent and truck barely fitting onto a small grassy knoll that sloped down to the edge of a slow-moving, deep stream. The water was crystal-clear and frigid. The colorful fall leaves on the trees danced and swirled in the breeze, gracefully dropping into the water below and floating away downstream. We could not have found a more perfect setting.

Our trip to the mountains was short and sweet. Ray and I enjoyed our time immensely and had shared conversations on many interesting topics over the sounds of the crackling campfire and the melody of the stream beside us. It was on the last day of our mini vacation that the conversation turned to a topic that I seldom discussed: my Grandma Lea. Ray listened patiently while I described my grandmother and our complicated relationship. I went into great detail about my love of the farm in Saskatchewan, and the joyful memories of numerous visits to the lakeside cabin my grandparents also owned. I spoke of the valuable lessons I had learned as a child from my experiences with my grandparents and aunts and uncles on the farm. I spoke at great length and with fondness of my memories, surprising even myself at what was coming from my lips and where my thoughts were going. It had been many years since I had such recollections. It was such a rarity for me to mention my grandmother that even Ray found it unusual. When I had finished speaking, he looked at me and commented, "That was strange, where did that come from?"

I honestly could not answer him for I had also found it a little odd to be reminiscing about my grandmother and the time I had spent with her. The memories had come to my mind suddenly, without warning, and seemed to stop just as quickly. It did not take long for us to move on to other discussions, and the rest of the day passed quickly.

It was mid-afternoon before we were packed up and headed back to civilization and the reality of everyday life, and with that came the return of cell phone service. Imagine my shock when I checked my voice mail and heard the message left there by my mother. It was left on the same day we were coming home, September 26, 2002. My Grandma Lea crossed over that very morning, right around the same time that I had been chatting about her with Ray. Ray's eyes grew round with shock when I relayed the news to him, for he saw the correlation between the time of my grandmothers passing and the conversation we had very clearly. It had been no coincidence that she had come to my mind when she did, and I believe that her spirit was there that morning with me, if only briefly. Maybe she heard my conversation with Ray and realized how much I loved her, too. In hindsight, it was a beautiful, comforting experience.

That moment of connection I had with my Grandma Lea on the morning she crossed over was the only spiritual interaction I had with her for quite some time. I did not notice her presence at any time during the next few days, or while we were in Saskatchewan attending her funeral. I was not aware of her spirit at all in fact for at least six months after she had passed. When that day came to be it was quite uneventful, actually. I was standing at the kitchen sink tending to my daily chores, not really thinking of much at all, when I suddenly became aware of Lea's energy in the room behind me. In my mind's eye I could see her, but she was not as I would have expected her to be.

Most often my interactions with those that have crossed over reveal to me a spirit that is appearing younger than they were when they left this earth, especially if they were in advanced years when they passed. In my experience, this can be a result of that entity having had the freedom from the physical body, the chance to re-connect with loved ones, and to have experienced the love and forgiveness of our Creator. It is a time for further growth and opportunities, to swiftly change as they learn. Very frequently these lessons are involving forgiveness of self and others, and learning love on a whole other level. Their spirit will reflect the changes that they have experienced, which can manifest in their appearances, showing them to be content and happy and youthful. I am not ever surprised to see these changes, for they are very common, but I am quite often pleasantly surprised by the suddenness of it all.

How the spirit appears to me is also another means by which I can determine their lot in the spirit world. If the entity has died of unresolved, traumatic events, such as the murdered woman I met in spirit on the Highway of Tears, they will most usually appear to me as they were on the day of their death, at the moment they left the physical realm. That is because the trauma of those events, and their inability to resolve and let go of those moments, leaves them trapped in the same patterns they were experiencing here on earth. In no way does this mean that they have been abandoned. But there are times when the spirit traps itself, essentially. Unable to move forward or loosen its grip on the physical realm, because of the strong unresolved connections and emotions it holds to past events. God cannot force them to continue on in their journey, for all are granted free will, so, He waits. When the moment is right and their need for change is evident, God is always present through His holy spirit hosts to support that individual and release them from self-inflicted bondage. Sometimes He has to employ the use of human envoys to convey His messages to those who are "lost", as He has done with myself and the entities of Catharine or Carl, mentioned in my previous book.

At any rate, when I became aware of my grandmothers' spirit in the room with me, I found that I could hardly contain my surprise at the appearance she presented. Grandma Lea had barely changed at all since she had crossed over. Although she did not appear to me to be frail and ravaged from the effects of cancer, as she had come to be when she was physically alive, she presented herself at this moment looking only as young as she had appeared to be in her senior years, before she grew ill. Her hair was dark, though, no longer grey, and she stood tall and straight. But, despite that fact, the spirit that I was seeing was reserved, silent, and did not seem happy at all. Lea also did not appear to be sad, or angry, but there was no indication of joyfulness or serenity, either. I was momentarily stunned with shock at seeing my grandmother so unexpectedly, and then puzzled by the appearance she was presenting. Worse still, I found myself instantly pulling back emotionally from Lea and withdrawing from communicating with her.

This very human reaction came about as a result of our relationship issues from when she was alive, and, in this moment, I found myself unable to resolve these issues and allow any more interaction other than observing. Please understand that it was fear controlling the outcome of this meeting. Fear that I would somehow interfere with anything that Lea could possibly convey to me. You see, if my grandmother were to relay to me bitterness, hurt, or anger, I would naturally assume that I was interfering with the message because this is what I would *expect* from Lea if she were alive. I felt this way partially because she was so adamantly opposed to spirit communication previously, and now here she stood before me.

Contrarily, if Lea were to speak any words of happiness or mending our relationship, well, that is another comment I could expect to hear from her if she were learning and moving forward; leaving me to decide once more that I could be hearing what I wanted to hear in this matter, and I was fearful of making assumptions. The complicated interactions we had previously were now carried over into the spirit realms, and silence remained between us. I later joked to my husband that perhaps Lea had looked so reserved because she was angry that I had turned out to be correct about the spirit world and she was not. But truthfully, I did not believe it was the reason, even though I did not understand her stance.

Months turned into years and the rare, intermittent visits from Grandma Lea were always the same. She was stoic and silent every single time that I saw her. These appearances always left me mildly frustrated because I could not understand for the life of me why we could not seem to knock down the walls that left us unable to communicate. I was confused that her spirit never seemed to change, that alone would have been a good indicator that she was progressing upwards in the spirit realms, but change never came about. As time went by, I grew accustomed to the silence of her presence, and although I always acknowledged her when she was in the room with me, I too remained silent.

I chose not to mention Grandma Lea to any of my family members other than Ray. I felt that it would be too hard to explain that I was certain my grandmother was stuck emotionally and not progressing forward past a certain point. I could not understand what could be holding her back, nor could I find the words to make any one else understand. There were also moments when I would be in communication with other family members who had crossed over and I would see Lea present with them, but she always chose to remain in the background, silent as ever.

To complicate matters even more, my aunt Colleen, one of Lea's daughters, had asked me on more than one occasion if I had been in contact with her mother, to which I could only vaguely indicate that I had seen her, but not much more. It was painful to hear Colleen tell me that she had made a pact with her mother before she had died; they agreed that Lea would let Colleen know somehow that she was okay in the spiritual realms, but that message had not ever come to her. I have always been taught that such a visit is permissible in God's time and when it is right for the entity to come forward, not when we will it to be, but still, this explanation was hard for Colleen to accept. Even more frustrating for Colleen was the fact that she had gone to visit several mediums in the hope of communicating with Lea, to no avail. It seemed that no one could contact Lea, all attempts resulted in silence.

Fast forward to the year 2018. One of my uncles gave me a wonderful gift, a surprise Christmas present, to be able to stay on a houseboat that he owned, for 4 nights any time during the off-season of the upcoming year. This houseboat was located on the huge Shuswap Lake, located in British Columbia. After consulting with my family, we decided on September 2019, after the long weekend holiday. My uncle had also suggested that time of year because the water was still warm, the fall colors were beautiful, and the lake was far less busy with pleasure-craft on the water than it was in the heat of the summer months. The houseboat was equipped with 3 bedrooms, a loft with 2 beds, and 2 additional fold-out beds in the living area, so I was able to include my entire family: my husband, all 3 of my boys plus one of their girlfriends, and both of my parents (divorced for years). I also decided to invite my Auntie Colleen, who I have a very close relationship with. Everyone was excited about the houseboat excursion, an opportunity we might not ever have again.

Colleen called me a few months into the new year of 2019, ostensibly just to chat, but it soon became apparent her actual intent of the conversation. She was so sorry, but she had to inform me that she did not think she could make the houseboat trip. I was taken by surprise at this statement, for Colleen had seemed to be very excited about the prospect of the upcoming vacation. She had a difficult time explaining to me that she felt a strange discomfort about coming along with us, she couldn't really understand it herself, but she did not think that she should go. Although I was very disappointed, I did not try to change her mind, for I am usually very accepting of the fact that there are reasons beyond my control that people make the choices that they do. I did inform her that she was very welcome to change her mind if she would like to join us, however, and left it at that.

I was quite pleased when Colleen called me the next month to say that she had changed her mind and decided to join us on the Shuswap in September. She laughed about her uncomfortable feeling and she was determined to join us and have some fun with the family, brushing aside any unfounded trepidations. I was certain all was well when the conversation ended and I went about planning for Colleen to be present.

Perhaps you might be just as confused as I was to hear that Colleen called me again a few short weeks later, unwilling to attend the family vacation and remaining vague about what her problem was this time. Personal issues were making it difficult to get away she explained to me. I could not make any sense of Colleen's indecision to join us, normally she was very comfortable with the whole family and enjoyed herself immensely when we spent time together. My disappointment was evident, but once again I chose to end the conversation on a positive note, with the offer for Colleen to change her mind at any time. Which, to my astonishment, she did once more.

My head was absolutely spinning the final time that Colleen decided yet again she was coming with us. Nothing was stopping her, she stated to me, no matter what. I was becoming very curious as to the reasons why there appeared to be so much pressure on Colleen to stay home and not be with us on the houseboat. Was there a spiritual reason? Experience has taught me that whenever there is great opposition against me traveling a particular path, that is most often the path I *should* take, and I pondered this scenario for Colleen. I could see no good reason that my aunt could not be with us, I certainly did not feel as though God was trying to stop her, so I let the matter rest. The remainder of the summer was uneventful, and September swiftly arrived. I forgot about the unseen forces that appeared to be attempting to thwart our vacation with Colleen.

As our family group was congregating from different parts of Alberta, and my aunt from British Columbia, we agreed upon a time to meet at the houseboat facility in Sicamous, on the Shuswap Lake, for our check-in time on the 7th of September. Scheduling the houseboat for off-season turned out to be an excellent decision for the fact that essential paperwork was filled out quickly and boarding the houseboat was swift because we were the only vacationers present at that moment.

Staff members briefed us on houseboat protocol, especially how to land the boat on the rocky beaches and firmly secure it with heavy ropes. Metal rods were provided, which in turn needed to be anchored with a sledgehammer pounding the rods deep into the ground on shore, and the ropes were to be tightly attached to these rods. There were two ropes, one at either corner of the rear of the boat, and the ropes were positioned onshore in a manner that left little room for the boat to move out of its fixed position. It was explained to us that it was especially important to be moored properly in case of bad weather.

We were all very excited to explore the houseboat and settle in with our belongings, eager to pull away from the dock and head out into open water. Ray was the designated Captain of the boat, and the rest of us spread out across the top and main decks to watch the scenery go by as we pulled away from the dock. It was a beautiful, warm, sunny day. We encountered many other houseboats traveling on the calm, sparkling waters even though the Labor Day long-weekend had passed and most vacationers had ended their stay on the lake.

Because houseboats are not equipped with night time running lights it was expressly stated that we had to be off the lake and moored onshore long before dark. This was a rule for all houseboats, regardless of who the owner or operator of the houseboat was. We found a suitable beach covered in small, smooth rocks to drive the boat up onto, thankful that we were the only occupants of the small cove we had discovered, grateful for the privacy. The Shuswap Lake is very deep, with only a small portion of land stretching out under the clear waters from the beach, before dropping off steeply into impenetrable depths. This allows the front of the boat, the bow, to be grounded and moored while leaving the back end of the boat to float freely, with its motor partially submerged and the propeller ready to be engaged. Ray and my three sons Wayde, Adam, and Zach had taken responsibility for mooring the boat, with extra care taken to ensure that the metal rods were pounded down into the ground as far as they could go. The ropes were tight and at the appropriate angle from the boat to keep it firmly in place.

We prepared a quick meal for our supper and with the advent of evening skies we began to drift into separate little groups. Wayde and Adam were in the upstairs loft preparing their beds, Zach and his girlfriend Becca were at the front of the boat deep in conversation, and my parents, Glen and Pat, had retired to their separate berths to organize their belongings. Ray, Colleen and I were standing outside on the back of the main deck of the boat, chatting amicably and watching the sun make its gradual descent over the horizon. Some distance away, but moving swiftly, were rolling thunderclouds of an approaching storm. We observed them without concern, we had been warned that storms could form quickly over the lake but we felt confident that we were well prepared. Even as the air grew heavy and the wind picked up speed and began rocking the boat, we remained outside. We were enjoying the display that nature was providing, all while watching the twinkling lights of the houses on the opposite shoreline appear in the rapidly approaching darkness.

Suddenly the swirling, black clouds were overhead of us and shards of lightning began to illuminate the skies. In between the flares of electricity making our surroundings bright as day, the only perceptible light to be discerned through the storm were the pinpricks of light still visible on shore. Then, in all the confusion of the wild weather, I gave my head a shake as though to clear my eyes, for the lights suddenly appeared to be *moving* across my line of sight. My brain was momentarily stunned as I tried to fathom what I was seeing. Reality slapped me hard in the flash of an instant as I realized with horror and some panic that indeed, the shore lights weren't moving, *we were.*

Somehow, in the crazy rocking of the waves on the lake, our boat had slipped its moorings and was most certainly moving, swinging sideways in the water. The whole length of the boat was headed for the shallow water of shore and some large, jagged rocks that had been visible in the water to our right when we had beached. Shocked as I was, my reaction was swift, and I was already turning to run and alert the rest of my family as I was yelling to Ray and Colleen about our dire circumstances.

Comprehension jolted Ray into action and he pushed past me, running to the engine controls as quickly as he could, frantic to get the engine and the propeller out of the water before it was smashed and rendered useless against the rocks in the shallows. Not a moment too soon we could hear the whine of an electric motor pulling the propeller and shaft up from the pounding waves, followed almost immediately by a sickening scraping noise as the pontoons of the boat made contact with the solid, unmoving rocks below. The entire length of the houseboat was now beached, rocking back and forth in the crashing waves as it was being constantly pushed against the shoreline by howling winds. Miraculously, the motor was unscathed and remained intact.

The motor was saved from harm, and we were also safe even if we were completely disabled and at the mercy of the storm. It appeared that only one line had let go, on the left side, (port), of the boat, which is why we had swung to the right, (starboard), as we were still attached there. All nine family members huddled together in the living quarters of the boat, helpless and unable to correct our situation, listening to the sickening sounds of rocks hammering against the hollow pontoon below us as the waves rolled. The wind was wailing and bolts of lightning illuminated our surroundings in split-second bursts.

Ray turned on the two-way radio so he could alert the emergency crew at the rental facility about our predicament and request aid. The airwaves came instantly alive with the sounds of distress calls from many other houseboats in the area, in far worse condition than we were in. Some boats had been moored in proximity to other houseboats that had slipped free, and were now literally crashing into each other. Another boat had precariously floated out to the dark, deep waters of the lake, trailing the moorage lines and was unable to start his engine for fear that the ropes would entangle the propeller. Some boats had experienced breaking windows, and appliances such as refrigerators were falling off of the walls in the violence of the storm. We felt fortunate that we were in the situation that we were in, obviously it could have been much worse.

Although we were able to get a response to our call for help, we were informed that it would be some time before we would be able to receive any assistance at all, given the plight of so many other boats on the lake. The gale around us persisted and we resigned ourselves to a long night of waiting for help. We could do nothing with the unsecured rope floating in deep water and our boat hung up on rocks, parallel to the shoreline.

Then, without warning, the craziest thing happened.

While the storm outside remained unrelenting and the winds were still pinning us hopelessly against shore, the boat suddenly, of its own accord, began to *move*. We all stared at each other in total amazement as the boat began to float off of the rocks and, completely against the force of the wind and waves, swing out to deep water and realign itself head-on with the beach.

Impossible. But true.

It was as though a giant hand had come out of the sky and positioned us in the perfect spot, regardless of the weather, as easily as that of a child with a toy.

The shock of what had just happened was momentary, however, and Ray and the boys sprang into action quickly. Wayde, Adam and Zach leapt off of the front of the boat into the churning, shallow water before them, scrambling to shore with the loose rope somehow captured and firmly in tow. Ray started up the electrical motor responsible for lowering the main motor and propeller into the water. Once submerged, the primary engine roared into life, and as quickly as possible Ray drove the boat up onto shore to properly beach it.

The night sky was pitch black, but somehow, with the aid of a small flashlight and the bursts of searing lightning illuminating the surroundings, the boat was once more secured to the metal post that had been pounded down into the ground as far as it would go. Unbelievable. It was as though nothing had ever happened. The boat was completely intact, the propeller undamaged, and our journey could continue on in the morning. Not one of us could come up with a rational explanation as to how the boat had moved like it had and positioned itself so perfectly. But of course, in my heart, I knew. Thank you, God, for your protection. Amen.

The next morning was calm and sunny, the scenery was beautiful, and we were all very grateful that our trip had not been ended before it had even started due to the events of the previous night. Listening to the calls on the radio, we surmised that many vacationers had ended their trip abruptly with heavy damages sustained to their boats. We found ourselves amazed that we were not one of the casualties, and mentioned more than once how unusual it was that the boat had turned, seemingly on its own, in the middle of a severe storm while it was grounded. There were no damages at all to the boat that we could see, which also seemed incredible. Our holiday was able to continue, yay!

Shuswap Lake is absolutely huge, boasting a surface area of over three hundred kilometers and consisting of four arms that connect together in such a way that the lake appears to have the shape of an abstract letter H. There is no possible way that one can travel the entire length of four arms in four days, and we were not about to try. We spent the day of the 8th slowly travelling along the shoreline of the Salmon Arm of the lake, in awe of just how many Bald Eagles we could spot roosting in the trees. Although there were many lakeside homes to view, they were only in specific areas that were easily accessible by car, leaving countless kilometers of untouched forests stretching alongside the shorelines of the lake to observe and enjoy. It was so calming and peaceful. We were fortunate enough to find another secluded cove to moor in and explore, and we enjoyed soaking in the hot tub on the top deck afterwards. The guys were also diving off of the back of the boat into the depths below, thoroughly enjoying the camaraderie. I am beyond grateful that I was able to enjoy the company of my family while experiencing such peace and solidarity during that trip.

The morning of the 9th was calm and uneventful, although a little cloudy and wet. We were in no rush to push off from shore and start our travels anew. The morning meal had been prepared and cleared away, and most of the family was gathered in the front of the boat in the living area, chatting. I had retreated to my room at the rear of the boat to tidy the bed and dress for the upcoming day.

As I turned to exit the room and rejoin my family, I was suddenly overcome with the urge for solitude. I found myself turning instead to open the sliding glass door that led to the rear of the boat while grabbing a warm shawl to cover myself with. Stepping out onto the small back deck, I glanced around and chose to settle on the only available surface that was not soaked from morning rains, a hard plastic seating platform that was tucked into the corner. With my back to the wall and my knees drawn up to my chest I settled in to observe my surroundings and enjoy the seclusion. The rhythmic sounds of water slapping the sides of the pontoons beneath me were the only accompaniment to my wandering mind and random thoughts. I felt as though I had no specific purpose regarding my desire for some momentary quiet and was enjoying myself thoroughly.

My gaze was directed at the opposite shoreline for the most part, and up at the grey, overcast skies above me. The serenity I was feeling at that moment was comforting. I glanced down at my lap to adjust my shawl so that it better covered my legs, and was quite astounded when I looked up once again and discovered that the majestic scenery that was before me had disappeared from my line of sight. Obscuring my view was a vision of a beautiful woman with dark hair that was loosely pulled back and secured at the nape of her neck. Although I could only catch a glimpse of the hair curling up behind her, I could see that her hair was styled in a fashion that reminded me of an earlier era, perhaps the 1940s or 50s. Her eyes were sparkling and warm, her lips curved into a gentle smile, and she was emanating a peaceful vibration. It was with considerable surprise that I was struck with the sudden understanding that the entity before me was my Grandma Lea!

I barely had a moment to begin to recover from the shock of seeing Lea and to register how well she was looking, before I was overwhelmed once more with the presence of yet another spiritual being, one whose energy I am very familiar with. It was my Auntie Carole, Lea's sister. I must admit, at that moment I was in complete amazement to be blessed with this very unexpected visit. My heart was overjoyed to see how well Lea was looking, and that she was with Carole. I barely had time to register their presence, however, before I was overcome with a barrage of emotions and words that were not my own. It seemed as though I was receiving information from both of the women almost simultaneously, although the communication was concise, clear, and delivered calmly.

Simply put, I was reminded once again of the reasons why Auntie Carole had to learn about forgiveness before she crossed over. I was also informed that not only did she have to learn about love and forgiveness in her own heart, she also needed to progress to that state of understanding so that she could help her sister, Lea, once they were reunited in spirit. Lea had been unable to let go of bitterness, hurt, and possibly hatreds, for a good portion of her life on earth. As stubborn as she was, Lea had also carried these belief systems with her when she crossed over.

I know from her former spiritual appearances to me that although she had shed a good deal of earthly considerations after she crossed, and while she had obviously moved forward at least somewhat, Lea was not very happy. And although she had appeared to me looking younger than she was on the day she died, she hadn't looked youthful. I did not understand why at the time.

Carole was able to assist Lea in further understanding and healing, because of her own experiences with that very issue. Carole had held a life-long *hatred* for a man that had crossed over decades previously, to her emotional and spiritual detriment. She experienced forgiveness for this man before she crossed over in 2017: a monumental task. The grudges that Lea carried with her when she crossed over remained with her because of her refusal to let matters go. Sometimes bitterness runs deep within our soul and clouds our vision, hindering our ability to move forward.

I have no doubt in my mind that my grandmother was a God-fearing woman and a devout Catholic. But I also believe that she was extremely angry or disappointed with herself, as well as others, and that she was experiencing a very difficult time moving past that. These would not have been small, petty grievances that she was carrying in her soul. These would have been issues of the most deeply felt, large-scale matters. She might not have ever shared this grief with another person in her lifetime, as Auntie Carole had also done. I was not told about what her issues were, for that was of no concern to me and would remain private, but the explanation that was being shared with me made perfect sense. I was astounded to see the consequences of Carole's ability to forgive manifesting in Lea's progression in such a massive way. What a beautiful legacy.

Although the message from Carole and Lea was brief, it was impactful. For the first time ever, I could see that Lea was looking youthful and very happy. She was radiant with love. I could also feel the love that she held for her two daughters and other family members that were with me on the boat. I knew that she had truly experienced forgiveness and was at peace. I could feel the joy that she felt to be with her loved ones in the spiritual realms, as well as with her family in the physical realm. I understood that all was well.

In the flash of an instant Carole and Lea departed from me and I was left once more in full view of the shoreline across the lake with its hills and forests. I was experiencing utter joy at having learned about my Grandma Lea and the progress she had made. I made sure to describe in a voice recording on my phone what I had seen so as not to forget it, and then proceeded into the houseboat where the rest of the family had remained. I understood that this message would be of great importance to Colleen, who had waited so many heartbreaking years for a message from her mother, but I also understood that the time was not right at that moment. I chose to be patient and wait for the inevitable pull that would guide me to speak.

Our journey down the remainder of the Salmon Arm that day was lovely, even if it was overcast with low-hanging clouds and a heavy mist in the air. We continued straight down the arm of the lake we were on and stayed our course in the same direction after crossing the connecting channel of water that linked all four arms. We had now begun traveling the length of the Anstey Arm of the lake, which also happens to be the shortest arm. Part of the way down that arm, on the northern shore, and around mid-afternoon, we discovered an interesting-looking cove that was dotted with small man-made rock formations along the stony beach. We decided that this was a great place to have some fun exploring and to set up for the night.

Once our feet hit land we discovered, upon closer inspection of the cove, several little inuksuit and various other offerings and monuments. They were built of rocks, mosses, branches, feathers, pinecones, bark, string and any other little treasure that could be found on the shoreline. Various tokens that were displayed in an effort to leave behind small gifts for the next traveller to find and marvel at; marking a memory of the peace that could be tangibly felt. We were in awe of the wonderful energy that emanated from the area, quite happy with our decision to moor there.

The next morning arrived with no change in the weather. The mist was cool but easily overcome with a light jacket or shawl. The majority of the family had taken the time to beachcomb and really enjoy themselves not only the day before, but on this morning as well. There were so many interesting things to see, and the rocks in that area seemed especially colorful and sparkly.

Wayde and Adam decided to build a tribute of their own out on a small outcropping next to the water. It was a pyramid of small boulders stacked waist-high and then decorated with driftwood and tiny rocks with a little help from me. We discovered after we had set back out on the water that the pyramid could be seen for quite some distance away given its position on the beach. It was heartwarming to realize that some small part of our energy now served to mark an area that was so special to us and would most likely become special to many others.

We reached the end of the Anstey Arm right at the beginning of the afternoon. It was a majestic sight. Completely uninhabited, the shores were contrived of the same sandy-colored pebbles that most of the beaches had been covered with, and they arched in a graceful curve from shore to shore that marked the end of our travels on this part of the lake. We were surrounded by tree-covered hills. The water in the cove was as still as glass, although a small river could be seen emptying directly into the lake a short distance away. The sun was breaking through the clouds and reflecting off of the water below, causing it to sparkle and shine in an especially eye-catching manner. I felt a deep sense of contentment inside my soul in the serenity of that moment, alone as I was on the top observation deck of the boat. The rest of my family remained on the main deck below. To add to my peace, Ray had turned the engine of the boat off and we were gently drifting in the quiet seclusion. No one else was around.

It may come as no surprise to you to hear that at the very moment my body had begun to fall into a deep state of relaxation, my throat began to tighten, as though I had a great need to speak. I then felt overcome with some urgency to do just that. I realized in a flash of a second that "now" was the time I had been waiting for, the guidance that I sought concerning the best time to speak to Colleen had come. There was to be no more waiting.

I knew that Colleen was sitting outside on her own as well, just below me on the main deck. We had been equally appreciative of the tranquility before us and felt no need to join each other in conversation, remaining comfortably apart in the company of our own thoughts. My voice broke into the silence of the moment as I requested that Auntie come up to the observation deck to be with me. She told me later that my voice had taken on such an unfamiliar tone that she understood the importance of that request immediately, and did not hesitate to join me. Amazingly, the remainder of the family stayed inside, preparing a light lunch and conversing amongst themselves, allowing me the privacy that I was desperately in need of.

As Colleen settled in front of me, Lea and Carole were also present once more. I could feel the space around us bustling with energy and activity. I began to explain to Colleen the events that had taken place the morning before as I had taken refuge in the stillness of the morning, and I replayed the recording that I had made describing what I had seen and heard. Colleen was sitting quietly and listening intently, a little shocked I was sure, at the unexpected events taking place.

Then Lea herself began to speak, and I could hear her words in my mind, words I relayed to Colleen as quickly as I could. Lea confirmed the message that had been delivered the day before, and she began to elaborate and expand upon that subject: her need to experience forgiveness, and how her inability to do so had hindered her spiritual journey. The importance of Carole's role in Lea's progression was explained to Colleen, as well as the correlating reasons why Colleen had been unable to contact her mother. Lea needed to resolve her issues with forgiveness in order to experience the spiritual freedom that she had been seeking. The gift of communication that was granted between mother and daughter at this moment could only be allowed because Lea had set herself free with love and acceptance of her past. True forgiveness in every aspect.

It was as though Lea's burdens had weighed so heavily upon her that she found herself *unable* to communicate previously, even though she had been present with all of us at some point in our lives since she had crossed over. And although seventeen years of our life had gone by, time is but a blink of an eye in the spirit world. The changes that needed to be made can seem to be a lengthy process in our comprehension, but not so much in the spiritual realms. I could see comprehension and relief flooding over Colleen's face with these words; her mother had not been lost to her all of these years.

Although Carole was present at the conversation Lea was having with Colleen, I don't recall specific words from her. She relayed through emotions her love and support for us, and then faded into the background while Lea spoke. Once Lea had fallen quiet and I understood that the message was ending, I also assumed that the interactions from the spirit world were finished. But I was wrong. God had yet another gift for Colleen.

For over fifteen years my Auntie Colleen was a care-giver and support worker with the elderly, before moving on to a position as a supervisor in the same industry. Serving as a care-giver was a position that she enjoyed immensely, she has a deep love and respect for seniors in general. It was very important for her to see that they had the best quality of life possible, and for them to be given the respect and dignity that they deserved while they were alive. I can say for certainty that I *know* Colleen excelled at her job and was as dedicated as I have mentioned, because of what I was now seeing.

In my mind, appearing brightly against a black background, I was quite astounded to be observing a huge group of individuals. They were positioned off to the side of where we were seated, in a large semi-circle in three rows, one row behind the other. Most of the people in the back two rows were standing, but the majority of the people in the front row were sitting. In wheelchairs. My mouth was almost hanging open once again, from the shock of seeing individuals appearing to me in hospital gowns, seated in wheelchairs, standing with the aid of walkers, and leaning against I.V. poles with bags of medicine hanging off of them. Most every one appeared to be elderly and quite frail, but what I found to be very interesting is the fact that I understood immediately that these spirits were appearing to me to be as they were when they were *alive*, for the purposes of identification. They could not appear to me as they now were in the spirit world, because Colleen would not be able to identify them or connect with their presence if they did. I certainly would not have been able to understand the message at all if I had seen a large group of happy, youthful-looking people. So, while these spirits appeared to be very aged and ill, I knew that this was not so. This comprehension was followed by a sudden, overwhelming barrage of emotions and thoughts, all directed towards Colleen from the group of seniors before me. Strong emotions such as gratitude and love, heartfelt words of thanks, all of these things echoed in my mind as I began to relay to Colleen just what exactly I was experiencing.

I truly was astonished to see such a large gathering of spirits all present for one person. Colleen had made a monumental impact upon each and every one who had appeared, and they all wanted her to know this without a doubt. It seemed as though the air around Colleen was positively glowing with all of the appreciation, joy, and love being sent her way. If Colleen had ever felt that her role in life was insignificant, she was truly realizing this was the exact opposite of what was her reality. Colleen was not just loved by these people, she was cherished. And not only when they were in physical form, but now, and always.

Colleen had tears in her eyes as I described everything I was seeing and feeling. I have to admit that I had tears in my own eyes, for this was a beautiful, heartwarming, celebration of souls reuniting, even if only briefly. What an amazing gift. Thank you, God.

It was almost amusing when Ray appeared on the top deck merely minutes after the elderly spirits had departed. I could appreciate how well this moment had all been planned out, the peaceful surroundings, the boat motor turned off so we could drift in silence, the entire family occupied on the main deck so as not to disturb us. Ray could see that the conversation we were having was important, and most likely of a spiritual nature, so, unwilling to interfere, he stayed standing in his position at the top of the stairs and announced that lunch had been prepared before retreating. Almost immediately after that, we could hear the sounds of the rest of the family spreading out into separate groups and some of them were heading up to the top deck where we were seated. Our time with the spirit world was finished.

In hindsight, I can see clearly now why Colleen had felt so plagued by doubts about coming on the houseboat vacation. I know with certainty that the message from Lea, Carole, and the elderly spirits, had been planned long in advance of our trip. I do believe that evil was trying to interfere with the message ever coming through for Colleen and that it was nothing holy that was trying to stop her from coming. What better way to thwart the plan than to torment her with doubts? Evil would not want Colleen to be released from the pain of losing her mother. Or to experience the freedom that was granted to her soul upon the news of Lea's presence, and the explanation of her absence for seventeen years.

I believe that this message was so important for Colleen to receive, that evil used to its advantage the terrible storm that would have cut short our visit immediately had the boat been damaged; stopping the gift that was to be delivered from ever coming. I also have no doubt in my mind that the miraculous turning of the houseboat into open water while it was beached on rocks and still in the throes of a severe storm, was the aid of holy spirit hosts determined to see God's will be done. And I believe it was done. The gratitude that I feel for being able to witness such a wonderful reunion is immense. To see the effects of this visit upon Colleen makes my heart swell even more. I am in awe.

Immediately after the mid-day meal was consumed and the kitchen was restored to a state of cleanliness, we were underway once again, headed back down the Anstey Arm and continuing to the Salmon Arm of the lake. This was our last night on the houseboat and we were all a little sad that the vacation was coming to an end. It was truly one of the most enjoyable times I have ever had, and I like to think that my family feels the same way. I also wish I could say that our last night was a peaceful one, but it was actually quite the opposite. You see, when we moored our boat for the final time on a rocky beach, within a short distance of the rental office, we were aware that we were very, very close to a set of train tracks. As we had not observed any trains going by in the short time we were in that area, we thought it might be a good place to park. We discovered that we could not have been more wrong, for in actuality there was a locomotive going by on average every thirty minutes or so, all that afternoon and throughout the night.

It was very entertaining to watch a specific, unnamed person in my family standing outside on the front deck of the boat in pyjamas, gleefully waving a spatula at every conductor to be seen, much to the delight of most of the conductors that observed this hysterically funny behavior. Although, no one got much sleep once we retired for the night. The rumble of the freight trains could be heard on a deafening level from some distance away. But somehow, in the end, the interference only added to our adventure and made it more memorable. I could not have had a more amazing time, and my journey back to Alberta was completed with a grateful heart filled with wonderment at all of the events that had taken place.

Lea (picture supplied by Trudy T.)

Houseboat fun! (Picture supplied by Shannon H.)

ASHES THE CAT

For the last eighteen and a half years our acreage has been blessed with the constant presence of our beloved Ashes, the cat. Or, she could be more aptly described as the Porch Kitty, for more often than not, Ashes could be found sitting on the front steps leading to the large porch entry of our home, ever observant and watchful from her elevated position there.

Ashes was a medium-sized cat, with a tortoise shell pattern on her back and a white patch that ran from between her eyes and around her mouth, down her chin, and onto her chest. Her dainty front paws resembled socks with their coverings of white fur, and her back legs continued with that theme, although the white ran past her paws and further up her leg, like a stocking.

Ashes came to our home in the spring of 2004 as a kitten, christened with her name by our son, Wayde, who was eleven years old at the time. Ashes arrived with a littermate we named Mittens. Mittens came by his name quite honestly as he was a large, grey cat with white paws that had extra toes, giving him the look of one who is wearing mittens. It was a genetic anomaly that identified him as a polydactyl cat.

Together they were raised as outside cats, but were well-fed and had shelter any time they wished through a small door leading into the garage. Once inside, they had access to the entire structure. The mouse population declined rapidly when the cats moved in, and we were most grateful. Both cats turned out to be marvelous hunters.

The acreage was an idyllic place for cats to grow up. Chicken coops and a fishpond full of koi were highly entertaining to observe, especially for a young feline on the loose. There were trees to climb, and all kinds of nooks and crannies to explore. A good game of pounce was easy to instigate with any little object blowing across the yard in the wind. And, if you saw one cat, the other was bound to be nearby. Mittens and Ashes were inseparable.

Mittens vanished one night in the year of 2006, never to be seen again. While we were never positive of what the circumstances were that lead to his disappearance, we were certain that Ashes witnessed the event in question because she vocalized her distress loudly, constantly, and in varying pitches every time she saw us, for days. We had never heard her speak in such a manner before or since. It was heartbreaking to witness. We speculated that Mittens had been picked up by a neighboring Great Horned Owl, as whenever coyotes were nearby our beloved cats had always sheltered in the garage, and we weren't aware of many other predators that could catch a cat unawares in our yard during the night-time hours. Because the cats were so well fed, and spayed/neutered, we had not ever had problems with them straying, either. Ashes changed after that fateful night. She was still a loving, faithful cat, but without the same carefree manner she had before Mittens disappeared.

Sometime later that year, Ashes literally marched into the garage where Ray and I were standing, spat a pair of small feather-covered legs with feet attached on the ground in front of us and then turned, head held high, and marched back out the door again. They appeared to be the legs of an owlet. I felt as though my theory about the owl killing Mittens was justified. An eye for an eye. That was the first and last time we ever saw Ashes bring home a dead bird.

We tried more than once over the years to introduce a new kitten to Ashes so that she wouldn't be alone, but she flat-out rejected every one of them with extreme hostility. What we could never understand was why she would tolerate the numerous strays that were dumped on our acreage over the years. These poor creatures were always wild, starving, and too terrified of humans to come near us or make friends, but we fed them anyway. Ashes would not chase them away, but steadfastly refused to accept another tame cat into her territory. It was very frustrating, but Ashes had made her choice clear.

Ashes was an unusual cat in the sense that she did not often seek out human companionship, even though we loved her dearly and she was always acknowledged whenever we were outside. Ashes loved to greet us all and reach out an inquisitive nose to say hi, but rarely made herself a nuisance by insisting on being in our lap or rubbing up against our legs. This was a trait that endeared her to many who were not naturally cat enthusiasts: her willingness to receive affection and not become a pest at the same time.

From very early on, Ashes assumed her role as our protector, ever watchful from her position on the front step, and she was as diligent as she could be in performing her task. It was an extremely rare occasion indeed that a passing rodent would survive her intent gaze and hunting prowess. Much to our surprise, Ashes has caught not one but two weasels lurking near our chicken coop, and more gophers and mice than we can count in the span of her life-time. I doubt we shall be so fortunate as to find another who could rival her skills.

Not only did Ashes guard our entryway, she also made it her duty to observe and follow us most of the time whenever we were in the yard. She reminded us more of a dog than a cat with this behavior, for it was no surprise to find her hot on our heels no matter where we would wander on the acreage. More often than not one of us would have the irresistible urge to pick her up and carry her about the yard on our travels, with loud purring and a few snuggles being the ultimate reward for our efforts. Once Ashes had perceived our whereabouts and what task we were accomplishing, once she had determined that we were going to remain in one area, she would eventually wander back to her step and curl up in a circular ball of fluff, waiting for our return.

Ashes was a constant presence in our lives. She was a dependable sight no matter the season, the weather, or if it was day or nighttime, she was almost always at our door or in our garage. We marked the passing of the years with Thanksgiving and Christmas celebrations, birthdays, graduations, weddings, funerals, and numerous dogs that were raised here and who died here, all under the watchful eye of Ashes the cat. It felt as though it would always be that way.

The years seemed to pass by at the speed of sound, and in the blink of an eye, we were in the year 2019. It became evident around this time that Ashes, now fifteen years old, was slowing down and her age was beginning to show. She was even becoming cuddly, which was not a term one could normally use to describe her. Her forays patrolling the acreage were shorter in both distance and duration, and the mouse population in the garage had been returning with a vengeance for some time.

Evidence of just how out of control the mice were getting became very clear the day I pointed Ashes in the direction of a live mouse trapped in a bucket. She just sniffed at the cowering rodent and sauntered away, leaving the mouse untouched. I was shocked, for never before would Ashes have allowed such a creature to exist right under her nose.

Mice were one of her favorite treats, however. So much so that she loved to wait beside the chicken house when we were doing chores, because any mice unfortunate enough to have drowned in the water bucket the night before were unceremoniously dumped onto the ground the next morning, only to be eagerly scooped up into her jaws and devoured on the spot. Ray called them "mousecicles." Ashes loved them so much that she would beg for them with loud yowls whenever we were tending the birds. Her disappointment would be clearly evident if the water bucket happened to be empty some mornings. She would sniff around on the ground in apparent disbelief, practically shaking her head in annoyance as she stomped away, unappeased.

It was early in 2022, during the cold winter months that marked our eager anticipation of spring, that Ashes began to shake her head in irritation while she scraped a paw over an offending ear that appeared to be driving her to distraction. It was obvious that this was more than just a fleeting annoyance, and it did not take long before I could hear a sound that imitated water gurgling in a bottle whenever she did shake her head. I packed Ashes into a travel kennel for a much-hated car ride into town for a visit with our favorite veterinarian, where we discovered unfortunate news. Polyps were growing inside of her ear canal, causing the discomfort, and surgery was our only option.

I understand that there are many individuals in the world who would have put the cat down right then and there with her age and the cost of surgery. Indeed, the cost was a concern for me, but my vet, who also had a soft spot in her heart for our aging cat, volunteered a discounted rate for the procedure. She understood that our options were limited without that assistance, and she also understood that we were not yet ready to say goodbye to our dear, sweet Ashes. With grateful tears and evident relief, I accepted that offer, and Ashes soon had a spot on the surgery schedule that week.

The surgery was lengthy but successful, although the vet carefully explained afterwards that the polyps were found to be cancerous and they would most likely return. Ashes had a slow recovery that required an extensive stay at the veterinarian's office, and it was evident that she was very happy to be returning home to the outdoors that she loved, as soon as she was able. In true cat style, upon her arrival, Ashes leisurely strolled out of the kennel as though she was a fashion model on the catwalk, flopped herself down onto her pillow on the porch, and surveyed her surroundings with her head held high. It was as though she had never left. All was well, once again.

Spring seemed to disappear in the blink of an eye, and summer arrived as swiftly as a hurricane. Such is the passage of time when one is counting the precious minutes remaining in a life-time that is obviously measured, and waning. The changing of the seasons was bittersweet; joyous with the arrival of each new leaf on a tree or bloom in the garden, but painful for the inevitable ending to come. Ashes grew slower by the day, preferring to languish on the porch steps most of the time, rarely venturing further than the back yard pond for a drink of water. Cuddles and pets were high on the list of her favorite things to do, and we were more than happy to oblige at every possible opportunity.

As fall was rapidly approaching, I found myself growing concerned about Ashes' well-being during the cold winter months ahead. What on earth was I to do with a cat that had lived all of its life outside, and a house full of plants and breakable ornaments, not to mention two very boisterous dogs? It was not an ideal situation, and I felt that Ashes would be very unhappy trying to navigate new surroundings with so many obstacles in her way – literally and figuratively.

Upon hearing of my dilemma, and despite severe allergies to cats, my son Adam stepped up to the plate and offered to take the old girl in for the winter. I was overjoyed. Adam worked from home during the day which meant that Ashes would rarely be left alone. Plus, his home was not full of plants and breakables, let alone pesky dogs. It was an almost perfect solution, if only there were no allergies involved. We agreed that Ashes would remain with us out at the acreage until it was getting to be too cold, and that I would take her in for a complete check-up with the vet beforehand just to be sure that all was well. Adam was preparing to stock up on allergy medication in the meantime.

September arrived in a flurry of activity with harvesting the garden and yard clean up. Leaves were beginning to change color, the weather was fantastic, and Ashes continued to maintain her position on the step, observing her surroundings from the comfort of her pillow. I was extremely content with my life except for one small, slightly alarming occurrence: Ashes was shaking her head again.

My logical mind knew full well what the head-shaking meant, but my heart was not ready yet to deal with reality, so I set about continuing my plans for Ashes to move in with Adam. I even made an appointment with the vet for a physical exam of the cat, in preparation for that move. I had become very determined to see these plans go forward. Ashes would be so happy in a warm house for the winter, and even happier to return home in the spring. At least, this is what I was telling myself.

A couple of weeks before her vet appointment, I began to notice some swelling underneath Ashes' ear and down into the side of her face. Stubbornly refusing to admit the obvious, I tried to pretend it was not serious, but the swelling persisted and so did the head-shaking. By the time the day of her appointment had arrived, I knew I could no longer hide in denial about Ashes' situation, it was only a matter of time. There would be no winter home with Adam, there would be no retirement on a cozy couch. There was no need for a physical exam to confirm her ability to move off of the acreage. The vet could only confirm what our hearts already knew. The cancer had spread and there was no stopping it. Ashes would remain at home; winter would not arrive for her this year.

The vet was surprised, however, to see that Ashes remained in excellent health despite the incessant swelling. Her temperament, her appetite, and her behaviors had all remained the same. She was happy to have attention, and her loud purring only confirmed it. She would even lean into your hand when her ears were scratched or when you touched her swollen cheek. I almost cried with relief when the vet informed me that Ashes did not appear to have any pain, and was well enough to go home and spend some time with her family members for a final farewell. I understood these last days were precious, and I could not help but ask how many more did the vet think Ashes had left? My heart jumped with joy when I was told that Ashes had anywhere from four to eight weeks, which was far longer than I could ever have hoped for.

It was five days after the vet had made her final diagnosis concerning the cat that I found myself sitting at the kitchen table alone, drinking my morning cup of coffee, and playing a popular word game on my phone. The stillness of the early hour was peaceful and enjoyable, and my whole focus was on the game I played. Only the loud clattering of doggie nails on the kitchen floor, headed for the basement, momentarily broke my concentration. Still engrossed in my word game, I hardly paid attention to the sound of clicking nails that ran into my office downstairs, then ran across the hallway into a guest bedroom. I became very aware when the sounds entered the adjoining laundry room, however, and most especially when I heard the nails click out of the laundry room, but then reverse and enter once more. Every once in a while, my dogs like to drag an old towel or two off of the laundry room floor and make short work of them by chewing them to pieces, and that was something I did not want.

I took a deep breath, filling my lungs with air in preparation to holler at my dog, Farley, the most obvious choice of culprits who would be in the laundry room. As I lifted my head from my phone and opened my mouth to yell, I saw that Farley was actually laying on the floor near my feet, fast asleep. Obviously, it was not Farley in the basement, so I called out for my other dog, Brandy, to come upstairs. My call was met with silence. I yelled a second time, louder, for Brandy to come up, and waited with some impatience for her to appear. No response.

I began to push myself away from the table in an effort to rise to my feet and head down the stairs to chastise my dog, who I was certain was in the throes of ecstasy chewing on a dirty dishrag and in no mood to listen to me. I was in no mood to deal with the dog. Movement caught in the corner of my eye as I turned towards the stairs, and I glanced back over my shoulder to see what had garnered my attention. My brow furled in surprise as I realized that it was Brandy walking towards me, coming from the living room on the main floor with sleepy eyes and big yawns, having just been awakened from her slumber by my annoyed tone. Neither of my dogs was in the basement or had run down the stairs. But there was a dog in my basement for I had heard it clear as a bell. Suddenly I heard one word flash through my mind: Amy. Then I heard it once again, louder. *Amy*. Amy was my little dog who had crossed over in the same twenty-four-hour period as my other dog, Mystique, in 2016. I then realized, without a doubt, that we were not alone. The dogs were here for the cat. My spirit dogs. They knew. Ashes would not be alone when it was her time to cross over. My heart cracked a little as I swallowed a lump in my throat.

Ashes lived a good life in her final weeks. All of the people who loved her came to say goodbye and lavish as many hugs and kisses upon her as she would tolerate. Quiet moments in the yard were spent with her folded into our arms, the only sounds being her contented purrs. We had countless conversations with her, over and over again she was reminded of what an amazing cat she was. The Best. Ever. Never to be replaced by another, for none could equal her. If only she did not have to leave us. It was a heartbreaking situation to experience.

I struggled with making the decision to call the vet for that final visit. The only indicator that anything was wrong with the cat was the large mass that was now unmistakably obvious, the right side of her face was extremely puffy and oddly shaped. We had started feeding her soft, canned food so as not to cause her pain while chewing, and Ashes thought that this was one of the best things that had ever happened to her. It took exactly one time to be fed moist food and she was almost clawing at the door for her breakfast and supper in anticipation every day since. Nothing else about her had changed. She was happy, she was still wandering the yard, and she was still purring and asking to be held. How could I let her go?

Winter weather was forecast for the second week in November, and I knew that I could no longer stall. Ashes would not be subjected to snow and frigid temperatures, no matter how badly I wanted to keep her with me. The fateful day was scheduled, it would arrive on November 4th, 2022.

It was agreed that my vet and her partner would make the drive to the acreage late in the day to tend to Ashes, so that she could be spared the stress of a kennel and the dreaded car ride to town. The weather that morning was amazingly warm, and I stood in the yard and swayed to and fro in the sunshine, all while holding my purring cat and crooning in her ear. It was a beautiful moment, one that I cherish. I thanked my dear friend, over and over, for her fierce loyalty and protection, and for her love. I held her for as long as I could, with the intent of returning to cuddle one last time in the afternoon. Ashes was also fed all the wet food she wanted, including a tin of tuna fish. Wayde was home to spend extra time with her the night before and say goodbye; we were as prepared as we could be.

The afternoon cuddle that I had promised my cat did not come about. When I went to visit with Ashes she was curled up in her kennel in the garage, and very unwilling to be removed from it. She was not purring, she was not interested in the last of her food, and she did not stay very long in my arms before she asked to be put down and returned to her bed. Her whole demeanor had changed. She was letting me know, for the first time, that she did not feel well physically, and I swear that she also understood her journey was about to take a different path. She was tired, and she was ready to go. I was now truly grateful her day had come, even though a tear escaped my eye and trickled down my cheek as I walked away.

Ray was with me when the vet arrived, and he stood by me as I held Ashes close. Unable to contain my grief any longer, tears were streaming down my face as I spoke aloud every single word I could think of to tell my cat. I closed my eyes as the vet prepared to administer her merciful concoction, openly sobbing as I stroked her fur. In a matter of mere minutes the vet spoke, her voice cracking, as she whispered that Ashes was gone. My eyes were still closed, but a smile formed on my lips as she informed me, and I lifted my face towards the sky.

"I know," I replied, for I could see her.

I could see Ashes clearly, if only for a moment. The scene, to me, was so glorious that it made my breath catch in my chest. Gathered before me in a small cluster were all of the dogs who had lived with our family, that had crossed over before Ashes. Eight dogs in total, tails wagging and teeth showing through delighted grins in a joyful greeting. Best of all was the sight of Mittens, patiently waiting, sitting in front of the rambunctious group that frolicked behind him, doing his best to ignore them, as only a cat can do. I observed Ashes walking towards them before the scene faded, and as I opened my eyes, I was sending prayers of thanks, grateful for the confirmation that Ashes was not alone.

Before she left, the vet relayed to us an interesting fact. Because of hazards such as predators, vehicles and adverse conditions, the average outside cat only lives to be around the age of five years, and quite often less. This was also the case with Mittens, who died young. Ashes was over eighteen years old when she died, closer to nineteen in actuality, for she must have been born no later than February or March 2004, in order for her to come to us that spring as a tiny kitten. This was truly a remarkable feat, achieved by a remarkable cat. We were in awe.

Ashes was buried with her dog family in our little plot on the acreage. As Ray was digging her final resting spot I could see her in spirit, winding around and between his legs, tail high, trying to show him that she was okay. It was a comfort to observe.

She came to me in the quiet of the evening hours, as I was in the kitchen trying to tidy up after supper. With my focus on the task at hand, I was somewhat surprised when I heard a simple statement spoken in my mind. “It was an honor to serve you.”

I remember thinking to myself with a chuckle that those words were just exactly what a cat *would* say, although I understood it was her guide speaking for her at that moment. Then, without warning, my mind was vividly recording scenes suddenly flashing before me. Ashes was communicating with me, without the need for words, by sharing her memories in pictures so that I could understand.

She showed me her memories of always being held by one of us and carried around the yard, visions of each of us in the family with her at different times. I also saw her following Zach outside as he turned and bent down to encourage her to run to him. I saw her walking down the driveway and sitting with the boys, day after day, waiting for the school bus to whisk them away; something I had totally forgotten about as it was so long ago. She understood somehow that Adam was willing to take her in for winter, and she was grateful - I could feel it. She loved Wayde's last cuddles. She showed me a vision of herself and Mittens, playfully interacting with the kids when they were much younger. She had been very happy here, and much loved, and she knew it. A heavy sigh escaped my lips when the vision stopped. I did not want it to end.

Sometime in the early hours of November 5th as I lay awake in the dark, I became aware of Ashes, sitting on the front steps with her back against the door, scanning the night for any threats. I could see her beautiful countenance framed with moonlight, her eyes were wide and shining, her ears were pitched forward. I understood that she was doing what she had always done; guarding the home and its inhabitants, caring for us all. For a brief moment I could also comprehend that Ashes was aware of the fact that the cold night air could no longer be felt through her luxurious fur coat, although I am not so sure she understood why. I turned onto my side and drifted back into slumber, comforted by the fact that Ashes was nearby, if only for a while.

I observed Ashes periodically, throughout the weekend. I always saw her outside, most often close to the house, and occasionally in the backyard near the pond. Despite being reunited with her animal family she had remained focused on what she felt was her duty, and that was watching over us. I wondered how long she would stay. I knew in my heart that it would not be for long.

Monday, the 7th, was a day of terrible weather. The snow was falling heavily, and the wind was mercilessly whipping across the prairie fields that surround our property. Ray had remained home that day as his work site was shut down, and we were spending a lazy afternoon in front of the television. My idle mind was absently following a home improvement show and I was wrapped in my favorite blanket with a cup of tea, when my view was suddenly obscured by a new scene that lay before me.

It was Ashes. She was walking outside through the snow, between the garage and the garden, headed for the bare field behind the house. Her tail was held high as it gently waved in the air with each step. She stopped once, at the edge of the field, to look over her shoulder back at the house (and me), then she turned and kept walking away into the blowing snow until I could no longer see her. The scene before me blurred, then became crisp and sharp as I focused on dark green grass and shining sun. There was Ashes, small in size, as a kitten in her first year of life. She was leaping to catch a butterfly between her paws, but she missed. Then I watched her chasing dandelion fluff across the grass, her front paws were scrabbling to catch it as it bounced in the breeze, just beyond her reach. Lastly, I observed another kitten playing nearby, it was Mittens. As I viewed this scene, I was blessed with the understanding that even though they were presenting themselves to me as younger cats, they still carried their shared experiences with us in their hearts and memories. The love we had lavished on them remained imprinted upon their very souls. What a comforting, beautiful scene. But still, it brought me to quiet tears as the vision began to fade, and I understood that it was time for me to let Ashes go.

Goodbye, my dear, sweet kitty. You will be missed. It was an honor to have you in our lives. Goodbye for now.

Ashes in 2022. (Photo by Shannon Harwood)

INSPIRATIONAL WRITING

I have kept, for many years, several journals containing messages that have been received by me from my holy spirit guides. Although a great deal of them contains personal information concerning matters of my own spiritual growth, the following is a message that I wish to share. I refer to it as inspirational writing, meaning that the message was delivered to me by means of strong thoughts which were inspired upon me, which I then wrote down as I heard the words. The message was received on a day that was set aside for a small group of people coming together to rejoice in a communion ceremony; a remembrance of our Lord and Savior Jesus Christ and a celebration of his love for us. It was a very spiritual, revered gathering. The message was, in actuality, a prayer to God. The date was November 8th, 1989 and it reads as follows:

Dear Heavenly Father, Greatest above All.

May you please grant, through your grace and truth, the strength for your servants upon this mortal realm to continue to refine their thoughts and their ways towards the perfection of your Divine Will. Oh Lord, we thank you for the days spent in your love and filled with the realization of your grace, we lift our eyes to Thee, in exaltation and worship, to praise you everlastingly.

May we seek to further understand your gift of humble Love, and to practise this fully and completely, in accordance with your wishes. For 'twas you, Lord, who gave your Son to die for us to set us free, and for this we thank you.

And so, on this communion day, may we begin to realize that your Love shall never stop and never end, but continue; perfectly, evenly, and unconditionally, forever, throughout time. Our thanksgiving shall be always to you, Lord, for our redemption, bought through love, through Jesus Christ our Lord, your Son, Amen.

MOVING FORWARD

Life, be it in this realm or any other physical or spiritual realm, is always in a constant, ever-changing pattern of growth and rising momentum. We advance as we learn, moving forward and expanding our capabilities for love, forgiveness, spiritual enlightenment, and development. It is our choice to continue to evolve and grow upwards; it is also our choice if we wish to stagnate and plant ourselves in the murky waters of agitation, deceit, anger, and the misery of choosing to hold hate. As with every decision, there is a consequence, or a universal reaction, to the choices we make and the energy we exude. Our influence reaches much farther than most would anticipate, affecting both the material and ethereal worlds surrounding us, which, although separate, are so very intertwined and connected.

As is often the situation, some leave this realm and find themselves having to acknowledge issues and take responsibility for their actions, or lack thereof, once they are residing in the spirit world; despite making efforts to avoid doing exactly that when they were in the flesh. I believe this is a rather shocking outcome for some individuals who carried with them the opinion that the afterlife simply does not exist. Or that all will be sunshine and roses in the spirit world once they cross over, regardless of any measure of harm they may have inflicted without care during their lifetime.

God does not cast us away to an everlasting hell to suffer excruciatingly for all eternity merely because we are unbelievers, or if we were unable to achieve all of our tasks assigned to us on earth. Not even because we suffered from terrible character flaws and committed unspeakable acts. God is just and righteous, however, and He does hold us all to stand the test of Truth, like a flame that illuminates our way, or burns us if we do not respect its heat.

It is our choice to acknowledge Truth; it is also our choice to cast it aside for as long as we desire in the hopes that it shall not ever see the light of day. No matter what we choose, a painful day of reckoning shall surely come for those that stubbornly refuse to admit the part they played in the game of life. God is patient, however, and will not force anyone to be self-aware and responsible. That will come in time, as each is able to process their reality, see the outcome of their choices, take responsibility, and learn.

The struggle here on earth to strive for goodness can be a challenge. Quite often our reaction to important events, especially the difficult ones, will determine the path our life will follow. If we have developed the ability to step outside of our situation emotionally and analyze without *reacting* to events around us, we are left in a far better position to succeed with our decisions and our personal growth and understanding. I am not suggesting that we become aloof and unresponsive, but merely that we choose to see all sides of the circumstances first, without the coloration of offense, rage, emotional injury and so on. It is far easier to heal oneself from a position of calm and security, it is almost impossible to succeed and move ahead when swimming in a sea of turmoil.

Some of the most aggressive and distrustful people I have ever met are also those that were extremely traumatized and emotionally injured at a particular time in their life. The aggressiveness is carried as protection from fear. Fear of ever being hurt again. It is far easier to project anger and defensiveness in an attempt to keep all possible harm at arm's length, than it is to let boundaries and guards relax and chance being harmed or deceived again. "I will hurt you before you hurt me" is a very common, subconscious reaction to harmful situations from the past that some people continue to cling to.

It can take monumental effort to be self-aware enough to recognize this mindset within our own psyche and do the emotional soul-searching necessary to release these fears and aggressions; to trust that we are "safe" enough physically, and spiritually to make that effort. Trust can be hard to develop, and, depending on your own journey, it can be hard to make the leap to trust in anything, even yourself.

Because I was one of those extremely aggressive people early in my life, full of hurt and distrustful of most individuals around me, I can understand the viewpoint of excessively hostile people. I am not easily intimidated by them. I have done a lot of hard work to overcome my past and my traumas, and although I can still fall into fight or flight mode, (most often I am a fighter, a survivor, in any challenge), I seldom have the need to do so. I came to the point in my life some time ago where I understood that I am the product of my past and my upbringing, but also of my former and current behaviors and my choices. I am willing to bear the responsibility of such. I am also willing to overcome the obstacles in my path, work through them, and continue on my path.

My personality can still be described as "intense" or "passionate" to this very day. I suspect that I always will be, but I am no longer out to prove to the world that I am an island of hostility and you need not come near me because, in reality, I am fearful. Those issues are gone. I know that in many instances, especially spiritual matters, I have become fierce and will walk into any situation and confront it head-on, but without the need to overpower and dominate. I have acquired this attitude not only because life has been difficult and made me tough, but because I humbly understand that God walks with me, protecting me through His holy spirit envoys constantly surrounding me. As we are all protected. It is a strength and guidance to heavily rely upon, and I do so gladly.

I have learned, over many years, that God will put important people in my path as He sees fit. Most often these people are not only struggling with serious issues from their past which affect their daily living, they are also very ready to do the hard work needed to bring about important change. Sometimes these folks are not quite consciously aware that they are ready for transformation, but God knows. And that is where I come in.

There have been situations where I am encouraged to interact with certain individuals, and I receive a message to relay at that same time. Then my work with that person is done and we go our separate ways. Other times I am not only guided to assist, but I form permanent bonds with people who have become friends for life; cherished and valuable family members in my heart. I am very fortunate to have a large "extended family" from all walks and colors of life, with various beliefs and a wide variety of cultures. I am as grateful for their love and support as they are for mine.

One friend of mine, known as Cheryl G. when I first met her, (not to be confused with Cheryl Y. in my first memoir) came into my life in the late 1990s under rather comical circumstances, almost immediately after my arrival into the small rural community we were both a part of. It was not a meeting by chance, but rather outside influences, that brought us together in the first place.

I had gone into the local post office, situated in a tiny town in Southern Alberta, to establish a permanent mailing address for myself and my family upon purchasing what can only be described as my dream property, located a few miles out of town limits. At that time I was married to my first husband, and my name was not what it is now. However, I was rather taken aback when the Postmaster informed me that I couldn't have a "new" post office box assigned to my name because I already had a box.

This was a very puzzling statement to hear. I most certainly did not have a box number there or at any post office nearby, and I smiled as I tried to correct him. Repeating my first and last name, I assured him that I most certainly did not have an address at that location. Just as pleasantly, with twinkling eyes, the mild-mannered gentleman repeated my name, and then affirmed his first remarks: I couldn't have another box because I already had one.

Now I was thoroughly confused. How on earth could this be so? I repeated my first name, Shannon. "Yes," he said. I repeated my last name again, which he also confirmed with a nod to be correct. My brow was furled and I was obviously perplexed, which got me a rather odd look from him in return. In an effort to clear up the confusion, the Postmaster turned towards the open-ended row of postal boxes into which he had been sorting the mail. Pausing for a moment, he carefully made a choice and reached his hand into one of the boxes, retrieving the envelopes contained inside. "Look!" he exclaimed triumphantly as he began to read the name inscribed on the paper in his hand, but his voice trailed off almost immediately as he began to speak. My last name was most certainly correct, but the first name was *Cheryl*, not Shannon.

With an awkward chuckle, the Postmaster offered me a new post office box number, which I graciously accepted through the sound of my laughter. I wondered briefly who this woman named Cheryl was, especially since we shared the same surname, but had little time to do much else other than speculate, as my next objective was to go to the local bank and open an account there.

I had no problems opening accounts at the bank or enrolling my boys into the local school, and I soon dismissed the confusion regarding my last name at the post office.

Less than a month had gone by since moved into our new home, but we were settling in rapidly. Despite the frigid winter weather and unbelievable winds of Southern Alberta, I found myself quite busy exploring our property in detail every chance I got, all while raising three young children, and trying to keep up with household chores. Most of the time it seemed as though I was juggling two or three tasks at once, and such was the case one afternoon as I sat opening bank statements and utility bills at the kitchen table. With hardly a glance at the address labels on the outside of the envelopes, I had begun emptying the contents inside and sorting the paper. The statement from my local bank almost dropped from my hands in surprise, however, when I looked at the balance and the transactions that were recorded. Nothing that I saw was familiar to me, and I realized almost instantly that this bank statement could not be mine. I was embarrassed to have to look in further detail at that statement, but I continued to unfold the entire thing until I could see the name and the address at the top.

It might not be a surprise for you when I say that although the post office box number was my own, the name inscribed there was not. The name happened to be specifically that of Cheryl G., not Shannon.

With a heavy sigh, I did the only thing that I could think of to do, and I called directory assistance and inquired for the phone number of this woman with my same last name, living in the same area. I then called her and explained the situation and the obvious confusion. Cheryl was very understanding about my mistake and her personal information, and we agreed that I would leave the statement at the bank for her to pick up when I went in to try to amend the situation. That was my only interaction with Cheryl for about a year.

1999 was not a bad year for me, but it was difficult in many ways, and I found myself in need of employment by summer of 2000 in order to assist with household finances. Because my youngest child was just over three years old at that time, and my oldest was only seven, I was reluctant to have to get a day job and leave my children with sitters. The only option that I felt I had was to go to work during the evenings so that my husband could be with the boys at night, thus eliminating the need for child care outside of the home. The local bar was the perfect solution.

Some of you reading might question why I went to work as a server in a pub with my strong spiritual beliefs the way they are. I can tell you that my children and my home were of the utmost importance in my life, and I felt that this would be my best opportunity to provide for them. I was willing to do whatever I had to do. Also, my upbringing involved being around alcohol, and my mother worked in a bar for many years. I have mentioned before of my own struggles with liquor. Therefore, I can tell you that I am quite comfortable being around alcohol and people who drink. I try very hard not to be judgemental in situations involving excessive use because I have been one of those people many times, for varying self-destructive reasons. And I also know that God is with me no matter where I am.

As is so often the case, the bar was a central hub for many of the locals who wished to socialize and catch up on the news around town. It was inevitable that I would meet the woman who shared my last name, and that happened in the first week that I worked there.

When Cheryl came striding into the building, I observed her to be a short, average-sized woman with closely cropped light-brown hair and glasses. Her head was up high, her jaw was set, and I was very surprised to observe such a strong personality, that I can say. She was meeting up with her husband, already seated on a bar stool, and she looked like she was not very happy. Cheryl and her husband did not stay long after her arrival. I got the impression, after they left, that some of the patrons did not seem to agree with her overall demeanor. This only left me curious to discover more about her.

Aggressive was really the only way to describe Cheryl back in those days. I soon learned that she was forceful in her opinions, extremely outspoken, and had no problem challenging anyone who might want to take issue with her, man or woman. Alcohol did not fuel her moods or her sharp tongue; Cheryl had no problems voicing her opinions stone-cold sober. In fact, she rarely drank to excess.

Because I am a very strong woman and not easily intimidated, Cheryl was not a problem for me. I very much enjoyed her company and her conversation, even if she could come across as quite cranky some days. I never took it personally. It was obvious that Cheryl was always in offensive/defensive mode, although it was impossible to determine why. I also noticed that Cheryl triggered strong reactions from other people in the bar, and she was a woman who was, quite often, either loved or hated on sight.

My relationship with Cheryl began to slowly develop into friendship, partly because I saw a lot of her while I was at work. One of the reasons I saw her so much is that Cheryl lived on the same street as the pub, a very short walk away, actually. Which made it a convenient location to socialize in. But the other, more significant reason is that Cheryl's husband, Ed, also liked to socialize. A lot. And more often than not, when Cheryl couldn't locate Ed, it was because he was sitting in the local bar, enjoying a cold beer and a cigarette. There were days that I could understand why Cheryl was a little short-tempered with Ed, due to his frequent visits.

Ed was a short, slim, dark-haired man sporting a neatly trimmed moustache and glasses. One of his most distinguishable features was the large cowboy hat always perched upon his head. You never saw Ed outside of his home without his hat on. In a large part it was his identity, for Ed was a genuine cowboy in his day, riding the range on horseback, tending cattle and mending fences, etc. Ed was a pleasant man to talk to, mild-mannered, quiet, and calm. The only time I ever saw him get agitated was when another man tried to swipe the hat off of Ed's head. That man backed down quickly when Ed started getting red in the face. Ed and Cheryl appeared to be an odd couple, however, opposite both in personality and behavior, although they were an extremely hard-working pair who got a lot accomplished in a day.

There was another reason that Cheryl and I formed a bond, and obviously it was because of our last names. We found it quite comical that we were both married at that time to short, dark-haired men with similar personality attributes and the same last name, but were not related. There were actually three families in town that year with the same last name who were not related, impressive with a population of fewer than 500 people.

Not only did Cheryl and I have similar spouses, we have similar personalities, despite the fact that we are very different from each other. Both of us are passionate about our viewpoints and we stand strong in our beliefs and values. Honesty is very important to us, and don't ask us for an opinion if you don't want to hear the truth. We discovered that we were born in the same year, and we also found that we have shared very parallel, major life events, often during the same period of time, even though we did not meet until the year we each turned 33 years old.

Our relationship stayed mostly within the walls of the local pub for the first year and a half that Cheryl and I knew each other. Which meant that although we enjoyed each other's company, we didn't really have much time to get to develop a close connection. I was usually busy with customers, and seldom did we have a chance to chat without someone being able to hear our conversation. As we are both quite private, this was somewhat of a hindrance to further deepening our friendship and opening up the channels of communication.

Had we been able to do so, we would have understood that both of us were desperately in need of a friendly, sympathetic shoulder. We also might have realized that we were not at all as alone and isolated as we both felt we were. We would have been able to support each other. If only we had known that our very similar lives happened to be unfolding in synchronicity once again. Alas, this fact we would later discover to be true only once all of the turmoil had settled down.

Neither of us was aware that the other was also enduring the most difficult, tumultuous, moments in our marriages. Oh, there were obvious signs that weren't hard to miss, so, in that sense, we "knew." There was the gossip repeated in the pub, and uncharacteristic behaviors were occurring with us both, signs of serious fractures in our lives. But we did not confide in each other back then, nor did we disclose to very many people at all just how serious our respective issues had become. No one actually knew what was taking place behind the closed doors of our homes, or what was triggering the breakdown of our marriages. People could only speculate on the rumors they heard. Suffice it to say, Ed and Cheryl's marriage survived the fallout. Mine did not.

It wasn't until after I had quit working at the bar, moved on with my life, and relocated to a neighboring town with my new love, Ray, that I began to share a really serious friendship with Cheryl. Over countless cups of coffee and many shared hours together, Cheryl's life story began to emerge. It was not hard to understand why Cheryl struggled so much with trust and anger, and I listened intently to every word she spoke.

Cheryl was born fourth in line out of a family of five children. Her parents, Dorothy and John, raised their family in a small town in central Saskatchewan, and, by all appearances, they were as normal as pumpkin pie is to turkey dinner. Unfortunately, this was not the case, and "normality" was not Cheryl's reality. For the sake of those still living today I will not go into a lot of detail, but suffice it to say, all was not well at home. Dorothy was a very meek and mild woman, and John was the extreme, polar opposite of that. He was an angry man, whose behaviors were very mentally and emotionally traumatizing to his entire family. Cheryl grew up watching disputes between her father and her mother regularly, and in many different ways: physically and verbally. As a child, the circumstances in which Cheryl was raised created a ton of anxiety and fear for her. She learned very early on not to trust. She witnessed what happened when her mom was overpowered, and she vehemently decided that this situation was not going to repeat itself in her adult life. In an effort to protect herself and disguise her fears, Cheryl also became fierce and aggressive. No one was ever going to be in a position to hurt her in the same manner her mother had been hurt. No one. Vulnerability was not her style.

Despite the fact that Cheryl appears to be hard as nails to those that don't know her well, Cheryl is a very kind and loving individual. She has no problem rolling up her sleeves and pitching in whenever there is a task at hand to be performed. She loves her community and tries hard to be of service. She takes pride in her home and her yard. She is extremely generous, talented and creative, with a quick wit and a hearty laugh. It was the hard exterior shell that she surrounded herself with that made it difficult for most people to get past. Once you have Cheryl's trust, however, she is at your side through thick and thin.

That ride-or-die personality characteristic, the extreme loyalty, although admirable in most instances, was a serious hindrance in Cheryl's only other significant relationship with a man besides her father. That man was Ed. Unfortunately, although Ed had some wonderful traits when Cheryl met him, he was also a very injured man emotionally. I believe that it would be fair of me to say that his past, and the choices he made in that time period, haunted him. Not that Ed had committed crimes or anything of that sort, but he definitely had regrets and carried a whole lot of emotional baggage. This baggage affected every aspect of Ed's life and shaped his behaviors, which were often totally irresponsible, selfish, and hurtful. Another result of Ed's emotional issues was a heavy dependence on alcohol. Cheryl, at the early age of eighteen, and with the trauma of her own past, could not recognize these issues in him until it was too late. Once she had committed her heart to Ed she stayed, and she would not go no matter what the circumstances were.

By the time I met Cheryl she had been with Ed for fifteen years, and her father had crossed over a few short years beforehand. Although Ed was not ever physically abusive, the repetitive cycle of narcissistic behaviour and trauma from the two most important men in her life had been almost unending, and she could not see beyond the hurt in her heart. All of her life Cheryl has been in that fight or flight mode, and her best defense was to strongly react to any situation that she found to be even mildly uncomfortable or threatening to her personal space. Cheryl was not inwardly calm, and neither were her reactions. She was unable to see how the behaviors of both her father and her husband had affected her deeply, leaving her feeling rejected emotionally and spiritually.

This in no way means that Cheryl was blind to the fact that her life had been very difficult, or that the behaviors of her father and her husband were unacceptable. She knew very well the difference between right and wrong. But, in an effort to protect herself, she had put up emotional walls, huge walls, that did not allow her to look past that pain. At one point in our chats, while we were discussing the importance of forgiveness, Cheryl informed me that she could hardly stand to think about her father most days, and when she did it brought about an almost physical reaction from her: disgust.

One thing that I truly appreciate about Cheryl is her willingness to try. And Cheryl was completely open and ready to try to shed the weight that had held her spirit in chains, at least where her father was concerned. We began the slow and sometimes painful process of self-examination and identifying raw emotions. There is no sense denying your true feelings or trying to hide them from yourself. Those feelings exist for a reason. One needs to understand them and accept that they are there before you can rid yourself of them. Do not hate or judge yourself for your reactions to life events that have shaped you, for that is even more harmful than the actions others commit against you. Do not deny the person you have become, for that is the only way to recognize that you need to change. Be willing to lay down your weapons in this fight, take a step back, and breathe.

Slowly, over time, we peeled back layers of grief, hurt, and anger. Cheryl was surprised to discover that she was struggling with self-loathing because of the way her father had treated not just herself, but the whole family. She felt as though she must not be worthy of love because of his incapacity to love and care for them. She had, unwittingly, begun to reject herself because of his rejection. She believed she did not deserve better, that she must be flawed. This, in turn, caused her to choose a mate that would also reinforce these emotions within her. Once again, her needs would be denied, causing her to feel insignificant and unlovable. All of this hurt had to go somewhere, and it would creep out now and again in short bursts whenever something would trigger and emphasise this wrongly-held opinion of herself.

Cheryl also began to understand how her inability to forgive and let go of the pain from her childhood was holding her back spiritually, harming her capacity to love herself and make better choices. She no longer wished to drag around that anchor. She did not want to be connected to John in the next life because of that negative energy.

In order to have a better understanding of what motivated John to behave the way he did, we also began to piece together John's history and upbringing. It was not a surprise to hear that John also came from an abusive, heavily controlled home, and Cheryl made the connection quickly in regard to her own childhood. John was merely following the path he had been initially led on. She began to understand that having empathy for John's situation and forgiving John for his transgressions because of her knowledge, did not mean that she was condoning his actions in any way. It did not make the past "right." But it did make it understandable. Cheryl did the hard work needed to step out of her past and analyze it without the coloration of emotions. She began to see her father in a different light, one that exposed his weakness, insecurities, and vulnerabilities. She saw his anger and felt his rage from a different perspective. A perspective that allowed her to be free for the first time in her life. Freed from emotional and spiritual bondage because of love and a newfound understanding. Freedom from hate. It was as though she had rid herself of a thousand pounds of weight upon her shoulders in regard to her childhood.

Let it be said that this achievement was not attained overnight. Cheryl worked on herself and opened up to me about her emotions and experiences over a long period of time. We talked, we laughed, we cried together. Small steps were taken every day that brought about huge results. Her effort was impressive. There were many instances in which Cheryl felt that her progression in this area was slow and painful, but she did not give up.

Although John had crossed into the spiritual realm in the '90s, I had not ever noticed him or any other family members around Cheryl in all the years up to that point that we had known each other. Whenever we talked about the past it was without the benefit of further guidance from John's viewpoint. I understood that in all likelihood John would not be permitted to be near Cheryl if he would be harmful to her at all. If he had not experienced a change of heart, if he was stuck in the same hurtful patterns, he would see Cheryl from afar. I didn't give much thought to his whereabouts.

The fall of 2005 arrived swiftly. Cheryl and Ed were seldom home due to the fact that they had to travel for work. I was in charge of checking on the house and watering Cheryl's plants while they were gone. It never took very much of my time and I was usually in and out in less than fifteen minutes.

One day in particular I was in a real rush to check the house and continue on with errands. Ray was waiting outside in the truck, and I was looking forward to enjoying my time with him while he was home from his job working in the oil patch up north. I unlocked the door and hurried inside, pausing long enough to stop at the kitchen sink to fill a container with water for the plants. It never occurred to me that I wasn't alone.

As I came around the corner to enter the living room, the jug of water I was holding almost flew out of my hands as I came to a complete stop, mid-stride. My eyes must have looked owlish, wide as they were from surprise to observe the spirit of an older man, merely sitting at the end of the sofa. He was dressed in a bulky, dark winter coat and a dark-colored winter hat with ear flaps. Even his pants were dark. His open hands were held with the palms up, resting on his lap. His shoulders slumped a little as they curled forward, and he looked very serious. He did not look at me, but was examining his hands.

I have to say, I was at a bit of a loss as to what to do. It felt strange for me to be witnessing what looked like a quiet, introspective moment for a man I did not know, in the privacy of an empty home. I almost felt intrusive, especially since he did not acknowledge me in any way, and I had literally walked in on him, not the other way around. Because of that, as strange as it may sound, I chose to do nothing. I had no push to intervene in any way, so I did not. I respectfully averted my eyes and quietly completed my chore before locking the door and retreating.

Admittedly, I was intrigued by the appearance of this older gentleman. Why was he in Cheryl's house? Who was he? He did not look in any way like one who has been progressing and leaving his past behind, he looked stuck in time, as though he had the weight of the world on his shoulders. I contacted Cheryl that same evening, I felt like the curiosity would kill me if I waited any longer.

Cheryl was also very surprised to hear of the visit from the aged man. Especially because she was able to recognize him immediately upon hearing his description. It was her father, John, who had been sitting in her living room alone. And, from the sounds of it, he was still looking much like he had before he crossed over. I surmised that my earlier observation was correct: John was stuck. My best guess, from experience, was that he remained unable, or unwilling, to take accountability for his previous actions when he was a mortal being. I wondered to myself if his arrival in her home meant that he was experiencing a change of heart, even if just a tiny bit. I felt that God would not have allowed him to be close if he had malicious intent. Was it possible that the emotional and spiritual progress Cheryl had been making regarding her father was allowing him to come near? Could he understand, could he feel, that Cheryl no longer rejected him in every manner possible, but was working on acceptance and understanding?

John did not make his presence known to me in Cheryl's home ever again. The months flew by with the changing seasons, and eventually his visit became a dim memory that I gave little thought to.

Cheryl continued to try to work on her personal issues with Ed, but had little success. Ed simply was not interested in self-examination and working through emotional matters. Nor was he interested in changing his patterns and behaviors. There were some days that this attitude almost drove Cheryl insane. She found it particularly painful to have the strong urge for change, with the inability to bring about any change at all. This left her feeling as she always had: with no control over her life. She simply could not bring herself to leave her husband, and he absolutely refused to deviate from his self-destructive path.

Because Cheryl felt that she had very little control over her life, from childhood onwards, she also struggled with the need to fight quite desperately for every ounce of control she could gain, to make her feel at least somewhat empowered. She had been this way ever since I had known her. It might be a strange concept to some, that a woman as aggressive and intelligent as Cheryl actually felt powerless, but it is true. Not that Cheryl tried to control other people, but she was *rigid* about her surroundings, the one thing entirely within her power to maintain to perfection. Her house was spotless, day or night, every day of the week. You could probably eat off of her floors, and while you were at it, lick the walls - they were that clean.

Admirable, yes, but the reasons behind it were heart-wrenching.

The one thing that was awesome, however, was the fact that Cheryl had finally come to the point in her growth that she was able to understand her motivation for excessive housework. Not that she was able to change it much at that time, but she could see it, she was aware of it, and that was the first, most important step she needed to take to facilitate transformation in that area. It can be very difficult to let your guard down and relax while learning to love and accept yourself. It is hard to have trust and faith in God if it is something you have not previously comprehended. I was proud of her, and all the efforts she had made.

The messages and lessons that I receive from the spirit world are delivered to me in a wide variety of ways. I am blessed with the ability to see and hear those that have crossed over. I can also be overcome with strong emotions instead of words, which I then translate into speech so that others may understand. These abilities can also be categorized as clairvoyance, clairaudience, and clairsentience. There are other ways in which I can communicate with the spirit world, but these are the three most commonly used abilities I possess. Sometimes the spirit world engages me by making use of only one or two of those abilities, sometimes they employ every method of communication they have at their disposal. You are safe to assume that any message that comes through using sight, sound and emotion all at once can be very impactful. So impactful that it seems as though those particular experiences are etched upon my memory for eternity.

One specific encounter that I shall not ever forget occurred on an ordinary, unremarkable day in 2006. My home office is in the basement, and my desk was facing the wall furthest from the door, which put my back to the door when I was seated. I happened to be rather intently inputting numbers into an accounting program that morning, and this was my only focus.

Without any warning at all, the peaceful quiet in my office suddenly erupted into a flurry of activity. Over my right shoulder, almost directly behind me, was a very loud whooshing noise. It sounded like a large volume of air was entering the room all at once, as though an impending storm had arrived. I felt the energy in the room change instantly, and it was ominous and threatening.

I whirled around in my chair just in time to see the figure of a man, with dark, menacing eyes and dark hair swept off of his forehead to the side, enter my office! His skin appeared tanned, and he was wearing a white, long-sleeved buttoned shirt, and faded, well-fitting blue jeans. As he took a step towards me I had just enough time to register his appearance and the muscles in his upper thigh rippling through his jeans, when I turned away involuntarily in shock and horror. My hand was pressed against my chest to still my pounding heart, I was certain that this man was going to harm me, if not kill me. He looked absolutely furious, and the rage poured off of him in invisible waves.

Although I was truly terrified, it was only for a moment. As I was retreating in terror, experiencing sheer panic for my life and turning my back on the spectacle I was witnessing, the logical, rational, analytical part of my brain was already overriding the fear.

"Wait!" This word was loud in my mind. I stopped immediately. And then I realized: he had walked through the WALL!! This man was not physically alive, he could not hurt me, he was here in spirit and I was safe! He walked through the wall, not the door!

I swiveled around in my chair once more so that I could better assess the situation, grateful and confident that I was not about to die. But it was too late. I merely caught a glimpse of the spirit who had terrified me. He had continued striding behind me when I turned my back, and now he was swiftly exiting, disappearing into the wall on my left as though it were not there at all.

I have to say, this whole event took place in a matter of seconds. My brain was absolutely overwhelmed with sensory information that I did not know what to do with. For starters: who was that man?! Why was he so enraged? Why was he in my office, showing himself to me, of all people? Why?! It was a mystery that I was determined to solve.

I started off by calling immediate family members of my husband, Ray. Because the entity appeared to have light-brown or tanned skin, and Ray is of Native American descent, it was an obvious place for me to start. To no avail. It didn't matter who I talked to in the family, no one recognized this man. I tried asking my friends, at least those that I thought might have a connection to the stranger, but no one had answers and I was puzzled beyond belief. Perhaps even a little frustrated. I had been undeniably scared out of my wits for a reason, this much I knew, but for what purpose I could not say.

A couple of weeks passed by, and I was none the wiser in my search. I had all but given up, although I still recalled the story to anyone who would listen to me. I am sure that I repeated myself more than once to a few friends, like a broken record, but I couldn't help myself. I was a little obsessed.

Cheryl and I can go for extended periods of time without speaking to each other on the phone, only because we are so busy and most of our phone calls are lengthy. It can be hard to find the right time to chat. By the time we got around to discussing the mystery man, I am going to guess that about three weeks had passed by. Enough time for me to have almost forgotten him, and I mentioned him quite casually to Cheryl, it was almost an afterthought at the end of our talk.

Cheryl appeared to be quite interested in what I had seen, and she began asking me for details, which I happily relayed. I told Cheryl everything I had seen, how it had affected me, and about all of the people I had inquired of concerning his identity. When I stopped talking, silence was the only response to my passionate speech, and I was momentarily startled by such a lack of response. Then, Cheryl spoke. Although calm, she sounded somewhat stunned when she said to me, "Shannon, that sounds like my *dad*."

Now it was my turn to be shocked. What?!

My mind began to race. I couldn't believe my good fortune. I finally knew the identity of the scary man, and, as usual, the answer had simply fallen into my hands. I sent a quiet prayer of thanks before I dove into the conversation once again. Cheryl explained to me that when her father appeared to me in my office, he had shown himself to me as the man he was when he was younger. And, apparently, he was every bit as terrifying in person as he was in spirit. I had a momentary flash of empathy for Dorothy and the whole family. John was truly intimidating, even years after he had crossed over.

As we spoke, I found myself musing about John's recent appearance to me, compared to my sighting of him in the previous year. Quite obviously change had been taking place within his heart and soul, he looked so much better than he had before. His younger appearance told me that he was learning and growing, yet, he had been so furious he was almost spitting. I couldn't make sense of such an obvious contradiction. How on earth could someone be progressing rapidly enough to change so quickly, yet still be so mean and angry? What could be triggering such an overwhelming response?

I felt that there was more to the meaning of this vision than we were grasping, but the answers did not come.

I got a very sad phone call from Cheryl merely weeks after discovering who the angry man walking through my wall was. Her mother, Dorothy, had just been diagnosed with Alzheimer's. I felt truly awful for Cheryl and her whole family. However, I could not help the fact that my brain was immediately making the correlation between John's arrival and this diagnosis.

Could it be that John was showing himself to me only so we could understand that he was nearby? And, was he nearby because he was seriously working on his emotional and spiritual issues? Was his "physical" appearance showing that inner change, symbolizing that he was finally taking responsibility for his actions even though he still carried rage? Also – was John taking responsibility for his behaviours because he could finally *see* the outcome of his actions? Could he finally understand what he had done to Dorothy? Did he know her pain, her heartache, and terror? Could he finally admit to himself that his actions were wrong, could he now truly realize the effect his actions had upon his children, and see the trauma reflected back to him? Was this the cause of some of his rage, was it directed towards himself?

I understand fully that all disease, physical or mental, is an indicator of something seriously wrong within the corporeal shell that we have been granted for this moment in time, here on earth. I myself suffer from a genetic, chronic condition that affects my mobility, my internal organs, and, in actuality, all of my body. But, in all seriousness, I do also believe that there is a spiritual connection that goes hand in hand with our diseases. The connection between the physical body and the mind is powerful, and it can also affect the spirit, or, vice versa. I believe that in some instances what is lodged into the depths of our spirit, our soul, can alter the physical body.

In this specific case, for example, was it possible that Dorothy desperately wanted to forget her life with John? Could this have triggered the Alzheimer's? It was something to consider, given the timing of his visit and Dorothy's diagnosis. In no way do I mean to imply that every person with Alzheimer's wants to forget part of their past, nor do I trivialize the seriousness of this horrific, degenerative condition. I speak only of Dorothy here, and the possibility that this could be the emotional/spiritual situation that activated the physical decline in her brain, which brought about her mental deterioration. I was thankful to discover that Cheryl was able to understand where my train of thought was going in this matter, and she did not take offense to what might be an odd concept to consider. At any rate, there was no more contact from John.

A few years passed by, and other than the usual bumps in the road of life, all remained relatively uneventful for Cheryl and me. Cheryl continued to try to work on her personal issues, but she felt as though she was making very little progress in her marriage. Ed was not willing to invest much time and effort into changing. Especially since he was unable to see the correlation between his past (before, and also after meeting Cheryl), his self-condemnation, the present, and how it pertained to his alcohol use. Although Cheryl was more than willing to forgive everything that had come between them in their marriage, it was impossible to heal and let go, all because the behaviors of an out-of-control alcoholic continued and did not change. The real shame was that when Ed did not drink, he was a model husband. Hard-working, considerate, kind, honest, and loving. Regrettably, alcohol ruled most every day.

Unfortunately, as is so often the case with humankind, we continue on our merry, self-destructive path until life intervenes and gives us a reason to pause. 2009 dealt a blow that would see no deviation from its chosen path. Ed was diagnosed with stage 4 lung cancer on April 29th. This eventually metastasized to several parts of his body, until finally the cancer was detected in his brain. Although the fight was never-ending, and Ed was fighting his hardest, the outcome was not going to be what was desperately hoped for.

Ed lived almost an entire year after his initial diagnosis. I did not have many opportunities to speak with him before he passed away. I did not need to talk with Ed, however, to be able to understand the amazing transformation that was taking place within him. It was unbelievably obvious. There was more than one occasion when I would see Ed out in the yard as I was driving by, or I would have a chance encounter with him and Cheryl at the local gas station. It was almost astonishing to see the rapid change occurring in Ed, for he looked so radiant he absolutely glowed. I could see and feel the peace emanating from him every time I was near him. Without a doubt, Ed was battling and conquering his demons in preparation for the journey still to come. I believe he felt the importance of having a clean slate so that he would have an easy transition, with nothing to hold him back spiritually.

I happened to mention the phenomenal changes I was seeing within Ed during one of our many phone conversations, and Cheryl was able to affirm this. It was almost heart-breaking to hear her tell me how Ed had finally become the husband she had always dreamed of, now that he was not drinking and had made the choice to confront his problems head-on. He had completely changed. Ed was even picking up the phone and reaching out to the people that were important to him, some he had not spoken to for long periods of time. He had the urge to settle any grievances or grudges he felt were unnecessary. He called on his family and let them know he loved them. He was ready to meet his Creator.

Ed left the physical realm on April 6th, 2010 with Cheryl, and a beloved best friend of Ed's named Art, at his bedside. Ed had managed to hang on until the day after Cheryl's 43rd birthday, and his crossing was peaceful.

I wanted to be at Cheryl's side at this difficult time in her life, but my own life was in utter disarray and I was nowhere near my home when all of this took place. Ironically, our parallel lives were once again in sync. While Cheryl was busy dealing with Ed's final days, I was on the west coast of British Columbia at my girlfriend Cheryl Y.'s cabin on Digby Island, trying to cope with my Highway of Tears encounter which had just occurred on the drive out.

As it was, although I was completely rattled after witnessing the vision on Highway 16, and utterly exhausted by our return travels, I remained home only long enough to tend to necessary chores and important calls. In less than an hour I was once more in my vehicle, this time headed to Cheryl's house. It was the day after Ed's funeral, Cheryl was alone, and she was, understandably, a mess. So was I. There had been no time for me to process my own emotions and experiences after witnessing the horrifying murder scene, and I was at a loss trying to cope. My girlfriend was in worse shape than I was right at that moment, however, and I shoved my own issues aside as I walked into her home.

I have personally witnessed others, and experienced first-hand, intense grief. We all grieve, but we are all unique in our losses and our grieving process. For some individuals, the grieving is a painful, extremely lengthy, gut-wrenching experience that seems to be unending. Most of the time, in those situations, I have had to ask myself where the cause of such devastating grief originates. This in no way is meant to imply that we should not be sad, or lonely, or that we should deny any feelings that we experience. We are absolutely going to experience that and far worse when we lose a loved one.

I cannot speak for others, but I can speak from my own experience. I have noted two interesting observations. One is the fact that, after the initial shock of loss and the ordeal of the aftermath that follows, there are rare occasions that I continue to suffer traumatic, long-term grief. My prolonged grief seems to be directly tied to the guilt or responsibility I feel pertaining to the one I have lost, and I find myself unable to move forward. It matters not if the guilt and responsibility are justified, it is my outlook. One of the best examples I can give you is in the story of Holly

Berry (in this book) and what I experienced after her loss.

Secondly, I find I can really struggle with feeling sad for *me*. I might have abilities that allow me to be aware of an entity in the room, but, like you, I have to wait for that visit. I cannot command it. I can't pick up the phone whenever I want to chat, I cannot visit with my loved one in person at will. That is all gone once they leave this realm. I understand that my loved one is safe, that God is watching over them, and that they are no longer in any physical pain, but it doesn't make me feel any better regarding my own personal loss. I am very sad for me.

My grief becomes less intense, and less painful with the passing of time. As it does for most. But I have found that I move forward much sooner when I examine my role in the past, and forgive myself for not being perfect in my handling of certain situations. Such as with my dog Holly. Such as with my brother, Trevor, who crossed over in December 2010 by his own choice. I had to forgive myself for not being there for Trevor in the manner that he needed, and perhaps being able to intervene. I had to let go of that guilt in order to heal. The past is done, and it cannot be changed. No matter what.

In the situation with Cheryl and Ed, I observed a similarity. Although Ed had been terminally ill for a year, and Cheryl had begun grieving from the day of that diagnosis, the sorrow she felt when Ed passed was overwhelming. Through countless hours of phone conversations between us, and in-person visits, it became evident that Cheryl was struggling with far more than the physical loss of her husband, which in itself was bad enough. To add to the weight was Cheryl's guilt.

Cheryl felt guilt for all of the unresolved issues in their marriage, for starters. Even though Ed had changed so radically in the last year, much of what they had experienced as a couple together in their dysfunction, was still echoing in her mind. Ed and Cheryl had not spoken much of the baggage that lay between them before Ed crossed, despite Ed's transformation. Cheryl could not let go of the painful hurt that had been inflicted upon her when Ed was alive, nor could she forgive herself for her responses and actions in kind. She continued to struggle with questions of why Ed had behaved as he had, and why he could not find it in himself to find her worthy enough to change before his terminal diagnosis. What was wrong with her? The answers would not come.

Try as I might, I was having a hard time getting Cheryl to understand that it was Ed's own issues with worthiness that had been a driving force behind a lot of his behaviors. It had little to do with her. Ed didn't believe that he had much value to anyone because of his poor choices in life. The resulting self-hatred those choices brought about only drove him to even more outrageous behaviors. It was his inability to forgive himself, let alone her, that had continually widened the chasm between them. He had been stuck, quite literally. Cheryl was trapped in a continuous loop of guilt, self-recrimination and sorrow. She also came to realize that she still struggled with forgiving Ed for the past, and all of the baggage between them. It was hard to watch. I prayed often for enlightenment and strength for my dear friend.

In May of 2010, Cheryl finally found herself strong enough to return to work, even though she had not yet been able to come to terms with all of the emotional struggles she still endured. Her job required her to work away from home, as she was a seasonal worker in road construction, and it was my task to watch over her house while she was away. The summer months were quick to arrive, and seemed to be passing by just as swiftly. I made it a point to drive into town to stop at Cheryl's house every three days, checking on the houseplants and the general well-being of the home. Nothing ever seemed out of the ordinary and the empty house was always quiet, until one afternoon in August when all of that changed.

I had entered the house from the back door, as I normally did. Upon entering the kitchen area, I grabbed the plastic jug off the counter and began to fill it at the sink. A cursory glance over my shoulder into the living room behind me showed nothing amiss, and I began making my way slowly through the rest of the house, stopping at each plant to tend it. The layout of the home was such that I had to walk from the kitchen through the living room to get into the master bedroom, and from there across the living room once again to get to the spare room on the opposite side. All was well.

I exited the spare room with the intent to place the empty jug on the counter and lock up the house so that I could be on my way. My feet had barely stepped back into the living room when I was suddenly assailed by the very strong scent of cigarette smoke. Now, I must say that I had noticed, on rare occasion during prior visits, a faint whiff of cigarettes in some of the rooms. It always reminded me of Ed, and I questioned if it might possibly be him there in the house whenever I detected that odor, but I didn't think much of it. This time, however, the smell was very obvious and it made me stop instantly, frozen for a moment, while I considered what was happening.

My first thought was that Ed was with me. My next thought was a question: why? I began to ponder what his purpose might be. But then I thought to myself, no, I must be mistaken. Therefore, I am sorry to say that I dismissed this event with a bit of a shrug as I began to tour the house one last time before leaving. Except, I was not alone as I walked; I could feel an entity following behind me. I had to give my head a shake and admit that this was no longer my imagination as I decided to sit upon the loveseat and wait. I only waited a split second.

The air was almost crackling with electricity when my eyes beheld an amazing site. There was a man standing before me, and of course, it was Ed. But it was an Ed I was not familiar with. His countenance literally *glowed*, he was absolutely shining. He was surveying me with a grin that almost went ear to ear and he appeared to be delighted to be visiting me. To my surprise, Ed no longer sported a familiar moustache, he was clean-shaven. But the biggest shock of all, however, was the fact that Ed was not wearing a cowboy hat, or any hat at all. His head was bare.

Before Ed even had a chance to speak, I surmised that his progression upwards must have been swift once he crossed over. That cowboy hat had meant everything to Ed, it was, as I have said before, his identity in so many ways. It was very significant that he appeared without it.

There have been many times over the years that I have witnessed spirits who continue to hang onto the symbols of certain material "crutches" that they had here on earth. They often do so for long periods of time after they have crossed over; unwilling to lose that sense of self that remains attached to the very important object in question. Unable to see the need to shed those spiritual hindrances, such as cigarettes, or, a very special, extremely important hat.

I also understood immediately that cigarettes were no longer a part of Ed's identity, even though his arrival was foretold with the odor of smoke. The aroma had merely been a means of catching my attention and identifying him. There was no way possible that Ed could shine so brightly and continue to hang onto something so spiritually heavy and burdensome like a cigarette.

Ed was not finished with surprises for me. When he opened his mouth and spoke to me, my eyes grew wide upon hearing his words. I still know exactly what Ed said to me after all of these years, because I wrote it down as soon as I got home that day. I knew it was important. When Ed spoke, he was calm, assured, very happy and proud, but humble. Ed said to me, and I quote:

"The Lord is my Savior and my friend now, and I understand. You tell Cheryl I said that – Yep – I UNDERSTAND."

I could feel compassion emanating from Ed as he continued with his speech, but his words were to discuss a personal matter that I will not repeat. Nonetheless, Ed's words could be melted down into one specific message, and that was forgiveness. Ed absolutely understood what had gone on inside of his marriage. He saw the triggers, the reactions, and the consequences, on both sides. He could easily comprehend how his weaknesses manifested a tremendous amount of hurt and pain. He could see why Cheryl had behaved in the manner that she had. He *understood*, fully and completely. He had forgiven himself; he had forgiven Cheryl. He had welcomed Jesus into his heart and he had met with his Creator, God. He was at peace, that was very evident.

I remember quite fondly Ed's final words, for they were to me. He encouraged me not to give up on a particularly stressful situation that I was dealing with, in regard to my personal life. And before he departed, these words were left to echo in my ears: "Thank you for your integrity in my home." Then Ed was gone.

I was a little startled by his final comment. It had not occurred to me previously that when I smelled smoke on some of my other visits to the house, not only was it positively Ed that was with me, he was observing my conduct in his home. In other words, I was not snooping through cupboards and drawers where I did not belong, and he knew that. He could see me. A small smile plays upon my lips even now as I recall this memory. It was an honor to be acknowledged.

I know that Ed's visit lifted a lot of burden from Cheryl's shoulders that day. Receiving forgiveness is just as important as granting it, and I think Cheryl began to experience this upon hearing Ed's message to her. She was able to quit condemning herself, she was able to seriously work on her grievances with Ed, and at least begin the process of letting go of unnecessary pain. It was very gratifying to watch Cheryl learn and evolve spiritually. As she grew in acceptance and understanding, her temperament began to soften and some of the harshness left her words. Even the housework had lost its importance and was no longer a compulsion. It was beautiful to see. Cheryl's struggles with self-worth did not disappear overnight, however. It took a lot of work on her behalf to put her life into proper perspective, and to begin to view it without the stain of her emotions to influence her outlook and slow her down. Her progress was admirable.

An unexpected confirmation of my vision came to us quite by chance, many months after Ed's visit. Cheryl was on the phone talking with Ed's daughter, which was a rare occasion, and quite naturally the subject of their conversation was Ed. The young woman had a very interesting experience she wanted to share, regarding her dad. Something that had never happened before. Apparently, while watching television one evening, she noticed movement out of the corner of her eye. As she glanced towards the wall, off to the side and away from the bright screen, she was amazed to see standing before her, Ed. Her father looked extremely happy and very peaceful. Although he was only there for mere moments, the vision brought instant joy to her heart. But she confessed to Cheryl her confusion with what she saw. Was it possible it was her imagination?

Apparently, despite the fact that it was very clearly Ed her eyes had seen, and she was able to instantly recognize him, he was missing one really important thing: the only thing he was not *ever* without. His cowboy hat. Ed had appeared before her with a bare head. Could it be so?

Cheryl paused for a moment before replying, and then quite happily started off by saying, “Let me tell you about my friend, Shannon...”

Another person who was instrumental in Cheryl’s life was Ed’s best friend, Art. Cheryl had known him for years, ever since she met Ed. Art was a huge support for Ed and Cheryl both in the final months of Ed’s life, and for Cheryl in the days and weeks to follow after Ed’s crossing. It was no surprise to see, that over the course of many months, their shared grief developed into a strong bond that would eventually blossom into a loving, supportive relationship. Much to the approval of all who were closely involved in their lives, Art and Cheryl were married in 2013. I have no doubt in my mind that Ed would have approved and was very happy for them.

Unfortunately, 2013 would also mark the year that Dorothy, Cheryl’s mother, would cross over. Although her life with John was something Dorothy wished she could forget, that was one of the things that Alzheimer’s did not steal: her painful memories with him. More than once, Cheryl would comment on the irony of that situation.

The months prior to Dorothy's passing were also very difficult for Cheryl. It was emotionally exhausting watching her mother deteriorate and slip away mentally and physically, until finally she needed twenty-four-hour assistance in an appropriate facility. Dorothy resided in Saskatchewan, and Cheryl in Alberta, so it was impossible for Cheryl to tend to her mother in the manner in which she would have preferred, but Cheryl tried her best to provide for Dorothy despite the distance between them. It was a tremendous loss when her mother did finally pass, although I believe that Cheryl was very relieved that Dorothy no longer suffered.

Guilt is a terrible burden, and I believe it is one that we all shoulder, although to varying degrees. Why we, as humans, prefer self-hate and condemnation instead of love, acceptance and forgiveness of ourselves is beyond me. As a species, we seem to prefer torturing ourselves with our imperfections and our inabilities, which ultimately leads to rejection of self. Life is already difficult enough, without this added weight.

I struggle with the battle of perfectionism and guilt when I cannot live up to my own ideals and standards; most of us do. But it never occurred to me that in the months and years after Dorothy crossed, Cheryl would be fighting the same war in her own head. My dear friend, who confided in me almost everything that went on in her life, did not share this. I believe that Cheryl thought very poorly of herself for not being there in person to shower Dorothy with all of the nurturing love and care that Cheryl felt her mother deserved. She thought herself so horrible for not providing perfect living conditions for her mom, that she could not bear to expose her weakness and her failure to me out of fear. Cheryl condemned herself thoroughly, and could hardly tolerate the thought of more. This is a perfect example of how guilt alters perceptions, for I would not ever have shamed Cheryl, and logically, she knew that. However, because she was ashamed of herself, she assumed the same from others, and hid in silence.

Nothing is ever truly hidden and silent from God, however. He knows our hearts. He understands us better than we can understand ourselves because He also sees our past, since the beginning of time. Above all, God has compassion and love for His children even though He is a strict Father, and He wants to see them heal all wounds, from the smallest of cuts to the largest of tragedies. Thus, it was so with Cheryl. And finally, in the fall of 2017, God allowed Cheryl to receive the gift of healing, once again in the form of a spirit-visit, this time from Dorothy.

Cheryl and I were chatting on the phone one evening, casual and light-hearted. As the conversation was beginning to wane, there was a pause in the exchange of words, although the silence was comfortable. Before either of us had a chance to end the call, words began to echo in my ears and I found myself repeating them to Cheryl immediately. The message was not lengthy, but Dorothy spoke of the great burden of guilt that Cheryl was carrying. She could see that her daughter was punishing herself for her perceived imperfections regarding Dorothy's care. She wanted Cheryl to put this issue to rest, permanently. Cheryl was not at fault, and Dorothy held no ill will or blame. She spoke of the harm that Cheryl was inflicting upon herself, and the weight that was dragging her down. Dorothy wished for her daughter to be free, and to let her know once more how much she was loved. And then Dorothy was silent, and my voice fell still. The sound of Cheryl's relieved sobbing was all that could be heard.

I don't know who was more surprised by that visit, me or Cheryl. It was not the sudden, unexpected message that I received which caught me off guard. It was the content of the message which shocked me a little. Why and how did I not know about this previously? Cheryl had not ever said a word.

Cheryl was completely caught off-guard in every way. It had been four years since her mom crossed over, and this was the first time Cheryl had heard from Dorothy. That alone was an amazing gift for Cheryl to receive. But to have her mom reveal such a dark, hidden secret and then expose it to the light so that it could be seen, for Cheryl to receive absolution for a sin only she felt she had committed: that was enormous. My prayers of gratitude were immediate and heartfelt.

It has been my immense pleasure to witness, since the year 2000, the journey my friend Cheryl has undertaken. I am very proud of the effort she has made. Forgiveness, acceptance, and her love for God have allowed her to shake off so many of the chains that left her bound. Her willingness and determination to try her very hardest to bring about change has left her in a much better state of being, emotionally, spiritually, and even physically. Is Cheryl, to this very day, strong, independent, and outspoken? Indeed, she is. But these qualities are now tempered with love, not fear.

As 2022 was coming to a close, Cheryl and Art, myself and Ray, had gathered together in celebration. Eventually, the conversation began to naturally gravitate towards my favorite topic: spiritism and God. Cheryl had some news to share, she had been smelling cigarette smoke in the house that day. I found it very interesting to hear that when she smelled the smoke, she immediately thought of her father, John, instead of Ed. She asked me if this could be a possibility, but before I even had a moment to ponder that fact, I heard in my head, quite loudly, an answer to Cheryl's query. The voice simply stated "Spirit of Forgiveness." I was in awe.

Without a doubt, I could feel John's energy present in the room that same instance, and he carried with him the essence of forgiveness and love: it was a powerful vibration. I was hit with a flurry of emotions, not the least of which was the fact that John walked with forgiveness for himself and his past. He also arrived with forgiveness and love for Cheryl. He could see the consequences of his actions and the resulting choices she had made. No longer was John an angry, frightful man. I could hardly believe it was John that was with us, his energy was so changed. But although he was still a very strong presence in the room, John was at peace. I had no doubt.

Before the evening had ended the four of us joined in a discussion about hatred and negativity, and what happens when you harbor these emotions and direct them towards other people through your unforgiveness.

The resulting consequence of such actions leads to the one thing you probably don't want in the first place: your hate actually *binds* you to the one you despise. Let. It. Go!

Sever that emotional, energetic connection. It is a gift you give to yourself, let alone to the other person. Accept the situation, if it cannot be changed. Stop hurting yourself by refusing to surrender that useless baggage.

What a beautiful conversation to have during the conclusion of one year while entering into the next. How wonderful it is to be able to achieve closure on such a huge chapter in Cheryl's life, and to be able to see God's love and healing touch everyone involved. My heart is grateful for all of the guidance we have received, and I look forward to the next episode in our shared journey.

INTO THE SUNSET

As I sit at my desk, determined to write this final chapter, I am searching for the right words to describe the new direction my journey has taken as a daughter, a student of the Light, and as a medium. This year, 2023, is a time in which I have been challenged to learn and grow in ways I could not have foreseen, with the biggest change in my life being the loss of my father, Glen, in April.

I have endured sorrow as I witnessed my father depart from this life, and I have felt deep joy to see him continue into the next. I have suffered the agony of his physical separation from me, but also comfort in knowing that he arrived safely in the spirit world surrounded by loved ones. It has been a dichotomy of intense emotions, to say the least. Since his crossing, I am often aware of his spiritual presence as he supports me with love and guidance, continuing in his endeavor to fulfill his role as a father. What I have experienced drives my desire to share our story, and I understand that despite his quiet and somewhat reclusive life, he supports my decision to write about it.

I will start by saying that my dad and I were not always close, especially after I turned twelve. Our love for each other was deep, but our relationship was complicated. The fact that Glen came from a generation that had never learned to communicate well or express emotions did not help the situation between us at all. Glen was also struggling with poor life choices which were unintentionally affecting my life choices, and we had more or less grown apart, although we were not completely estranged. It was not until I was around the age of 24 that I decided to look past our difficulties, wipe the slate clean, and start anew. It was my choice to try to connect with my dad, and I knew I would have to put some effort into it, but he was important to me and I felt that it was worth a try.

Perseverance can be a wonderful personality trait, and in this instance, it served me well. I started by calling my dad on a Sunday morning while I was enjoying my morning coffee. It was not a lengthy conversation and we didn't have much to say to each other, but I sensed that Glen was pleasantly surprised to hear from me. I called him the following Sunday, and the Sunday after that, until many weeks of calls had gone by. Each phone visit lasted a few minutes longer than the one before, and my dad always seemed happy to hear from me. We never spoke during the week though, Glen always waited for me to reach out to him. I was beginning to wonder if we were ever going to have a comfortable, reciprocal relationship.

A few months after our first chat there was a busy Sunday morning where I completely forgot to call my dad. It never even occurred to me what day it actually was, and when my phone rang early that afternoon my absentminded hello belayed my multitasking activities. "Whatcha doing?" was the cheerful response to my subdued voice, and my shocked brain took a second to register what I was actually hearing. It was my *father*. I was thrilled! From that day forward my dad and I developed a bond that would only continue to strengthen and deepen over our lifetime together.

Weekly phone conversations eventually became twice-a-week, and in the last years of his life, we spoke every other day and quite often more. I will be forever grateful for the invention of the telephone. Once I left the Rocky Mountain House area in 1986 at the age of nineteen, I never returned to stay even though my dad remained there. If it were not for the telephone, my relationship with him would not ever have been what it was.

Glen was a man who was very small in stature, he barely stood five feet one inches tall. He never weighed much either, and in his prime might have weighed a hundred and twenty pounds soaking wet, far less as he grew older. His once dark blonde hair had deepened into a light brown color as he aged, and it was scattered with flashes of copper and red. He had unwavering blue-green eyes, and he was well known for his charming personality and his wonderful sense of humor. He was also intensely private and was seldom seen at large, public gatherings. Very few people were invited into his circle of trusted loved ones, although he was very recognizable in the town of Rocky, having lived and worked there for over forty years.

Glen became a proud grandfather with the arrival of my three boys, born in the 1990s. He tried hard to be present in their lives whenever the opportunity arose, despite the many miles that kept us apart more often than we wanted. Birthdays, holidays, special occasions and graduations, he was there for all of it whenever he could be. Although my parents divorced in 1979, quite often my dad would pick up my mom on his way through the city of Calgary as he drove to visit us in

Southern Alberta. Family was important to him, and he never missed an opportunity to chauffer anyone who wanted a ride in his vintage 1970 Chrysler 300 convertible. It was his pride and joy, with its beautiful red exterior and white leather top.

Despite the connection I had with my dad, and no matter how much my dad loved his children and his grandchildren, Glen had endured a life-long struggle with alcohol that remained a barrier between him and his loved ones and cast a cloud over most of his personal relationships. It was certainly a wedge that complicated ours. It was very hard to heal the wounds of the past when the figurative band-aid kept getting ripped off every time the cyclical behaviors continued. It was heartbreaking to watch the control that addiction had over his life, and hard not to be resentful of the alcohol that inevitably came first over everything else that was important to him. It robbed us of countless years together.

Imagine my utter joy when, after a lengthy but determined battle, my father became sober in 2008, and stayed that way for the remainder of his life. I was so proud of him then, as I am now. I am grateful. Sobriety gave me a father I could have only dreamed about previously. My dad became involved in my life in a way that I had never experienced before, and my brother, Trevor, felt the same way. Glen's emotional and physical support of family became even more evident as he tried to repair and make amends for damages of the past. Trevor and I were more than willing to move forward.

One of the most devastating situations arose in December of 2010, and that was the death of my forty-year-old brother by suicide. I cannot fathom how difficult it must have been for my father to abstain from alcohol during such a stressful time, but he did it. Glen was a very brave man, with incredible fortitude.

I have said before that my dad was an extremely private man, and one thing he rarely spoke of was his emotions, most certainly not anything sensitive or uncomfortable. Not only were painful or sad feelings never discussed, spirituality and life after death were other topics best left alone in my dad's opinion. It was not ever freely mentioned. Any efforts to engage in such conversation were abruptly ended by him, although I had no idea why he was so reluctant to open up about it. In my mind, I had delegated him as a non-believer, which was unfortunate, for this meant that I could not share with him the amazing knowledge that I have been blessed to experience first-hand, as a psychic medium. It was a topic we never discussed, not even once.

This also meant that although I had started writing about my spiritual experiences in the spring of 2010, I did not share them with my dad. It really bothered me that I felt I had to hide such a large part of my life from Glen, especially because we were so close. He had no idea I was even a writer until I dropped an unedited manuscript into his lap one day, in the fall of 2020 when Ray and I were at his house for a visit. I felt that it was important and respectful for me to allow him to read what I was about to share with the world, and to let him have an opinion before it was published. I felt awkward even bringing the subject up, but although

Glen was quite surprised at hearing my news, he seemed interested and happy to have the book. There was no scorn or scepticism regarding the subject of my spirituality, my beliefs, or the fact that I was a medium, for which I was greatly relieved.

The reaction my dad had to the book blew me away – he was proud! His absolute acceptance of the path I walked and the book I wrote astounded me, it was not the response I had been expecting. I was overjoyed and somewhat astonished when he asked me if a second manuscript would be started soon. I have to admit, we did not discuss much of what was actually written, that would have been crossing my father's boundaries of not speaking about emotional subjects. But I knew without a doubt that if Glen were unhappy with anything I had written, or if he felt that I was a charlatan, he would have made that very clear. And he certainly would not have been telling family and friends about the book. Not that he told everyone, but he told quite a few, which was impressive.

My father suffered on and off throughout his life with various health issues, some quite serious, but nothing had ever permanently affected his health, in the sense that it left him unable to function normally after taking time to heal. He was able to live alone and care for himself. We all noticed that Glen was incredibly cold most of the time, bundled up in sweaters and having the heater on even in the summertime, but we chalked it up to poor circulation and never thought much about it, for it had been ongoing for years and years. He started complaining about having painful feet that were uncomfortable to walk on sometime around 2019, but I never heard much about a diagnosis and I wondered if his doctor was doing anything to help him, or if something could be done. True to his nature, Glen stayed quiet about most of it.

By 2020 my dad, a heavy smoker for almost sixty years, had to admit that the doctors were strongly advising him to quit smoking because of the toll it was taking on his health. Thick plaque was building in the arteries which supplied blood to his lower abdomen and into his legs and feet, restricting circulation and causing his pain and cold issues. He knew he was most likely going to need surgery at some point. Unfortunately, despite the damage his cigarettes were doing, he found himself unable to quit.

By 2021 he was in serious need of surgery to open up his arteries. Unbeknownst to family and friends at the time, Glen's feet were a fiery red color, they had some open sores and bleeding, and he was in constant agony. But, for reasons we will never understand, Glen's doctors decided to withhold what would become critically important, life-saving surgery until April 2023. They even went so far as to book surgery for him in September 2022, but for no reason at all the surgery was abruptly cancelled mere days beforehand. And not rescheduled until seven months later when his symptoms had become unbearable. For two years my dad suffered tremendously, but hid the majority of his pain from everyone he knew and loved. Because he was so private, he refused all efforts to advocate for him and to accompany him into the doctor's office, so we had no idea just how poorly he was doing at that time. It was only after his death when I found pictures of his swollen, bleeding feet on his phone from two years previous that I understood how long he had suffered. I was horrified.

I am a four-hour drive away from Rocky Mountain House, where my dad lived. Because of my health issues and all of the animals we have, I rarely leave our home for overnight visits, preferring instead to return home no matter how late the hour. As a result, my visits are not usually lengthy, and such was the case in December 2022 when Ray and I drove up to see my dad before Christmas. I recall that Glen did not get up from his chair the whole time we were there, but as all of our visits were normally conducted at the kitchen table and the weather was cold and snowy, I thought little of it. We had just visited in October, and my dad was walking then, although not far and not quickly. I feel awful that I did not recognize or realize the depths of his pain at that time.

It is true that I was becoming more aware of some of the difficulties my dad was having with his feet, for he had started speaking more often about it, but as usual, the conversations were not lengthy. I was becoming deeply concerned about the situation, but Glen would always downplay it, as he did then, and refused all outside offers of help despite my obvious frustration. It did not matter that his beloved and trusted friends and family members felt the same way I did, Glen would not allow us to intervene on his behalf with his doctors, doggedly hanging onto the hope that the professionals would do what was best for him. We were all absolutely horrified at the obvious neglect Glen was suffering at the hands of the medical "experts", but without Glen's consent there was nothing we could do.

I wish I could have had the foresight to understand that visit would be the last time I would ever spend with my father at his kitchen table.

Alarm bells began to ring in my head in February when my dad refused to let us drive up to see him for a visit. His excuse was feeble, citing weather concerns, but he was adamant that we wait. When Glen was being stubborn a person had no choice but to listen because he could get a little cranky if you did not respect his wishes. March arrived, and again I told my father we would like to make the drive, but once more he refused, telling me to wait until after his upcoming doctor's appointment. The doctor finally agreed to perform surgery on Glen, scheduled in April, but that was yet another reason for my dad to put me on hold: "Wait until you pick me up for surgery. We will visit then."

My dad had an amazing community of close friends who did everything they could to care for him by bringing meals, running errands, and driving him to and from appointments. Any fears I may have felt about my father living so far away from me and being unable to assist him were alleviated with the knowledge that they were looking out for him, and always willing to stop and lend a hand. I could rest easy, knowing that those dear people kept a watchful eye over him. I will be forever thankful to all of them. It was the efforts of his friends that kept Glen as comfortable as he could be until April 4th, 2023. The day of Glen's surgery.

Ray and I arrived in Calgary early that day to pick up my father from a motel, not far from the hospital. Although it had been less than four months since we had seen him, we were absolutely dismayed at the shape we discovered my dad to be in. Glen was normally a slight individual, but he had obviously lost a lot of weight. His grim face spoke of the pain he was in. Much to his horror, he needed me to fully support him as we made our way to the car which Ray had pulled up to the entrance of the motel. At this point, his weakened, deteriorating medical condition had become life-threatening, but we had no true understanding of this. Our hopes rested upon surgery; we were sure all would be well in the days to come.

It was not to be.

Glen's surgery was unsuccessful in the sense that the repairs that needed to be made to his arteries were not fully completed in that operation. Glen still had plugged arteries in his left thigh when he awoke, a condition that the doctors were hoping would start to reverse itself with better blood flow to his leg as a result of the initial surgery. However, no one had prepared any of us for this outcome, and my poor father found himself to be in the same excruciating pain that he was in when he went to sleep. He was devastated to discover this. He had been hanging on to the strong hope and belief that he would be pain-free upon awakening. We all were. We were counting on it.

Glen's physical condition did not improve. He also began to waver in and out of delirium for reasons which were not specifically determined. It was finally decided that a second surgery would be performed to open up the remaining plugged arteries. That surgery was scheduled after the upcoming weekend.

Although we had almost a two-hour drive just to get to the hospital, Ray and I had been driving there and back daily. Whether he was delirious or fully conscious, my father was always aware that we were with him. I would like to think that my dad was also aware somehow of the other entities in the room with him, those in spirit form, and he took comfort in that. I say this because there were times when I could see quite clearly that we were most certainly *not* alone.

On more than one occasion I had seen in the hospital room various relatives of ours that had crossed over years before, most notably Glen's mother, and Trevor. Even a beloved friend of my dad's who had passed only months beforehand came into the room, fully recognizable to me in spirit although many years had gone by since I had seen her in the flesh. She approached Glen's sleeping form and lay her hand on his forehead, there was a beautiful smile on her face. There was also a comforting glow in the room whenever I became aware of Glen's spiritual visitors, and I was relieved by their presence. Much to my surprise Glen's cat, Misty, who had been suffering from old age and serious health issues and was put to sleep the day before Glen had surgery, strolled into the room looking healthy as can be and patiently settled onto his lap. Although she was a very reclusive animal while on this earth, she seemed not to care that we were in the room.

My aunt Colleen was not relieved, however, to hear this news. When she asked if I had been aware of any spirit activity in the room, and I told her what and who

I had seen, I also said that I was guessing they were there to support Glen. She responded by saying she hoped they were not there to take him home, back to the spirit realms. That was not a thought I entertained for long though, I was firmly of the belief that my dad would pull through this battle and succeed. My dad was tougher than nails in many ways. I had seen him very, very ill in hospital years previously, and he recovered. I believed that this situation would have the same outcome.

As it turned out, the second surgery would not be performed. Mid-way through the day on Saturday Glen began to complain of pain in his right leg, the leg that previously was pain-free. Despite the nurses checking his incision and determining there was not a problem with that leg, Glen continued to complain. Unbelievably, the staff did not discover that the artery repair performed on Glen's right side had ruptured and was bleeding internally. They did not realize their mistake until very early in the morning on Sunday, April 9th, when Glen's leg had a huge hematoma, the size of a pineapple, in his thigh. When I called to check on him at six AM that day, I was informed by a surgeon that they were waiting for an operating room to become available so that they could perform life-saving surgery. I was informed that surgery was risky in Glen's weakened condition and that he would have to be admitted into the Intensive Care Unit if he survived. I consented to the surgery with the understanding that there was no other choice if he was to live.

Glen survived. He was a fighter and would not give up easily. When we arrived at the hospital he had just been admitted to the ICU and although he was weak, he was aware of his surroundings and the fact that we were with him. Throughout the day Glen wavered in and out of delirium and he remained in the agitated state that he was in previously, but we remained hopeful he would improve. His left leg was still cold and without a pulse, but it seemed to be causing Glen less pain, for which we were grateful. There was no way he would be able to have surgery to repair that leg until he recovered from the surgery he just had.

Monday, April 10th brought about no change in my dad's physical or mental condition. I was grateful that he knew we were with him despite the situation. When we left the hospital that night, Glen was "okay" in the sense that he knew who we were, and he was holding on. He was somewhat aware of his surroundings. I remained firm in my belief that he was going to recover.

Sometime in the very early hours of the following morning, long before the sun would rise, I was unexpectedly jolted from my deep sleep without reason. I lay in the stillness of our dark room, pondering the reason for my wakefulness when, all of a sudden, I heard a strong, clear voice in my ear, it was instantly recognizable: Dad.

"I can't stay for much longer, Shannon."

His voice briefly echoed in my ear and then disappeared. I was stunned, barely able to comprehend what I had heard.

I stayed awake until the sunrise began to announce its arrival with a faint glow in the eastern sky. Reality did not hit me fully until I exited the bedroom, sat down at the table, and took my first sip of coffee. As bad as I wished it were, this was not my imagination. I knew what I had heard, even though I struggled to accept it. I knew I had to call the hospital to check on my father, but before I did so I shared with Ray the words I had heard earlier. As I spoke, a look of concern flashed over his face, and he waited patiently while I picked up the phone and dialed.

When Glen's nurse answered the phone, the news was not good. Sometime around four o'clock that morning, mere hours beforehand, Glen had become unresponsive and was placed on life support. The doctor was urging the family to gather at his bedside. Once more Glen's words played out in my mind, *"I can't stay much longer, Shannon."* I understood immediately my father's wishes and began to call our family members to prepare them for what was inevitably coming.

A phone call to my Auntie Sharon, Glen's sister-in-law, only confirmed what I knew to be true concerning my visit from him. As I began to relay the news of Glen's physical condition, followed by the words he said to me, Sharon began to quietly sob as she spoke.

"I understand, honey, he came to me too. Last night in a dream."

She then explained that Glen told her in the dream that he was leaving, he had to go, but he was so happy to be going and to finally be free from pain. Sharon was heartbroken to be losing a dear friend, but she gave him permission to move on and to let us go.

We both wept at the thought of losing him.

My immediate family members, as well as Glen's two nephews, were present at his bedside as quickly as we could get there. Although he was on life-support, everyone in the room felt certain that Glen was very aware that we were with him. He would squeeze my hand and move his legs, and he appeared to try to speak in response to my son, Zach, teasing him about flirting with the nurses. He looked like he was trying to make a clever comment in reply, the way his whole face scrunched up, and we all laughed in relief to see this. I found myself struggling, however, when a doctor I had not met before came into the room to ask the family if we would consider giving Glen a chance on life-support for a few days. He felt quite strongly that Glen might be able to regain function if his body was allowed to rest, and he was not so sure we should remove the breathing tube.

I found myself in a terrible quandary. How could I leave him in this state, hooked up to machines, when I knew in my heart that he did not want that? He had come to me in spirit only hours earlier to tell me he could not stay, and a short time later he became physically unresponsive. That was my answer, I knew this. Now I had a doctor encouraging me to leave my dad on life-support, telling me that there might be a chance, and giving the whole family hope. I could see the look in their eyes.

I felt torn right down the middle, my heart was breaking. What to do?

In the end, we decided together to hang onto that hope and take the chance that Glen might recover. I can honestly say that it was one of the hardest decisions I have ever had to make. The conflict that I felt deep within my heart was almost unbearable. I knew that my dad was going to be very angry with me if he survived but did not recover enough physically to live on his own. I also knew he was ready to go, he told me so. But yet, how do you turn your back on that last hope? How do you choose such a permanent outcome? How do you tell your family and friends, the people who loved him, that you would not take that chance, despite the doctor having optimism? How do you make that decision when you know that your dad is still present, that he can still hear your voice and seemingly knows you are in the room? I couldn't do it, although I knew I could not wait for long.

The end of the day arrived, and with it came the departure of our family from Glen's hospital room. One by one they wished him well, expressed their love for him, and said their goodbyes until only myself and Ray remained. We stayed for as long as possible, but inevitably the time also came for us to make that long drive home. We had to go. However, before we did that there was one more thing I needed to do.

My dad had suffered far more pain than I could have ever comprehended, but he hung on to hope for a better life as hard as he could. He struggled and he fought, and I know without a doubt that one of the biggest reasons he endured and survived was so he could be there for me. His love for me was such that he would not give up, and he would not leave, no matter what he had to go through. I knew that. And I knew that I had to grant him the freedom he so desperately needed.

I smoothed the hair from his forehead as I bent forward to plant a kiss on his brow. My words to him were simple and heartfelt. "I love you, Daddy. It's okay if you are too tired to fight anymore."

Tears blurred my vision as we departed from my father's bedside. My heart ached to see the golden glow that was once more filling the room, and the sight of my grandmother and brother standing vigil. Although I did not see any other spirits at that moment, I could feel them, and the room was full. Glen was not alone.

Less than six hours after I spoke those final words to my father, he suffered a massive stroke that would have killed him had he not been on life-support.

We did not actually discover this fact until we arrived at the hospital for what would be the last time, on the morning of April 12th. Scans only confirmed what was obvious to everyone in the room. Glen was no longer with us. The choice had been made for me, there was no debate, there was no hope. I could only accept the situation and prepare for what was to come.

To write about the impact of losing my dad is literally taking my breath away, and I don't think I can find the right words to describe it. If you have not had the misfortune to lose a parent, I am sure you can only imagine what that must feel like. It is all of those things and more.

However, I was calm and peaceful during this process. I did *not* accept the circumstances that led up to my father's passing, all of the years and all of the errors, but I did accept the final outcome. I accepted the situation as it was right then and there, I had to. I needed to be present in the moment, to let my father know he was loved and supported. I needed to be with him in a peaceful, serene setting. To hold his hand as his final physical connection was severed and he was free of the last vestiges of his earthly existence. And that is exactly what happened.

What has made this whole ordeal bearable is the knowledge that I was blessed with, and the vision that I was shown as Glen was finally being freed of the machines I know he detested. The vision came swiftly and with crystal clarity.

Glen was standing off to the side with a group of individuals gathered about him in a loose circle. I did not see their faces, but I could feel the love in the room and I understood that these were people who had crossed over before him, friends and family Glen cherished. My dad was laughing with joy as he conversed, his hands were stuffed in the front pockets of his blue jeans, and he looked forty years younger and thirty pounds heavier. He looked amazing. I understood immediately that he was ready to move forward, and that he was happy. As I observed this scene, I instantaneously became aware of one more extremely important detail. His feet.

Glen's feet were clad in a fine set of shiny, black leather cowboy boots that tapered and became pointed at the toe. The kind of boots he loved to wear as a young man. The kind of boots that can not be worn if your feet are swollen, infected, or painful. For me, those boots were the most beautiful sight I have ever seen. They symbolized his freedom. The weight of a thousand pounds was lifted from me at that moment with the understanding that my father was really, truly okay in every sense of the word. Thank God.

As one of the greatest loves of my life took his last breaths, and the physical bonds of this earth were severed from him as his heart beat its final pulse, I saw him once more. He was driving his precious red convertible with the white top down, his beloved cat Misty was in his lap, and my dog Mindy was nestled at his side on the white leather seat. Glen did not look back as he drove off into the sunset and the glorious scene stretching out before him. I could feel the peace and contentment that enveloped him as he drove away, and his eagerness to begin the next part of his journey. Goodbye for now. I love you, Daddy.

About four hours after he crossed over, I was overwhelmed with the strong understanding that Glen and Trevor had been reunited in the spirit world. This would have been one of my dad's greatest desires, and I am glad to have such certainty. I understood Glen had always held a deep longing to be reunited with his son.

The following day was, of course, extremely difficult for me. I did not have much time to process my loss, however, because we had no choice but to prepare for a trip to Rocky to check on my dad's house and make sure everything was secure. Glen experienced a frightening break-and-enter/robbery in December 2019 while he was in his bed sleeping. Before the thieves fled, they took his car keys off the hook on the wall beside the door. They returned less than an hour later and drove off in his vehicle, which they destroyed before it was abandoned. Because of this, we did not know if some important papers and possessions might need to be removed from the house immediately, in case of a repeat offence.

I was feeling quite numb from grief and exhaustion, and overwhelmed by yet another day of travel. I found myself staring off into space, trying to sort my thoughts. As I tried to shake off the melancholy that surrounded me, I cast my vision upwards towards the ceiling, only to find myself completely unprepared for the sight of my dad's intense blue-green eyes, quite close to mine. Those eyes sparkled with a look that forbade me to argue with him; I had seen that look many times before and knew it well. He spoke immediately, with forcefulness.

"Don't you be sad for me!"

He was gone as quickly as he had arrived, leaving me a little stunned. I don't know what I was expecting from my dad when he made first contact with me, but it wasn't that. I understood that I had just been given a parental order that was not to be disregarded, however, and I had every intention to try to heed it. I had no idea at that moment just how important those words would become to me in the days and months to follow. I did not realize at that time how strong the urge would become to drown in remorse as I began to comprehend more of my dad's health issues, and my loss, in the days ahead. That simple statement became my lifeline whenever I would find myself fighting back waves of despair and grief. I could also feel the concern my father had for me when he spoke, and I knew he did not want me to carry the heavy burden of guilt and sadness. Choices had been made that were out of my control to change, and I had to accept that.

There was one other thing that I noticed at the time my dad appeared, but I barely registered it as being out of place because it was familiar to me. My dad looked older than he had less than twenty-four hours beforehand, when he first crossed over. It never occurred to me at the time to question it, because he looked more like my father at that moment than he did when he looked so young. He didn't look haggard and skinny, he looked good, but he looked far more mature than he had only hours previously. Due to the circumstances, I am not surprised that I overlooked this detail, but it was truly the first time I had seen an entity go backwards, from youthful-looking to aged.

Our trip to Rocky was uneventful, and we found everything to be in order once we arrived at my dad's house. It was nothing less than surreal to be wandering aimlessly through a home that would never see the return of its current owner ever again. At least, not in the flesh. This was a home that had been loved and cared for. My father had so many hopes and plans for his house, plans that hinged on his return to health. It was heartbreaking to think that his dreams would never see fruition. It was absolutely crushing. *"Don't you be sad for me!"* Those words echoed once again in my mind. I gathered my resolve as tears stung my eyes. I was going to try.

I have mentioned before the vintage car that Glen loved to drive. It was a rare car, there were only two cars that were ever factory-produced that year with the specific motor it had. Everything about it was original except for the paint, which had been changed from blue to red. The car was stored in my dad's garage next to his house, and of course, it was of utmost concern to us that it be moved as quickly as possible to another location that would be safer. However, it did not take us long to discover that there were no keys for the car anywhere in the house. Nowhere obvious, that is.

As it turned out, there were no keys to be found for any of the vehicles that Glen owned. No garage keys or shed keys, either. Not only did he drive the convertible, he owned an old pick-up truck and a newer Buick SUV, both of which were parked in the driveway. I had a set of keys for the Buick only because of my dad's friend, who had driven my dad to the motel in Calgary and returned the car and the keys to the house. But the second set of keys, as well as any other keys, appeared to be missing. Gradually it dawned on us that Glen most likely was hiding his keys because of his experience with the break-in so many years before. Ray began a search of the kitchen; I began to search through my dad's personal belongings in his bedroom. Neither of us could locate the keys.

Finally, in desperation, I looked up towards the ceiling and called out to the quiet room, "Now would be a good time, Dad!" But the airwaves were still. Not that I was expecting an answer in the first place, although it was worth a try.

We left Rocky that night with the Buick, but no resolution to the missing keys. I called everyone I could think of who knew my dad well, but no one knew where they might be hidden. In fact, they were surprised to hear Glen had done that. Apparently, he had told no one his secret.

The next day I tried my hardest to figure out a resolution, but in the end decided that I had no choice but to call in a locksmith. I dared not leave the convertible in the garage any longer. It was very upsetting to think that there was a possibility of damage to the convertible when the locksmith tried to enter the car and take apart the steering column to make new keys, but I couldn't think of another solution. Plans were made to return to Rocky the following morning. I wondered what Glen would be surmising of my plan, and I was pretty sure he would be unhappy about it.

It didn't take long for my dad to let me know what I needed to do next.

Ray and I were relaxing on the loveseat in our living room after supper, watching television and discussing plans for our trip up to Rocky. We agreed that we needed to look for the keys one more time before the locksmith arrived. I had a strong inner pull to look in the kitchen drawers, which is something I had not done up to that point because Ray had already checked, and found nothing. Our conversation was ending, and our attention was returning to the program we were watching earlier, when movement caught the corner of my eye, off to my right-hand side. It was my dad.

He was perched on the edge of the seat on the recliner next to me, with one leg crossed over the other, and his hands were folded in his lap. His face still had the lined, mature look he had shown me earlier. As his bold gaze met mine, he leaned forward very intently and declared to me, "Kitchen cupboard, Shannon!"

Obviously, a locksmith was out of the question as far as Glen was concerned. He was not letting anyone ruin the beautiful condition his car was in. I was a little confused though, as I had that urge to search the kitchen drawers, and a drawer and a cupboard are two totally different things. I shared the message from my dad with Ray, as well as my conflicting desire to look in the drawers. We were very interested to see where the keys would be located.

As soon as we arrived at my father's house I ran inside, up to the first kitchen cupboard I saw as I entered the kitchen. It was a large cupboard, with double doors. Eagerly, I pulled open the doors and surveyed the scene before me. Everything inside, some canned goods and dry foods, seemed orderly and as though it were in its proper place. Everything, except for the margarine container tucked into the back corner. My dad would have kept margarine in the refrigerator, not in a cupboard.

I seized the small, plastic tub from its discreet position in the cupboard and squealed with delight when I opened it. The keys were there!

I discovered that all of the keys we were searching for, vehicles, garage, and shed, were in the margarine container. Each key had a duplicate set, also inside. I was puzzled to learn that there was no second key to be found for the Buick, however, and soon commenced searching the rest of the cupboards and checking inside of drawers. Imagine my delight when I found, nestled between a stack of folded kitchen towels placed in a drawer, the missing Buick key. The message from my dad, and my strong urge, had both been correct. I couldn't have been happier, and I am sure that at that moment, my dad felt the same way. The vintage car was moved that afternoon to my uncle's home out in the country, and stored safely in a secure garage.

My dad was an avid antique collector. His collection was extensive, and not limited to specific genres. As a child, I was fascinated by the "old" stuff both my mom and my dad liked to acquire, and I always understood that one day it would be passed down. In my youth I had no way of understanding that this experience would be bittersweet, to say the least.

One of the first things to be removed from Glen's house and brought to mine was an antique, hand-carved, wooden writing desk. It is very ornate, and delicate. It was one of my dad's most prized possessions, and he was very proud of it. It sits in my office now, and I find myself staring at it quite often as I muse while writing. When it first arrived in my home, though, I found it to be a rather painful possession to admire. All I could think about was the fact that my dad absolutely loved this desk, and now he was not here to enjoy it any longer. The surgery that should have saved his life had failed, and all future plans for my father were gone. His hopes and dreams were gone. My physical, earthly connection to him was no longer there. I couldn't pick up the phone at will and chat with him about my day. The desk he loved was with me now, but my father was not. Hot tears began to spill from my eyes.

"Take joy in my pleasures."

These words rang in my ears as I studied the desk. My tears were instantly halted as I considered what I had heard. I understood immediately what he was asking of me. Glen wanted me to enjoy what he had loved and see it through his eyes, he wanted me to see the beauty that he saw, he wanted me to appreciate the past. He did not want me to feel pain as I admired his possessions, he wanted me to feel happiness. He wanted my memories to be cherished and joyful, not despairing. Also, I clearly understood that these were only material possessions. While they were to be a beautiful reminder of my loved one and a connection to the past and my family history, they were not to be coveted and put before the most important things in life, which for me are God and my family. As well, I knew that Glen did not feel a connection to these possessions like he once had, I could feel it.

The car was a slightly different matter. Although it too was simply a material possession, my dad understood that his car would provide for me and my family when the time came to sell it. In that sense it was extremely significant to him, and worth the time and energy he had spent getting me to locate the keys. I believe the car was very important to my dad on many levels, for many other reasons, but it was not so important to him that it tied him to this world. He was willing to let it go. He knew I would have to part with it as well, he understood that. I was very sad when I discovered that I had no means to properly care for the car. We had no safe, affordable storage for such a large vehicle, and no real understanding of the maintenance involved or the ability to do it. I had to let it go.

My uncle, Garth, was an answer to my prayers in every regard concerning the convertible. Not only did he have the means to store the car properly, he is a vintage car owner and enthusiast as well, and very knowledgeable. He was willing to take on the responsibility of listing the car and talking to potential buyers, for which I am so grateful. I was simply too overwhelmed to even think about what had to be done to sell the car, and I knew next to nothing about it. Uncle Garth had the car sold in a week.

When it came time for Ray and I to pick up the car and deliver it to the new owner, I suggested to Ray that he drive it. I have driven the car many times and had also brought it to Garth's house. Ray has not ever had the chance, and it was now or never. I would follow him in my car to the city.

I discovered almost immediately that I could not have made a better decision in letting Ray drive, for I was far too emotional to have done so. The first thing that I saw as we set off down the road was my father, seated up front on the passenger side of the convertible, looking like a very young man once again. His excitement was obvious, for he had a huge, elated smile on his face and he was bustling with enthusiasm for the ride. I started weeping instantly. It was a relief to see him looking so wonderful, and above all, pain-free. But I missed him so much.

My dad thoroughly enjoyed the last ride in his beautiful car with Ray at the wheel. Glen loved Ray immensely and was thrilled to be spending time with him, too. Although I only saw Glen in brief flashes as we drove, every vision I saw conveyed how happy my dad truly was. My tears flowed freely. It was during this drive that I finally had the time to reflect upon why my father appeared as older and more mature when he was with me, yet he appeared to be so young when he crossed over, and when I saw him with Ray.

I knew that his aged appearance when he was with me was not an actual indicator of his spiritual growth and readiness to move on, as it has been in most other instances I have observed. Otherwise, he would not be able to appear so young and healthy when he was away from me. And then it hit me. Glen was my *dad.* For most of his life that is what he was: a father. It was one of his most important identities, especially as he got older. Glen didn't want to be free of that identity when he was with me, for that is how he sees himself to this day, as my father. And as we grew older together, as we aged, our bond grew deeper. That bond carried into the spirit world and shall continue evermore. But I do believe that Glen will always identify as being my dad no matter how he progresses, and that is largely how I shall continue to see him when he appears. Not as a young man, but as my dad. A dad with lines on his face and the wisdom of years imprinted upon it. A comfort, indeed.

There have been so many instances that I have been aware of my father at my side as I navigate the large responsibilities of managing an estate and seeing his wishes carried out. His visits are not lengthy but almost always I am left with a strong sense of love and support, and I have been so grateful to know with certainty that he is with me. When my dad appears in spirit, he is no longer restrained by an unhealthy body and the physical distance that used to separate us. He is thrilled to be able to move about at will, visiting all those that he loved and left behind, and trying to provide comfort.

Glen drops in for a quick visit in the most unusual moments. Occasionally I will hear his voice in my ear, admiring the scenery as we are enjoying a ride on our motorcycle. Sometimes he is beside me while I drive my car, drawing my attention to the beauty of the day and away from the overwhelming sadness I might be feeling at that moment. It is hard to remain crying for very long when you have the ability and the blessing to know without a doubt that your loved one walks with you and that he is fine. I think that is a huge reason that I am able to process and accept death fairly quickly, because I completely understand that their journey has not ended.

It is only the physical body that has broken, much like a vehicle or a vessel. When the body wears out, the spirit inside remains intact and transforms anew to start upon a different path. But that loved one is not gone. Perhaps not always able to be with me, but not gone forever. We will meet again; this I know with certainty.

The more time that has gone by, the less I am regularly aware of my father's energetic presence. Although his visits are not as frequent as they once were, I am sure it is because he knows that I am doing okay for the most part, and he also has many things he needs to attend to in the spirit realms. I understand that his concern and love for me are just as strong as ever and that it will remain that way. He continues to guide me when it is needed.

One of the things Glen found necessary to assist me with was preparation for his cremains to be interred in a small, out-of-the-way cemetery near his beloved hometown of Spalding, Saskatchewan. Time had passed so swiftly by that it was nearing August, and I still had not found an urn for him. I had not even a moment to think about it.

It was a dark and sleepless night that found me quietly contemplating the fact that I needed to find an urn, when I heard one word in my head.

"Blue."

I almost laughed out loud in delight when those words were spoken. I was quite tickled that my dad was going to be involved in the decision to choose the color of his urn. Okay, then. A blue urn it would be.

My search for the perfect urn began online, while I was on my desktop computer in the office. The first site I visited had plenty of handcrafted urns, and most were rectangular. There were several with blue epoxy highlights in the wood, but nothing that sparked my attention. I pondered if my dad would want a traditionally shaped urn, like my brother had, so I went to another site to look. There were several that I viewed which were traditional and blue, but nothing that grabbed me. I was considering a search elsewhere when I found myself clicking on yet another picture of a blue urn. Before my eyes could even register the details in the enlarged photo, I found myself suddenly bursting into uncontrollable sobs. In that same moment the energy of my father's spirit became overwhelmingly close to me, it was a very powerful vibration. It was this sudden, strong, energetic connection which had triggered my tears. Without a doubt, this was the perfect urn. I got the message, loud and clear.

It was a blustery day on the last Saturday of October when a small group of family gathered together to carry out Glen's final request. I had a very strong feeling that October was the month that he was insistent upon seeing this task completed, and we were determined to be there to honor that.

Glen's remains now rest beside his son and his parents, the only place in the world that he wanted to be. I am satisfied, knowing that I have done my best to honor him and be true to his wishes.

My final confirmation that Glen was content, that he was happy, came to me on our return trip home to Alberta. As I stared blankly into the endless expanse of snow-covered fields stretching alongside the rough highway, I found my view clouding over, as though a heavy fog had suddenly appeared. Before I could comprehend what was happening, the fog rolled and parted to the sides to reveal a radiant couple standing in the center. It was Glen and Trevor, standing side by side, and Trevor had his arm slung around Glen's shoulder. Glen looked like a young man in his early thirties once again, as did my brother. No words were exchanged, but the look on their faces said it all. Not only were they reunited in the spirit world, they were absolutely delighted to be together. They were at peace, and they could move forward supporting each other in their respective journeys.

I am grateful for this knowledge.

For now, I remain patient with a small, empty void in my heart. I wait, still longing for the day when I know we will be truly reunited. With every sunset I see, I know you wait for me, too.

Until we meet again.

Glen and Shannon. 2018
(picture supplied by Shannon Harwood)

Printed in Great Britain
by Amazon